Global Solidarity

Global Solidarity

Lawrence Wilde

EDINBURGH
University Press

For Joan Catherine and Frances Catherine

© Lawrence Wilde, 2013

Edinburgh University Press Ltd
22 George Square, Edinburgh
www.euppublishing.com

Typeset in 11/14 Sabon by
Servis Filmsetting Ltd, Stockport, Cheshire, and
printed and bound in Great Britain by
CPI Group (UK) Ltd, Croydon CR0 4YY

A CIP record for this book is available from the British Library

ISBN 978 0 7486 4029 4 (hardback)
ISBN 978 0 7486 4028 7 (paperback)
ISBN 978 0 7486 7454 1 (webready PDF)
ISBN 978 0 7486 7456 5 (epub)
ISBN 978 0 7486 7455 8 (Amazon ebook)

The right of Lawrence Wilde to be identified as author of this work
has been asserted in accordance with the Copyright, Designs
and Patents Act 1988.

Published with the support of the Edinburgh University Scholarly
Publishing Initiatives Fund.

Contents

Acknowledgements vi

1 Introduction 1

2 Evolution of the Concept 18

3 Theories of Solidarity 68

4 Radical Humanism 106

5 Social Division and Reconciliation 142

6 Culture 191

7 The Politics of Global Solidarity 218

8 Conclusion 255

References 259
Index 290

Acknowledgements

I would like to extend my deepest gratitude to Ian Fraser and Joan Melia for their meticulous and invaluable comments on an earlier draft of the entire manuscript and for discussing the issues with me over the past eight years. Thanks also to Tony Burns, Karl Haselden, Oli Harrison and Rick Simon, who have helped me formulate my arguments on solidarity in formal and informal settings.

A number of papers have been given on the topics in this book. I would like to thank participants for their comments on papers delivered at the Manchester Political Theory Workshops of 2004, 2008, 2010 and 2011. Thanks also to the participants who commented on papers presented to the Political Studies Association annual conference at the University of Reading in 2006, the conference on Recognition and Global Justice at the University of Nottingham in 2007, the International Utopian Studies conference at the University of Oporto in 2009, the Martha Nussbaum International Conference at the University of Nottingham in 2010, and the conference on the Relevance of Marx and Marxism to Contemporary Global Problems at the University of Newcastle in 2011.

Many of the ideas expressed here have been developed in teaching my final-year undergraduate module at Nottingham Trent University and I thank those students for helping me to clarify my arguments. I would like to thank Nicola Ramsey, senior commissioning editor at Edinburgh University Press, for her support from the outset. Finally, I would like to express my gratitude to Joan, Frances, and Scratch the cat for creating the loving environment in which this book was researched and written.

1 Introduction

The concept of solidarity has an elusive history. Emile Durkheim (1858–1917) brought it into the field of academic social science when he published *The Division of Labour in Society* in 1893, but although his distinction between 'mechanical' and 'organic' solidarity provides a seminal moment in our understanding of social solidarity, he famously does not provide a definition of the key concept itself. From the outset I would like to offer a normative definition of human solidarity as *a feeling of sympathy shared by subjects within and between groups, impelling supportive action and pursuing social inclusion.* There can be little doubt that the powerful subjective element of 'solidarity' deters conceptualisation, for as well as being realised in multiple forms of association, it is felt as an inward pull, as an empowering affective force. The tested tools of social scientific analysis struggle with this subjectivity, bringing to mind Henri Bergson's remark that attempting to analyse something that is essentially fluid is like a boy trying to catch smoke by closing his hands (Bergson 1913: 47). Nevertheless, towards the end of his book, Durkheim identifies the ideal that fired his work, the ideal of 'human fraternity', realisable only through the solidaristic division of labour. He clearly has in mind a social construction at the level of the nation state, but he also makes it clear that this could one day be achieved at the level of a 'single human society', however distant that possibility appeared at the end of the nineteenth century (Durkheim 1964: 405–6; Inglis and Robertson 2008).

International conflicts of the twentieth century appeared to mock that ideal of global solidarity, with two horrendous world wars and a 'cold war' that threatened human civilisation with nuclear destruction. Yet the century also witnessed the onward march of representative democracy, the eclipse of dictatorships, the end of colonialism, the establishment of the welfare state and the emergence of successful new social movements. A new discourse of globalization has conceptualised changes in economic, cultural and political life that have swept the world. Defined as 'the process of increasing interconnectedness between societies such that events in one part of the world more and more have effects on peoples and societies far away' (Baylis *et al.* 2011: 8), globalization poses a number of challenges for social and political theory. In particular, the development of economic globalization, dominated by transnational corporations, has limited the capacity of states to control their economic affairs, while increasing the power of technocratic organisations of economic global governance, such as the World Trade Organization (WTO) and the International Monetary Fund (IMF). The need to address this 'democratic deficit' has stimulated ideas about creating new forms of accountable decision-making that take responsibility for the welfare of all the peoples of the world (Held and McGrew 2007: 157–8). This opens the possibility that Durkheim's ideal of social solidarity in a nation state could now be applied to the world as a whole. *Global Solidarity* sets out to explore this normative goal, and, as such, it is a contribution to modern cosmopolitan theory.

The new cosmopolitan outlook is in fact the 'third wave' of cosmopolitan thinking, the first wave referring to the viewpoint developed by the Cynics and Stoics in the Ancient Greek world from the fifth century BC, and the second to the prescriptions of the great Enlightenment philosopher Immanuel Kant (1724–1804) in the late eighteenth century (Heater 2002: 26–52). The Cynics took their inspiration from Socrates (c. 469–399 BC), reputed to be the first to claim to be a 'citizen of the world' (Heater 2002: 39). Their position was anarchic, directed against all state authority, asserting the ability of wise men to live without the tutelage of political power. Diogenes, the most prominent Cynic philosopher, claimed that the only right state was that of the world (Barker 1970: 120–3). However, cosmopolitanism became a significant social doctrine through the later teachings of the Stoics, who held that human beings all belong to the same species and should be thought of as living in world society, governed by natural law and pursuing a goal of harmony (Heater 2002: 30). Unlike the Cynics, the Stoics saw no contradiction in being citizens of the world and proud citizens of their states, viewing life in terms of a series of concentric circles flowing out from self and family through cities and states until finally we see ourselves as part of common humanity (Nussbaum 1996: 9). The Stoics believed in natural law, applicable to all, to which all positive law should strive to correspond, a natural law that compels us to become citizens of the world with a duty to the common good above all considerations of narrow self-interest (Long 2001: 162–3).

The revival of cosmopolitanism towards the end of the eighteenth century is associated above all with Kant, who was deeply influenced by Stoic philosophy (Nussbaum 1997). His writings *Idea for a Universal History with a Cosmopolitan Purpose* (1784) and *Perpetual Peace* (1795) have proved inspirational to modern cosmopolitan theorists (Boucher 1998: 268–84). Kant was committed to the idea that constitutional representative government provided the means for rational thought to triumph, offering the promise of peace and prosperity. In *Idea for a Universal History* he states that the achievement of a perfect constitution within a state is subordinate to establishing the law-governed relations between states. He sees the competition between states as a spur to political perfection, for only the best states will prevail. Even war, the breakdown of politics, will eventually deter states from going down that path; tyrants will be found out and moral politicians will emerge triumphant. Kant sees this as part of a 'natural' development towards a rational world federation, arguing that the goal of reason is abandoning a lawless state of savagery and forming a federation of peoples in which every state, even the smallest, could expect to derive its security and rights not from its own power or its own legal judgement, but solely from this great federation, from a united power and the law-governed decisions of a united will. However wild and fanciful this idea may appear . . . it is nonetheless the inevitable outcome of the distress in which we involve one another. (Kant 1992: 47–8)

In *Perpetual Peace*, written after the French Revolution, Kant begins by outlining some guidelines which would make wars less likely. For example, peace treaties should not be set up with another war in mind, small states should be respected, standing armies should be replaced by citizen militias, there should be no interference in the constitutions of other states, and states should not be allowed to borrow to finance a war. In Kant's view, the civil constitution of every state should be republican and the right of nations should be based on a federation of free states. This commitment to the idea of a federation of sovereign states involves an acceptance that a world republic is unrealisable in the foreseeable future, as this is 'not the will of nations' (Kant 1992: 105). Nevertheless, Kant's vision of creating a 'universal community' in which 'a violation of rights in *one part* of the world is felt *everywhere*' has been a guiding light for modern cosmopolitanism (Kant 1992: 107–8, original emphasis).

Today's cosmopolitanism shares this commitment to the idea that we have a moral obligation to care for all human beings, without preference to those who happen to be our fellow nationals, co-religionists, or members of any other 'insider' group. As Gillian Brock and Harry Brighouse argue, the key idea of moral cosmopolitanism is that 'each human being has equal moral worth and that equal moral worth generates certain moral responsibilities that have universal scope' (Brock and Brighouse 2006: 4). The new cosmopolitanism has generated a wide-ranging discussion of the theoretical and practical issues involved in trying to achieve harmony in an increasingly globalized world (Vertovec and Cohen 2002; Beck 2006; Brock and Brighouse 2006; Fine 2007). Many of these ideas will be discussed in subsequent chapters, but here it will be helpful to flag up four main areas of this new cosmopolitan discourse in order to show where the consideration of global solidarity fits in.

The first area is the concern for global justice and global ethics from a variety of perspectives, which have been surveyed in several excellent texts (Tan 2004; Caney 2006; Hutchings 2010) and usefully excerpted in *The Global Justice Reader* (Brooks 2008). In the West, theoretical discussions of justice in the closing decades of the twentieth century were dominated by the work of John Rawls (1921–2002) and his critics, flowing from his 1971 publication *A Theory of Justice*, but there he pays only slight attention to international justice (Rawls 1999: 331–5). Rawls grounds his theory of justice as fairness in a hypothetical contract made between people in an original position in which each potential citizen knows nothing about the particular advantages or disadvantages of the others, conducting their deliberations behind a 'veil of ignorance' (Rawls 1999: 11). The outcome presents two principles of justice, the first guaranteeing that all have an equal right to equal basic liberties and the second, the 'difference' principle, that inequalities are arranged so that the greatest benefit accrues to the least advantaged (Rawls 1999: 266). However, Rawls was convinced that the same argument for justifying his theory of justice within a liberal society could not be applied on a global scale, and offers instead a theory of how different communities in the world can regulate their mutual political relations in *The Law of Peoples* (Rawls 2003). As this involves justice contracts for only two out of five types of society, liberal ones and 'decent' ones, it is not an approach that lends itself to theorising human solidarity (Cancy 2006: 78–85). Nevertheless, other theorists considered that it was possible to apply Rawls's original theory to the global community, in particular Charles Beitz in *Political Theory and International Relations* (Beitz 1999) and Thomas Pogge in *Realizing Rawls* (Pogge 1989). Pogge went on to make a highly influential contribution to the global justice debate in *World Poverty and Human Rights*, where he poses this moral question: 'Why do we citizens of the affluent western states not find it morally troubling, at least, that a world heavily dominated by us burdens so many people with such deficient and inferior starting positions?' (Pogge 2008: 3). He argues that we are morally responsible for breaching the negative rights of the millions who are harmed directly by the institutional arrangements that perpetuate vast inequalities.

Other approaches to global justice have come from the philosophical traditions of utilitarianism and neo-Aristotelianism. Peter Singer's utilitarian approach was originally expressed in his article 'Famine, Affluence, and Morality' (Singer 1972), and it has been expanded in a vigorously polemical fashion in *The Life You Can Save* (Singer 2009). Arguing that a relatively small donation from an individual in the affluent world could save a child's life in a less developed country, Singer builds on moral intuitions such as fairness, developed through the successful evolution of the species, in order to argue for redistribution that would eliminate world poverty. However, what Singer calls a 'realistic' means to achieve this rests on individuals pledging to donate sums calculated on the basis of varying proportions of income, a voluntarism that is not only unrealistic but also fails to address the systemic causes of the problems (Singer 2009: 151–74). The neo-Aristotelian approach to global justice has been developed in different ways by Martha Nussbaum and Amartya Sen, both of whom fix on the development of human capabilities as the measure of justice across the world (Nussbaum 2006, 2011; Sen 2009). Nussbaum in particular draws on Aristotle to defend an idea of what humans share in being human and what is required for humans to flourish (Nussbaum 1992). She identifies a number of essential capabilities that people need to be able to exercise in order to lead a fulfilled life and also specifies a number of principles for the global structure that would ensure that these capabilities could be enjoyed in a just global society (Nussbaum 2006: 71–6, 315–24). There is much in common between Nussbaum's approach and the radical humanist view adopted in this book, but there are important differences when it comes to conceiving human essence and confronting the structural limitations imposed by the processes of the world economy, and these will be considered in Chapter 4.

The radical humanist approach demands a more anti-systemic approach to building global solidarity. In general the concept of solidarity rarely rates a mention in the global justice debate, being completely absent from *The Global Justice Reader* mentioned above; theories of justice tend to focus on rules and principles rather than the subjective bonds needed to realise just outcomes.

The second area of new cosmopolitan thought is devoted to the normative goal of deepening and widening democracy on a global scale (Hutchings 1999: 153–81). The cosmopolitan democracy project was launched with the publication in 1995 of David Held's *Democracy and the Global Order*, in which it is argued that democracy needs to be 'recast and strengthened' both within states and across borders if it is to retain its relevance in an increasingly globalized world (Held 1995: x–xi). This can be seen as part of a general concern that issues such as ecological sustainability and chronic world poverty require new forms of global governance if they are to be addressed effectively. In the same year the Commission on Global Governance published *Our Global Neighbourhood* (Commission on Global Governance 1995), which reached the best-selling paperback list and revealed the extent of popular interest in the need to respond to these issues with new forms of global governance. Another report addressing similar issues, Richard Falk's *On Humane Governance*, also appeared in 1995 as part of the World Order Models Project, of which Held was a member. These contributions raised the question of the political processes required to tackle the range of global issues identified earlier in the 1980 Brandt commission report on global under-development and the 1987 report of the World Commission on Environment and Development (the Brundtland report), *Our Common Future*, which established the principle of sustainable development.

The cosmopolitan democracy model concerns itself with extending democratic process to decisions that affect us at the global level, proposing a union of states that is less centralised than a federal model but more transnational than a confederal model, as Daniele Archibugi is at pains to emphasise in his recent contribution, *The Global Commonwealth of Citizens* (Archibugi 2008: 101–12). Operating with a principle of 'subsidiarity', democratic control should operate at all levels appropriate to those affected by the decisions. Held's principle of autonomy holds that all persons 'should be free and equal in the determination of the conditions of their own lives, so long as they do not deploy this framework to negate the rights of others' (Held 1995: 147). From this principle flows the idea that all groups and associations have the capacity for self-determination provided that they guarantee certain rights and require certain obligations. These rights and obligations cut across each network of power, so that they could operate in particular areas of social interaction, such as the political, the economic, health, welfare and culture, as well as different spatial levels, for example the local community, the national state, inter-state organisations, regional formations such as the European Union, and the global (Archibugi 2008: 89–97). Overall, the collective priorities of cosmopolitan democracy are the defence of self-determination, the creation of a common structure of political action and the preservation of the democratic good. Clearly these are important issues, which will be addressed in Chapter 7, but here it must be noted that in the key texts mentioned above there is no consideration of the concept of solidarity.

The third area of cosmopolitanism is related to the second, but instead of focusing on possible new institutions of democratic accountability, the emphasis falls either on new processes of an emergent global civil society or on the development of global citizenship, as in for example Carter (2006), Kaldor (2003), and Keane (2003). The obvious objection here is that citizenship is inextricably linked to the state, so that in the absence of a world state it is misleading to talk about global civil society or global citizenship (Dower 2003: 142–3; Chandler 2005: 194). However, the processes of globalization have witnessed a growth in global governance, through economic steering institutions such as the WTO, the IMF and the World Bank, and through inter-governmental decision-making on a range of environmental and developmental issues. There may be no world state as such, but there are networks of global governance exerting immense power that need to be made politically accountable. John Keane, in *Global Civil Society*, refers to this as a 'cosmocracy', a spider's web of interacting and overlapping structures which have developed in a dynamic and unplanned way and which amount to the first-ever world polity (Keane 2003: 97). Cosmocracy is 'a conglomeration of interlocking and overlapping sub-state, state and supra-state institutions and multi-dimensional processes that interact, and have political and social effects, on a global scale' (Keane 2003: 98). In the absence of cosmopolitan democracy, the decisions that flow from this cosmocracy are only weakly accountable, but that is not to say that they are beyond politics. Inter-governmental meetings of the Group of Twenty (G20) may reflect citizens' concerns on major issues, but so far the G20 has tended to be responsive rather than reforming, and continues to exclude those states representing the poorest societies (Heywood 2011: 117).

The United Nations has created global forums for debate and action plans for interventions in social and environmental issues through its summit processes, and the targets set for the achievement of the Millennium Development Goals at least highlight the urgency of the choices that need to be made at global level (Black 2008: 92–5). Similarly, the adoption of the UN Declaration of Human Rights of 1948, although carrying no legal weight, offers a set of imperatives to which the peoples of the world can aspire. The legal adoption of the 1976 covenants on Civil and Political Rights and on Economic, Social and Cultural Rights can be regarded as laying the juridical foundation for legal, political and social rights across the world (Gareis and Varwick 2005: 144–5). However, despite progress at this formal level, the real movement for radical change in global politics has come from social movements in civil society, and this is where the idea of global citizenship comes in.

Civil society movements addressing global issues have multiplied since the 1970s, and these international non-governmental organisations (INGOs) have formal access as lobbyists to the UN provided that they are non-violent, non-criminal and non-commercial (Willetts 2011a: 19). One of the earliest attempts to argue that INGOs had a decisive role to play in reforming the world was Elise Boulding in her 1988 book, *Building a Global Civic Culture*, although she wisely qualifies her view by pointing out that transnational corporations will also grow to exert a different kind of influence (Boulding 1988: 54). There are about 7,600 well-established INGOs, with a similar number of ephemeral 'caucuses and networks' (Willetts 2011b: 328). Approximately 3,500 INGOs have consultative status with the UN Economic and Social Committee. Participation in such groups is not the only way in which interested citizens can act on global issues, for many activists operate within local or national political or social organisations on matters such as environmental protection, sustainability or ethical consumption. Nevertheless, in recent decades a dense network of international civil society movements has emerged, focusing on the environment, women's oppression, the exploitation of the less developed world and human rights abuses, amounting to a transformation of political activism (Della Porta and Tarrow 2004; Pleyers 2010). We shall return to this phenomenon in the discussions of new forms of solidarity in Chapter 2 and the politics of global solidarity in Chapter 7.

The practices of modern global citizenship range from protests against global economic governance to campaigns against greenhouse gas emissions and other environmental threats to sustainability, ethical consumer movements and human rights activism (Schattle 2008). The formation of global networks has been facilitated by the development of the internet, which has also broken through much of the secrecy beloved by administrative elites and enabled the dissemination of radical alternative ideas (Willetts 2011a: 84–113). Richard Falk concedes that 'most eyes glaze over' when cosmopolitans talk of the need for world government or a global parliament, but he argues that those citizens who are challenging the institutions of global power and demanding greater accountability should be regarded as 'citizen pilgrims' who commit themselves to 'transformation that is spiritual as well as material, that is premised on the wholeness and equality of the human family, and that is disinterested in devising technical fixes that will enable global governance to succeed as a functional project' (Falk 2002: 27–8). So, despite the absence of democratic control over global decision-making, it can be argued that activists grapple with the global issues in ways that look like 'good citizen' activity and carry with them an important aspirational component (Dower 2003: 141–53).

The fourth area of new cosmopolitan discourse focuses on cultural globalization, one of the first aspects of the new cosmopolitanism to attract academic attention with the 1992 publication of Roland Robertson's *Globalization: Social Theory and Global Culture*. The general argument is that although the world is not heading for some sort of homogeneity, it is increasingly the case that societies are becoming aware of and reacting to a new phase of inter-dependence (Robertson 1992). The terrain covered by the term 'culture' is vast, embracing 'high' art, popular entertainments and forms of recreation, religions and lifestyles, through which we experience the world in rapidly changing ways (e.g. Featherstone 2005; Hopper 2007). Some critics view the development of globalization as a threat to indigenous cultures through the imposition of tastes by transnational retailers, giving rise to concepts such as McDonaldisation and cultural imperialism (Tomlinson 1991; Barber 1996). In particular the mass international absorption of American television programmes and feature films is viewed with suspicion as a form of ideological hegemony (Hopper 2007: 88–9). Alternatively, it is possible to discern processes of de-territorialisation and hybridisation of culture that hold out progressive possibilities for cosmopolitan solidarity (Tomlinson 1999: 181–207).

The fear that globalization must provoke extreme reactions that will perpetuate conflict and division has been expressed in influential texts such as Benjamin Barber's *Jihad versus McWorld* (1996) and Samuel Huntington's *The Clash of Civilizations* (1997), whose homogenisation of distinct and incompatible world groups rules out in advance any possibility of global solidarity. More constructively, Ulrich Beck has emphasised the lived experience of developing cosmopolitanism and its potential as a community-building force to forge solutions across territorial boundaries and to create 'an active solidarity among strangers and foreigners' (Beck 2002: 78). He identifies a number of key indicators of cosmopolitanism such as the emergence of cultural commodities, the expansion of routes of communication, tourism and migration, dual nationalities, mixed citizenships, transnational ways of life, and common ecological problems. Globalization means not only more inter-connectedness between states but radical change to the internal quality of societies. Like Robertson, Beck also points to the importance of the growing awareness that we are part of one world, a 'reflexive cosmopolitanism' that draws people together. This opens the possibility of developing a cosmopolitan outlook through which we can constructively negotiate our differences, replacing the old idea of integration as a melting pot with the alternative metaphor of the salad bowl (Beck 2006: 92–5).

What is to be gained by adding a discussion of global solidarity to the list? Looking at the areas of cosmopolitan discourse it becomes apparent that these are relatively 'young' endeavours operating within established academic disciplines in which specialisation is rewarded and experimentation with transdisciplinary perspectives is discouraged. As Immanuel Wallerstein has long argued, academic disciplines designed in the nineteenth century are inadequate for dealing with the emergence of a post-national world (Wallerstein 1991: 237–56; Wallerstein 1999: 157–67). Frequently, work in one area pays scant attention to work in other areas. The contributors to the global justice debate may occasionally supplement their analyses with political proposals, but they are often found lacking in sound political and economic argument. Those focusing on institutional renovation tend to neglect the development of social forces that might carry the project forward. Archibugi rightly points out that the cosmopolitan democracy project is a thread that runs parallel with the debates on global ethics, but that 'the two research programs have interacted only to a limited extent' (Archibugi 2008: 147–8). Similarly, both approaches have tended to set aside cultural issues which are vital in the formation of social forces that may advance the cause of global justice and global democracy. Those focusing on the cultural dimension are unlikely to be found analysing the social and political forces that might achieve a harmonious multicultural world. Beck provides a good example of the perils of seeing different perspectives as *competing* perspectives when commenting on the work of Held, McGrew, Goldblatt and Perraton in *Global Transformations* (2001). Although he praises their work for its detailed analysis of global inter-connectedness, he criticises them for remaining within the bounds of 'methodological nationalism' because they take actually existing states as their point of departure (Beck 2006: 79–80). Clearly, however, if we were to take his advice, 'methodological cosmopolitanism' would ignore political developments at state level, thereby neglecting to examine social and political struggles of crucial importance for progressive social change at the global level.

Focusing on the normative goal of global solidarity touches on all the ethical, institutional and cultural dimensions of the future of world society. Jürgen Habermas's characterisation of solidarity as 'the reverse side of justice' serves as a reminder that normative principles of justice (and democracy) are intrinsically bound up with real social relations and social consciousness (Habermas 1990: 244). In a sense this takes us back to Durkheim, for whom 'social solidarity is a *completely* moral phenomenon' (Durkheim 1964: 64, original emphasis). So the focus on solidarity requires us to deal with a number of perspectives. First, there are ethical questions concerning the choice of principles to guide the development of social harmony. Second, it demands political analysis, to understand the successes and failures of solidaristic movements and the potential for institutional renovation that could promote greater solidarity. Finally, it requires cultural analysis to understand the production and reproduction of social identities, and the ways in which different identities may be harmoniously reconciled.

Before outlining the chapter plan, it is important to meet a fundamental objection to the normative goal of global solidarity, set down in by David Heyd in an article in a special edition of the *Journal of Social Philosophy* devoted to the concept of solidarity. Defining solidarity as 'a social force which contributes to the sustenance of the unity of a group of people', he argues that it is created in the course of struggles for a collective cause and is therefore necessarily exclusive, presupposing the existence of other groups to struggle against. It follows that solidarity cannot be universal, and 'the idea of a "human community" is as misleading as it is attractive' (Heyd 2007: 119–20). For Heyd, solidarity is in essence partial rather than universal, and always 'local and biased'. Heyd operates with a purely descriptive definition of solidarity, whereas if the normative one adopted at the outset of this book is used, struggles may be distinguished by the extent to which they promote or hinder social inclusion. This allows for the identification of progressive solidaristic struggles and holds out the hope for the achievement of social solidarity. This normative approach enabled Durkheim to theorise social solidarity as a realisable goal. Similarly, with the development of an increasingly globalized economy, it is reasonable to envisage the emergence of a globalized society that overcomes its major antagonisms and signals the goal of global solidarity, or 'human community'. These goals of social solidarity and global solidarity are not vitiated by the presence of groups or individuals who refuse the consensus, or who 'self-exclude'. The real obstacle to both social and global solidarity is the development of an economic system that accentuates social antagonism. Increasingly, therefore, solidaristic struggles will oppose the divisive processes that are presently driven by neoliberalism, a form of market fundamentalism that emphasises free markets, free trade and minimal state intervention that has widened inequalities of all kinds (Harvey 2009: 1–3; Peck 2010: xi–xvii). We do not have to wait for a 'War of the Worlds' scenario for humanity to unite against the alien invader (Appiah 2006: 98). Rather, the alien force is of our own making, unleashed by an alienating model of accumulation that reproduces oppression and exploitation and threatens us with ecological catastrophe. Movements that serve to eradicate social exclusions, on a global scale, can rightly be identified as movements for global solidarity. Breaking the hold that neoliberalism has exerted on global and national economic and social policies and replacing it with more humane governance will not, in itself, achieve global solidarity. However, it would constitute a decisive change of direction that would bring it in sight as an alternative, liberating, form of globalization.

Chapter plan

The concept of solidarity needs to be understood in its historical context, and this will be dealt with in Chapter 2. There appears immediately the paradox of solidarity: the word connotes unity and universality, but it is realised only in the course of struggles that entail antagonism and partiality. From Pierre Leroux's (1797–1871) original conception of solidarity in his 1840 work *On Humanity* (Leroux 1985: 157–72), the emphasis within nineteenth-century socialism and anarchism shifted constantly between, on the one hand, demands for solidaristic action to secure social inclusion within a democratic state and, on the other, demands for insurrectionary action to destroy the state and the economic system it protected, as a precondition for the emergence of a solidaristic society. The reformist tendency in socialism found its echo in the liberal espousal of solidarity in the closing years of the nineteenth century, with Durkheim's work as its intellectual pinnacle. The emergence of political democracy in the twentieth century gave rise to a major redistribution of resources in the Western democracies, culminating in the emergence of the welfare state, claimed by some to be the epitome of social solidarity (Baldwin 1999; Stjernø 2005). In recent years we have witnessed an erosion of the social forces that produced the welfare state consensus, and a weakening of the measures of social protection it had won. An important question to be addressed here is whether this means a weakening of solidarity *per se*, or whether it is possible for new solidarities to emerge around a variety of issues which may carry within them the impetus for the development of a broader, human solidarity.

Following on from this question, Chapter 3 engages in a critical discussion of the work of the leading contemporary social and political theorists who have helped to regenerate interest in the concept of solidarity. The theorists selected are all from the Western tradition, reflecting my own background, and I must leave it to others to bring in alternative ideas from different cultures. Richard Rorty, Axel Honneth, Jürgen Habermas, Alain Touraine and Carol Gould have offered valuable insights into the ways in which antagonisms may be reconciled and new forms of solidaristic practice may be developed. Understandably, perhaps, all these theorists are resistant to 'essentialism', a term often used derisively in social theory because of its past associations with exclusionary practices of the most vicious kind. Nevertheless, it seems to me that their contributions on solidarity are flawed by their resistance to the idea that there is something essential in human nature that can help us to overcome social division and promote human solidarity.

Chapter 4 puts forward a radical humanist view as a philosophical grounding for developing the idea of global solidarity as a real possibility. It draws on the tradition of virtue ethics, making use of the insights on human nature developed by the young Karl Marx and Erich Fromm. Rationality, compassion, productiveness and cooperation are taken to be key 'potentials' whose positive realisation would produce human solidarity. The chapter will also compare this perspective with the one which it most closely resembles, the capabilities approach of Martha Nussbaum mentioned above.

Chapter 5 deals with social division and reconciliation. Here the focus is on some of the most important issues that have historically divided societies and continue to act as sources of

Introduction

conflict, namely class, nation, race, religion and gender. It deals with strong allegiances and deeply ingrained predispositions, but this is not simply about describing obstacles to human solidarity. Rather, the aim is to show that the social struggles around these identities create the preconditions for reconciliation that can point the way towards greater human solidarity. Chapter 6, dealing with the culture of solidarity, follows on logically from the discussions in the previous chapter, for it is through culture that these identities are represented and negotiated. The chapter points to ways in which cosmopolitan ideas might be promoted, and then applies the radical humanist framework to show how ideas of solidarity are projected artistically in stories involving severe social stress. The texts selected are Barbara Kingsolver's novel *The Poisonwood Bible* and Walter Salles's film *The Motorcycle Diaries*.

Chapter 7 deals with the politics of global solidarity. It offers some positive scenarios that could produce a change of direction in global governance, involving institutional reform, redistributive policies and energised solidaristic movements. Together these could open the way to the democratisation of world society and real progress towards global solidarity. Chapter 8 will recapitulate the major themes discussed in the text, and reflect on the nature of the project undertaken.

2 Evolution of the Concept

The paradox of solidarity turns on its simultaneous appeal to unity and universality and its dependence in practice on antagonisms between particular groups. If a normative commitment to global solidarity is to be promoted, a clear distinction has to be made between group solidarity that reaches out to ever-increasing social inclusion, and that which is practised in defence of the permanent subjugation of rival groups. Examples of the latter include the open support of racism, sexism, homophobia, or national or religious supremacism. However, even where we can make a case that a particular form of solidarity aspires toward an ideal of human solidarity, its historical development may well subvert this ideal. In other words, its ends can be confounded by its means.

The task of this chapter is to outline the historical development of various perspectives on solidarity that have claimed to pursue a goal of ever-widening social inclusion, including, at the ultimate level, a commitment to universal peace and justice that can be equated with the idea of global solidarity. The chapter is divided into seven parts, beginning with the origins of the concept of solidarity in the work of Pierre Leroux (1797–1871), who adopted an explicitly ethical view that oppression and exploitation should be overcome in a fully inclusive democratic socialist society. The second part will deal with working-class solidarity from the mid-nineteenth century until the outbreak of the First World War in 1914, identifying three distinctive approaches. First, there is the 'ethico-inclusive' approach, which carried forward Leroux's initial position; then there is the 'redemptive' approach, which emphasised the solidarity of dedicated revolutionaries determined to sweep away all the economic, social and political manifestations of the current unjust society; and finally the 'class struggle' approach, which visualised solidarity developing in the process of struggles in mass political parties and trade unions, with the ultimate goal of a classless society. All three approaches carried with them a vision of human emancipation, but they had sharp differences over the forms of solidarity and the organisational strategy to be developed. The third part will examine the emergence of liberal solidarity towards the end of the nineteenth century, discussing in particular the contribution of solidarity's most eminent theorist, Emile Durkheim (1858–1917).

The fourth part will look briefly at the idea of national solidarity, first articulated in an idealist way by Giuseppe Mazzini (1805–72) as a commitment to liberty and democracy that could be generalised beyond borders and help to create a harmonious world. In practice, the national solidarity that asserted itself so forcefully at the outbreak of the First World War was focused on a sense of patriotic duty more likely to produce international conflict rather than global harmony. This leads us to ask whether modern theories of liberal nationalism are compatible with the cosmopolitan ambition to create a more solidaristic world.

The fifth part will look at one variant of the class-struggle approach to solidarity that cast a long shadow over world politics in the twentieth century – soviet communism, as developed in Soviet Union following the Russian Revolution of 1917 and in China and eastern Europe after the Second World War. The ideology behind this, which took the name of Marxism-Leninism, eclipsed the 'orthodox' social democracy that had been a powerful and unifying force in working-class politics before the First World War, but in dispensing with democracy itself it also dispensed with any realistic hope of achieving social solidarity. Ironically, the eruption of the Solidarity independent trade union movement in Poland in 1980 signalled the beginning of the end of the whole system of communist rule in Europe, a process completed by the dissolution of the Soviet Union in 1991.

The sixth part will examine the emergence of the welfare state in the affluent democracies of the 1960s and 1970s, as this has been regarded by some commentators as social solidarity in practice. However, the argument here will cast doubt on this view, suggesting that in important respects those societies remained insensitive to the needs of significant sections of society and found it difficult to accommodate newly developed interests. The final section will look briefly at the fraying of old forms of social solidarity embodied in the welfare state and the emergence of new forms based on the struggles conducted by new social movements since the 1970s. At first sight, the further development of individualism and the loosening of traditional social bonds suggest a weakening of solidarity, but we must consider the possibility that these new forms are reaching out beyond borders to develop transnational solidarity, opening the way for the radical transformation of global governance and advancing the goal of global solidarity.

Origins

'Solidarity' came into common usage as part of the lexicon of social struggles which also gave rise to 'socialism' and 'communism' in the 1830s and 1840s. There are, of course, forerunner concepts such as fraternity and brotherhood, with strong links to religious ideas (Stjernø 2005: 25–6; Brunkhorst 2005: 23–54), but the word itself has its origins in Roman and feudal law (as *solidum*), referring to common liability of a group for a debt incurred by any of its members (Brunkhorst 2005: 1–2). There has been some disagreement as to when its modern usage was established in print. Although Steinar Stjernø credits Charles Fourier (1772–1837) as the first theorist of solidarity, with the publication of *Theory of Universal Unity* in 1822 (Stjernø 2005: 27–9), Fourier himself prefers a variety of other words such as 'association', 'unity' and 'harmony' and makes no mention of 'solidarity'. His followers began to use 'solidarity' instead of 'harmony' in the 1840s (Pilbeam 2000: 116), inspired by several editions of Hippolyte Renaud's *Solidarity*, a short book on the doctrines of Fourier, first published in 1842. However, the title is misleading because there is no reference to solidarity in the text itself.

The first theorist of solidarity was Pierre Leroux, in *Humanity*, published in Paris in 1840 (Leroux 1985: 157–72; Wildt 1999). *Humanity* became a founding text for what became known as the 'humanitarian' movement, committed to the peaceful development of a democratic form of socialism embracing worker cooperatives. Leroux deplores the vast inequalities of wealth and power associated with private property and the market, but he is firmly convinced that progress towards socialism requires an explicitly ethical movement. The basis for this is to be a purified Christianity based not on the example of the modern churches but rather on early Christianity, with its radical egalitarianism and its emphasis on redemption in this world rather than the next. Leroux attempts to reclaim the appeal for human liberation that he takes to be implicit in Christ's life, with Christ represented as the embodiment of the unity of all humankind (Leroux 1985: 646–9).

Leroux conceives solidarity as the humanistic alternative to the shortcomings of the Christian virtue of charity, so that rather than helping others out of duty to God, people need to express the love of God through embracing their fellow human beings in mutually supportive relations. Christian charity presumes poverty to be unavoidable and views life as a 'vale of tears' which we unworthy mortals have to endure (Leroux 1985: 163). For Leroux, the driving ethic of 'love thy neighbour as thyself' has been developed through religion and needs to be elevated over the bleak views of human nature propounded by individualists since the writings of Thomas Hobbes in the seventeenth century (Leroux 1985: 25–9).

The goal of solidarity was universal social inclusion through peaceful means. During the French Second Republic (1848–51) Leroux worked tirelessly on behalf of the working class. When the government suppressed the workers' uprising of June 1848, Leroux denounced the government's ferocity and opposed all its subsequent repressive measures. He continued to call for democratic reform, proposing for the first time in history a bill to extend the franchise to women, shortly before the National Assembly was dissolved by Louis-Napoleon Bonaparte after his *coup d'état* of December 1851. Leroux argued for solidarity to be rooted in workplace associations that were to be international in scope (Sewell 1997: 274). This internationalism was an important feature of early socialism, marked by the formal establishment in 1846 of the Society of Fraternal Democrats, comprising members from a number of European countries. Its programme, formulated by the English socialist Julian Harney (1817–97), declared that 'our moral creed is to receive our fellow-men without regard to country, as members of one family – the human race, and as citizens of one commonwealth – the world' (Braunthal 1967a: 66).

The early socialist conception of solidarity sought to fuse the particular interests of the working class with the common good of the whole society. The workers were conceived broadly as all those who laboured to make a living, including independent urban workers and poor peasants. In this conception, the demand for social inclusion followed the spirit of the great French Revolution of 1789 with its appeal for 'liberty, equality, fraternity'. It was accompanied by an international vision of liberation, often legitimated by a form of Christian egalitarianism (Pilbeam 2000: 39–53). One of the most prominent socialist leaders of the period, Louis Blanc (1811–82), viewed socialism as 'the gospel in practice' (Blanc 1966: 257). In the 1845 introduction to his popular work *Organisation of Labour*, he explicitly addresses his work to the rich, appealing to them that the cause of the poor is also 'your cause' (Sewell 1997: 235). Few of the rich agreed.

Working-class solidarity (1848–1914)

The concept of solidarity developed by Pierre Leroux can be characterised as 'ethico-inclusive', in the sense that the demand for social inclusion was grounded and expressed in explicitly ethical terms. However, two other forms can be identified as having developed out of the experience of the upheavals of 1848. The first I term the 'redemptive' approach, one that viewed the prevailing social structures as totally inimical to human freedom and demanded they be swept away. Here the goal of social solidarity was one that could be achieved only after an apocalyptic revolutionary change, and the solidarity practised to achieve that goal was exercised in small groups of dedicated revolutionaries. The second approach is the 'class struggle' model outlined by Karl Marx (1818–83) and Friedrich Engels (1820–95) in *The Communist Manifesto* of 1848, based on building mass working-class social and political movements striving for a classless society, through peaceful means where possible, or through force where necessary. In order to understand the development of these three forms we need to revisit the revolutionary events of 1848, particular the French experience.

The workers' uprising in Paris in June 1848 was a pivotal moment in shaping these distinctive forms of working-class solidarity for subsequent decades, not just in France but in Europe as a whole, and it is important to understand the significant issues it raised. In the February revolution of 1848, a broad popular movement of middle-class and working class Parisians overthrew the monarchy of Louis Philippe and installed a provisional government. As so often happens in revolutions, the momentum of the revolution carried it in a more radical direction than initially envisaged by the moderate republican opposition. Instead of a limited extension of the right to vote, universal male franchise was established for the first time in history, and National Workshops were created to provide work for the poor. The historian William Sewell conveys the change in expectations that this inspired, commenting that although the majority within the provisional government intended the National Workshops as nothing but rechristened 'charity workshops', a temporary expedient to rescue workers from destitution in a time of particularly severe distress, the wording of the decree itself conveyed a radically different message:

> But the decree that established the workshops did not base them on charity; it based them on a solemnly proclaimed right of all citizens, the right to labour ... As interpreted by the workers of Paris and the other cities of France, it established the right to labour as a fundamental right of man. (Sewell 1997: 246)

At a stroke, Leroux's vision of the triumph of the principle of solidarity over the principle of charity appeared within reach.

The original idea for the workshops had come from Louis Blanc, who used his position in the provisional government to push for radical reform. In reality the workshops were a long way from his ideal of the 'social workshop', poorly resourced and organised with little enthusiasm, but for the workers they symbolised the goal of a 'social republic'. However, when a general election was held at the end of April, a large majority of the deputies returned to the Assembly were either conservative republicans or monarchists, reflecting the power of rural elites to control the vote in a socially conservative country. The radical forces, concentrated in the major cities, did not have the organisational power at that stage to mount a serious threat to the majority (Price 1975: 31, 71). Blanc was excluded from the new government, which, on 21 June, decreed the dissolution of the workshops. Thousands of workers in Paris took to arms in a rebellion that lacked leadership and clear goals, and in four days of fighting approximately 1,500 workers were killed and 12,000 arrested and imprisoned (Sewell 1997: 272).

The violent suppression of the workers' uprising was followed by repression of socialist clubs and publications, and eventually by the abolition of the universal male franchise. Nevertheless, this was not the end of the ethico-inclusive approach to solidarity. In November 1848 the first political movement bearing the name 'solidarity' was formed, and Republican Solidarity (*Solidarité républicaine*) quickly organised across the country. After winning more than 200 seats at the election of May 1849 the deputies called themselves 'social democrats' (Pilbeam 2000: 190–1). However, the state intensified its repression and the socialists in the Assembly lacked the power to resist it. Most of the leaders were arrested at various times during the Second Republic and many of them fled France even before Louis-Napoleon Bonaparte assumed total control in December 1851. The new dictator arrested or expelled the majority of the socialist leaders and imposed a ban on independent workers' movements that was tightly enforced until the late 1860s. This quickly led to the marginalisation of the ethico-inclusive model of solidarity, and the development of 'physical force' movements that were clearer about what they wanted to destroy than they were about the social arrangements of the post-revolutionary future.

Forms of the ethico-inclusive model of solidarity developed strength in Britain and also in Germany. In Britain, the Chartists campaigned for the extension of the vote to all men and other democratic reforms, petitioning Parliament three times between 1839 and 1848, to no avail. Although this mass movement had a 'physical force' element to it, which involved talk of insurrection and the military drilling of activists (Charlton 1997: 60), it was fundamentally a peaceful movement pursuing reform within legal limits. Indeed the sole Chartist Member of Parliament, Feargus O'Connor, refused to move acceptance of the third petition in the House of Commons in April 1848 when scrutineers claimed that many of the five and a half million signatures were bogus (Thompson 1984: 325–36). The last great national demonstration of 80,000 Chartists passed off peacefully at Kennington Common in London in 1848, but in the months that followed almost 300 leaders were arrested and imprisoned, and the movement collapsed (Thompson 1984: 328–9). However, the capacity for solidaristic action had been established and was to develop in new ways, through trade unions, in cooperatives, in discussion groups and, eventually, in independent political parties. The extension of the franchise in 1867 and 1883 created the opportunity for the representation of labour and put pressure on the Liberal Party to introduce the first major welfare reforms before the First World War. In this case a link is evident between a tradition of working-class ethico-inclusive solidarity and liberal ideals of social solidarity, despite some tensions (Taylor 1999). Nevertheless, British trade unions were active members of the socialist First International (1864–72) and the Second International (1889–1914), often allying with the Marxists and openly supporting the peaceful class struggle.

In Germany, the first national workers' movement, Ferdinand Lassalle's (1825–64) General Union of German Workers, founded in 1863, emphasised the role of the state in assisting workers' cooperatives and addressing major social problems (Geary 1992b: 118–19). Although the German Social Democratic Party (SPD) adopted a Marxist programme with a strong revolutionary rhetoric in 1891, the party in practice was committed to democratic reform of the constitution to enable it to achieve power. A move to acknowledge its gradualist and reformist position was proposed by Eduard Bernstein (1850–1932), but even though his 'revisionism' was formally defeated at the SPD's 1899 congress, there were no expulsions and the reformist position remained influential in the party and the unions (Steger 1997: 66–88). Although the SPD was less inclined to parliamentary compromise than, say, the British Labour Party, it also steered well clear of confrontational action (Steenson 1991: 91–107).

In contrast to the reformism implicit in the ethico-inclusive model of solidarity, the redemptive approach to solidarity viewed the existing social order as totally oppressive and corrupt, and sought deliverance through a complete revolutionary transformation. This action was conceived as being led by dedicated groups of clandestine revolutionaries 'on behalf of' the victims of injustice, and only occasionally engaged in solidaristic action among the mass of workers. Two of the leading advocates of this approach in mid-nineteenth-century France were Pierre-Joseph Proudhon (1809–65) and Louis Auguste Blanqui (1805–81). Proudhon refused to countenance participation in constitutional politics or in trade unions designed to improve pay and conditions through negotiation. Instead he advocated 'associations' dedicated to replacing the existing social system with a stateless society based on spontaneous forms of self-management (Woodcock

1977: 122–8). Proudhon was vague on how revolution was to be accomplished, envisioning a form of 'bottom up' economic transformation that would circumvent political processes to produce the triumph of 'universal brotherhood' (Proudhon 1971: 99–122), an idea that was later taken up by the revolutionary syndicalist movement in France. A different and more direct tactic of redemptive solidarity was pursued by Blanqui and his supporters, who saw themselves as heirs to the Jacobin tradition of the first great French Revolution (Gildea 1996: 43–4). Blanqui, who originated the idea of the 'dictatorship of the proletariat', conceived the proletariat as comprising the vast majority of dependent French workers and peasants. However, before the people could wield power and create socialism, it would be necessary for dedicated full-time revolutionaries to seize power by insurrection and hold onto it. He spent a lifetime gathering such groups of conspirators together, and also many years in jail as a result of his insurrectionary activities (Braunthal 1967a: 46–7).

The followers of Blanqui were a major political force at work in the great rebellion that produced the Paris Commune of 1871, along with other Jacobins, disciples of Proudhon, and relatively small numbers of anarchists and communists associated with the First International (Braunthal 1967a: 153–5: Horne 2002: 290–303). The Commune may have lacked ideological coherence, but its solidarity rested on a shared sense of the injustices of the past and a conviction that a more just society could be created without the privileged elites. A flavour of the sharp difference between this vague redemptive commitment and the ethico-inclusive reformism associated with Leroux and Blanc can be gauged from the Commune's reaction to Leroux's death (from natural causes) in the city on 14 April. The Commune sent two delegates to his funeral, having grudgingly resolved

> that it rendered this homage not to the philosopher who was the partisan of the mystical school that we are suffering for today, but to the political man who the day after the June rising courageously took on the defence of the vanquished. (Bakunin 1976: 221)

This curmudgeonly tribute indicates just how much the early 'inclusive' use of solidarity had been rejected by militant workers, shocked by the violent defeat of June 1848 and the suppression of their movements during the Second Republic and the Second Empire (1852–70). But the Communards were to pay a high price for their defiant stance. After ten weeks of independence, between 18 March and 28 May, the army of the national government marched from Versailles to destroy the Commune, slaughtering an estimated 25,000 people in the process (Edwards 1973: 158; Horne 2002: 418).

The ferocity with which the state suppressed the revolutionary working class was decisive in marginalising appeals to a social republic forged out of compromise with the ruling class (Sewell 1997: 275–6). In the late nineteenth century, working-class solidarity in the French Third Republic expressed itself in revolutionary rather than reformist terms, for despite the extension of democratic rights, militant workers were unwilling to trust parliament and the state. Although a reformist socialist party eventually emerged, the French trade union confederation, the General Confederation of Labour (CGT), was dominated in the early years of the twentieth century by revolutionary syndicalists who placed total reliance on the general strike as the means to sweep away the existing order (Magraw 1992: 54–100). The clearest expression of this apocalyptic commitment was Georges Sorel's (1847–1922) *Reflections on Violence*, first published in 1908, in which he extols the virtues of the 'terrible nature of the revolution' and 'its character of absolute and irrevocable transformation' (Sorel 1999: 154). In this conception, planning for the future form of society is a surrender to the existing relations of power. He considered that the proletariat's task is to prepare itself for the great battle, with the sole aim of 'expelling the capitalists from the productive domain' without needing 'to make plans for utilising its victories' (Sorel 1999: 161). Sorel's intellectual defence of revolutionary violence eschewed all ideas of social reform or reconstruction; the myth of the general strike was carried along with the emotional and irreconcilable power of redemption (Vout and Wilde 1987).

In Europe as a whole, anarchism was the leading doctrine operating with the redemptive notion of solidarity. One of its leading proponents, Mikhail Bakunin (1814–76), committed himself early in his career to the idea of sweeping away all institutions of power in order to achieve freedom, famously declaring that 'the passion for destruction is a creative passion, too!' (Bakunin 1973: 57). In *God and the State* (1871) he makes clear his refusal to compromise his demands by engaging in legal political activity:

> In a word, we reject all legislation, all authority, and all privileged, licensed, official, and legal powers over us, even though arising from universal suffrage, convinced that this can serve only to the advantage of a dominant minority of exploiters against the interests of the immense majority in subjection to them. (Bakunin 1973: 231)

The redemptive nature of Bakunin's conception of solidarity is well illustrated by his response to the defeat of the Paris Commune, in which he pledges his commitment to a liberty that would 'shatter all the idols in heaven and on earth and will then build a powerful new world of mankind in solidarity, upon the ruins of all the churches and all the states' (Bakunin 1973: 262). After talking about the massacre of the Communards as 'Paris drenched in the blood of her noblest children' and the crucifixion of 'humanity itself', he promises that the coming international revolution, 'expressing the solidarity of all peoples, shall be the resurrection of Paris' (Bakunin 1973: 264–5). Bakunin rejected the view that there would always be antagonistic interests to prevent the 'universal solidarity of individuals with society', but he recognised that the Commune, isolated and lacking experience, had been unable to produce a socialist society (Bakunin 1973: 265–70). Later, in an unpublished denunciation of Marx, he decries the 'Marxian solidarity' that was decreed from the top down, but extols the watchword of solidarity as 'the confirmation and realisation of every freedom, having its origin . . . in the inherent social nature of man'. In his view, this solidarity can only be 'the spontaneous product of social life, economic as well as moral'

(Bakunin 1973: 284–5). In this conception, solidarity is primarily focused on the future, with the anarchist movements acting in a guiding role.

For the Italian anarchist Errico Malatesta (1853–1932), solidarity was the 'law' governing the future of humankind:

> Solidarity, that is the harmony of interests and of feelings, the coming together of individuals for the wellbeing of all, and of all for the wellbeing of each, is the only environment in which man can express his personality and achieve his optimum development and enjoy the greatest possible wellbeing. This is the goal towards which human evolution advances; it is the highest principle which resolves all existing antagonisms. (Malatesta 1974: 24–7)

However, the determination of the anarchists to maintain their anti-authoritarian purity was such that they opposed the development of political parties willing to participate in constitutional politics. They were also critical of trade unions that operated within legal limits and with hierarchical structures. This was to prove decisive in limiting the effectiveness of anarchism as a movement, leaving the major organisations of the working class in the hands of reformists or Marxists. The political abstentionism of anarchism tended to confine solidarity in practice to the membership of marginal and often conspiratorial groups. There were notable exceptions to this, as in the case of revolutionary syndicalism in France and the anarchist movement in Spain, but for the most part anarchism preserved the purity of solidaristic libertarianism at the expense of building it in reality. Nevertheless, the redemptive notion of solidarity conveyed a burning sense of the injustice of prevailing social relations, and also preserved the important idea that non-state solutions to social division are possible.

Let us turn now to the 'class struggle' approach to solidarity. This refers to the revolutionary theory of Karl Marx and the practice of Marxism during the period of the Second International. Although Marx accorded no theoretical significance to the concept of solidarity, the empirical development of working-class solidarity was vitally important to the fulfilment of his vision of the capture of the state by a class-conscious mass of workers determined to wrest economic power from the bourgeoisie and extend the social revolution across the world. Unlike other socialist theorists of the time, Marx recognised the objectively progressive aspect of capitalism in developing the productive forces and creating a working class, who were tasked with placing the means of production under social control and putting an end to class rule. The class struggle for Marx was always international, and he played a leading role in the formation and operation of the First International, an alliance of European socialists, anarchists and trade unionists. Following the Hague congress of the International in 1872 he delivered an important speech in Amsterdam in which he declared that it was entirely possible for workers to achieve their goal by peaceful means in countries that were moving towards democracy. He explicitly invoked solidarity as the 'basic principle' of the International, declaring that 'we will only be able to attain the goal we have set ourselves if this life-giving principle acquires a secure foundation among the workers of all countries' (Marx 2010c: 325). The organisational framework to develop this foundation was to be supplied by trade unions and mass parties, using legal methods to subvert the status quo.

Marx's conception of class struggle contained a universal element, in the sense that the emancipation of the working class was also conceived as the emancipation of humanity from the long history of class oppression. In abolishing private productive property, the working class would abolish the basis on which classes arose and open the way for classless societies in which human solidarity could flourish on a global scale (Fraser and Wilde 2011: 181–2, 121). Marx was more specific than other socialist theorists of his day in defining the working class, which, for him, comprised those who sold their labour power to the owners of capital. It did not include the self-employed – the petty bourgeoisie – or the peasants, although Marx proposed that the working-class parties needed to devise policies that could attract the support of these sections. Although he encouraged the development of legal trade unions and working-class political parties, he was critical of them when they limited themselves to seeking reforms rather than embracing the need to win state power and transform the economic system. In his work in the First International Marx argued that the trade unions needed to convince the world at large 'that their efforts, far from being narrow and selfish, aim at the emancipation of the downtrodden millions' (Marx 2010c: 92). His involvement in the development of a unified German socialist party (the SAPD) showed his determination that it should remain completely committed to class struggle, insisting uncompromisingly that capitalism must be replaced by communism as part of an international social revolution (Marx 2010c: 339–75). In a sense, the class struggle offered a middle way between the ethico-inclusive and redemptive approaches to solidarity. It offered the goal of a classless communist society in which the whole people exercised full democratic control, but it resolutely refused to argue for this in moral terms. And in contrast to the redemptive model, it sought mass support for a strategy of building a viable social alternative, using all available means to ensure that the working class achieved victory in 'the battle of democracy' (Marx 2010a: 86).

The class struggle model involved a number of dilemmas, many of which were openly discussed in Marx's lifetime. Marx was well aware that engaging in legal forms of political and economic struggles might lead to the dilution of the commitment to social revolution, with socialists lured into compromises within the existing social and political structures. He spoke witheringly of the ineffectiveness of the 'parliamentary cretinism' of the French socialists in the Second Republic (Marx 2010b: 211), and warned the German socialists against becoming seduced by a 'servile belief in the state' and a 'democratic faith in miracles' (Marx 2010c: 357). Effectively, the achievement of democracy and the advancement of social reforms offered the promise (or illusion) of achieving social inclusion within a capitalist system, albeit one regulated by the state. Eduard Bernstein wanted the German Social Democrats (SPD) to officially endorse this approach in

1899, and although he was defeated, his 'revisionism' reflected the reality of the position that the party had arrived at (Sorel 1999: 213). When the SPD voted to support the war effort in 1914 it showed just how far this process of cooptation had gone. It was a problem that neither Marx nor Engels had fully considered (Calhoun 1982: 230).

One reaction to it was to offer an alternative interpretation of Marx that argued that he was prepared to support a 'dictatorship of the proletariat' by any available means, irrespective of democratic support. This was the view of Georges Sorel, effectively claiming Marx for the redemptive insurrectionary tradition (Sorel 1999: 129–30), and later, more fatefully, of V. I. Lenin (1870–1924) in *The State and Revolution* (1917) (Lenin 1992: 22–51). But the idea of the 'dictatorship of the proletariat' in which the proletariat did not constitute a majority created another dilemma for the class struggle model, for it necessitated a dictatorship of a party leadership *over* the people, thereby subverting the emancipatory goal. In order to justify his revolutionary seizure of power in Russia in 1917, Lenin emphasised Marx's defence of the Paris Commune of 1871 as the ideal political form of revolutionary government, but while Marx did indeed extol the virtues of the participatory democracy of the Commune, this should not be taken as an endorsement of insurrection led by a minority movement. Indeed the discrepancies between Marx's public and private pronouncements on the Paris Commune reflect the deep dilemmas involved in the class struggle approach. In public, Marx defended the Commune without reservation, but several months before the Commune was declared he had warned against the 'desperate folly' of an insurrection against the provisional government (Marx 2010c: 185). Ten years later he wrote in a private letter that the Commune had had no chance of success but could have reached a useful compromise if its leaders had a used a 'modicum of common sense' (Marx 2009: 642). This discrepancy between public and private statements reflects a genuine ambiguity in Marx and many of his followers on the strategy for social revolution.

Marx's conception of the state also contained a major ambiguity. Like the anarchists, he preached the virtues of self-government and hated bureaucracy, and in *The Civil War in France* (1871) he praises the proposed national model of communes that reserves only a few but important functions for central government. However, in a national state these 'few' functions will have to include the regulation of national production by a common plan, clearly an enormous and unprecedented endeavour. Marx had defined the state as the machinery of class rule, so it followed that if private property were abolished and a classless society ensued, the state would thereby be abolished. However, this merely evades the key issue of what forms of administration would be adopted (Fraser and Wilde 2011: 193–6).

The class struggle model, with its ambiguities, triumphed within European socialism in the years between Marx's death and the outbreak of the First World War. The Second International was convened in Paris in 1889, and, following the formal expulsion of the anarchists at the London congress in 1896, a massive international body comprising rapidly expanding socialist parties from all the major European states represented the official 'Marxist' line, with an infusion of radical reformism from the British delegation. However, beneath the surface unity of international solidarity a fissure had developed. The particular goals of working-class solidarity, such as political inclusion and the redress of social grievances, had become uncoupled from the universal goal of human emancipation. Just how far the class struggle model of solidarity failed to develop that wider universal goal became clear in 1914 when virtually all the socialist parties of Europe voted to support the war efforts of their respective states. When it came to war, national solidarity trumped socialist solidarity. The historian of the Socialist Internationals, Julius Braunthal, mourned the decision of the French and German socialists to support their governments, describing it as a 'mortal bow' to the International:

> It fell, the first victim of the world war. It had been conceived of as a brotherhood, uniting the workers of all countries in a spirit of solidar-

ity for the joint struggle against the ruling classes. Now the Socialist parties of the belligerent countries were making common cause with their own ruling classes, which bore the sole responsibility for the war ... The bond of brotherhood between the nations had been broken and the spirit of international solidarity of the working classes superseded by a spirit of national solidarity between the proletariat and the ruling classes. (Braunthal 1967a: 355)

The consequences of this debacle were shattering for international socialism and for the class struggle model of solidarity, which linked the particular goals of the working class with the universal aim of human emancipation.

Liberal solidarity

It is to France again that we turn for the first explicit liberal theorisation of social solidarity, in the work of Emile Durkheim, and the first major liberal political movement to make the call for solidarity its key theme, the Radical Party, led by Léon Bourgeois (1851–1925). Durkheim, a founding father of the discipline of sociology, taught at the University of Bordeaux and later at the Sorbonne in Paris. His book *The Division of Labour in Society* (1893) was based on his first course of lectures in 1887–8, and was written and published at a time of intense social conflict in his native France. Durkheim argues that social solidarity, the binding together of individuals in society, is a normal product of the increased division of labour (Durkheim 1964: 353). The argument sounds counter-intuitive, for the research question he posed himself asks how an individual could become more autonomous and yet at the same time more dependent on society, more individual and yet at the same time more solidary:

> This is the problem we are raising. It appears to us that what resolved this apparent antinomy is the transformation of social solidarity due to the steadily growing development of the division of labour. (Durkheim 1964: 37–8)

There are in fact two questions here rather than one. That the division of labour produces greater inter-dependence is hardly at issue, but that it produces social solidarity is more questionable. In making this case, Durkheim to some extent follows the argument of Auguste Comte (1798–1857), but also makes a decisive innovation (Lukes 1973: 140–4; Crow 2002: 12–18). Comte accepted that the division of labour increased inter-dependence by physically bringing people closer together, but he also considered that it had a natural tendency to weaken the bonds of community. Durkheim goes further than Comte in suggesting that the division of labour *naturally* produces social solidarity, and that the social divisions of modern society were abnormalities that could be overcome.

Durkheim contrasts what he terms the 'organic' solidarity of modern societies with the 'mechanical' solidarity exhibited in pre-modern ones. Mechanical solidarity is based on 'likeness' (Durkheim 1964: 70), that is to say, on shared life experience, beliefs and sentiments, enforced by strict moral codes. It is reflected in repressive law which punishes refusal to comply with custom and belief. Durkheim uses the term 'collective conscience' to denote the totality of beliefs and sentiments common to the members of a society (Durkheim 1964: 79–80). 'Conscience' in this sense combines the meaning of consciousness, indicating knowledge and awareness, and conscience, indicating a pre-conscious moral feeling for right and wrong. In mechanical solidarity the collective conscience developed around an incontrovertible revealed religion (Durkheim 1964: 92–93). In modern societies the development of a complex division of labour leads to greater individualism, and although this tends to weaken the collective conscience, it does not mean that the social will be sacrificed on the altar of egoism. Durkheim explicitly rejects Herbert Spencer's (1820–1903) idea that social harmony flows solely from contracts which regulate particular interests, arguing that 'if interest relates men, it is never for more than a few moments' (Durkheim 1964: 203). A society based on contracts can work only in so far as it establishes and develops a regulatory framework that is essentially social, drawing on custom, negotiation and coordination by the state.

In Durkheim's view, acting for the social good, or altruism, is the fundamental basis of social life, and 'men cannot live together without acknowledging, and consequently making mutual sacrifices, without tying themselves to one another with strong, durable bonds' (Durkheim 1964: 228). Although Durkheim uses the term 'organism', society does not comprise cells with defined and immutable roles as in nature, but develops dynamically, expanding the liberty of the individual and society's own 'suppleness' (Durkheim 1964: 329–30). Respect for individual dignity means that individuals choose to enter into solidaristic relations, for example in the family as well as in voluntary and occupational groups, and this infuses the collective life of the community. Individuals become conscious of their inter-dependence and actively support institutional frameworks which develop the vitality of social solidarity. Ultimately, Durkheim affirms the Aristotelian principle that human beings are rational because they are sociable (Durkheim 1964: 347). This organic solidarity, although based on the development of the division of labour and of individualism, has to be worked for, or built, as it is threatened by a number of 'abnormal' developments.

The final part of the book is devoted to a consideration of these abnormal forms of the division of labour which block the emergence of social solidarity (Durkheim 1964: 353–95). Durkheim depicts three abnormal forms – anomie, inequality and inefficient organisation. Anomie is best understood as loss of morale (Sennett 2012: 257), either at an individual or at a social level, and he uses it to describe the consequences of the anarchy of the market, an anarchy manifested in recurring industrial crises and class struggles between capital and labour. Implicitly, Durkheim assumes that this strife can be resolved by social regulation. In the absence of regulation, new conflicts will continually reappear (Durkheim 1964: 365). Additionally, the strict demarcation of roles in class society means that the worker risks being turned into an automaton with no prospects of developing his or her potential. Education is one way of addressing this, but more generally Durkheim saw the need for much greater social mobility (Durkheim 1964: 371–2).

The enormous inequality that existed in contemporary industrial society impeded the development of social solidarity. Durkheim was not impressed by the appearance of fair exchange in the labour contract, regarding it as immoral that exploitative contracts were forced on the weak (Durkheim 1964: 388). The implication is that the state would have to organise redistribution through taxation, or ensure fair contracts through legislation. Finally, Durkheim says, while the division of labour normally produces greater efficiency, there are times when it can hinder social solidarity because it is restrictive and wasteful. Restrictive practices of various sorts reproduce inefficiency, hierarchy and wasteful bureaucracy. Despite these powerful causes of social division, Durkheim felt confident enough to conclude that the division of labour produces solidarity, not only because it encourages exchange and inter-dependence, but because 'it creates among men an entire system of rights and duties which link them together in a durable way' (Durkheim 1964: 406).

Although Durkheim was at pains to present his work as scientific, the empirical evidence in the book is slight and selective, and to the modern reader it appears to be a straightforward normative appeal to construct the mediating institutions and symbols necessary to redeem the assertion that social solidarity was a 'natural' development of the division of labour. In the preface to the second edition of the book, in 1902, he proposes a key role for occupational corporations as 'one of the essential bases of our political organisation' (Durkheim 1964: 27; Giddens 2006: 17–20). These associations are to act as coordinators of good practice, mediating between the state and the individual, 'a whole series of secondary groups near enough to the individuals to attract them strongly in their sphere of action and drag them, in this way, into the general torrent of social life' (Durkheim 1964: 28). In his professional life Durkheim worked hard to contribute to the development of a collective conscience around social republican principles, playing an active role as a public intellectual and being particularly influential in shaping higher education and training schoolteachers for the new secular educational system (Lukes 1973: 320–91).

Solidarity has been described as 'the official social philosophy of the Third Republic' in the period leading up to the First World War (Hayward 1961), but although the solidarist movement enjoyed a brief taste of power when Léon Bourgeois became Prime Minister for a few months in 1895–6, the government was not able to secure even the introduction of income tax to begin the redistribution required to move towards solidarity (Cobban 1974: 67). Solidarism was an attempt to overcome class antagonisms around a programme of social progress for all, so that individualism could be reconciled with a sense of collective responsibility (Hayward 1959: 269). Bourgeois produced its programmatic text, *Solidarity*, in 1896 (Bourgeois 2009), but the concrete achievements of the movement were limited. In fact, Durkheim's connections with the solidarists were not strong, and his political position was closer to socialism than political liberalism (Lukes 1973: 172–8; Stedman Jones 2001: 94; Giddens 2006: 46)). Durkheim objected strongly to the rampant inequalities and social injustices of his day, but in declaring these problems to be 'abnormalities' he was clearly setting himself against the 'class war' position that saw such phenomena as the inevitable outcome of capitalist relations of production. Durkheim argued his case against one of the leaders of revolutionary syndicalism, Hubert Lagardelle, in 1905, stressing that there was no incompatibility between patriotism and working-class goals, and that it was entirely possible that the political and legal institutions could evolve in such a way as to regulate the economy and remove the injustices (Lukes 1973: 542–6). The revolutionary syndicalists thought they had thoroughly rejected the entreaties of Bourgeois and his solidarity movement to embrace reform, as Georges Sorel makes clear in *Reflections on Violence* when he writes that 'the proletariat replied to him by denying, in the most brutal fashion, the social compact, by denting the duty of patriotism' (Sorel

1999: 183–4). Sorel's conviction that the workers had turned their backs on patriotism proved to be misplaced, however, and the enthusiastic response to the call to arms in 1914 confirmed Durkheim's insight that there was a collective conscience, manifested in the conviction that the integrity of France had been violated (Gildea 1996: 143–4).

This issue of nationalism is an important one for the theme of this book. Durkheim quite clearly saw it as vital in strengthening the collective conscience, and was greatly impressed by the national solidarity displayed in France during the war. It was vitally important for Durkheim that France was fighting for democracy against the regimes of Germany and Austria that were 'established and maintained by force'. Indeed, he argued for an 'abominable paradox', namely, that war, apparently spelling the death of the pacific ideal, could really constitute its triumph if it resulted in victory for the democratic states (Lukes 1973: 547–54). So, even though Durkheim's focus is on the nation state in his work on social solidarity, the possibility of extending it across nations is present. In *The Division of Labour* he notes that 'strict nationalism always results in a protectionist spirit . . . a tendency of peoples to isolate themselves from one another economically and morally' (Durkheim 1964: 281). He openly talks in the book's conclusion about the possibility of the formation of a single human society, commenting that the greater expansion of 'higher' societies tends to overcome what he terms 'moral diversity' (Durkheim 1964: 406). At the Paris Universal Exposition of 1900 Durkheim declared that while we have special obligations to our country, beyond the country 'there is another in the process of formation, enveloping our national country: that of Europe, or humanity' (Lukes 1973: 350). David Inglis and Roland Robertson have argued that it is possible to detect an embryonic global project in Durkheim's work, and although the evidence is sparse, they point out that in the final part of his *Elementary Forms of Religious Life* he talks about forms of religious thinking that transcend societal boundaries and contribute to the creation of wider societies and, ultimately, an 'inherently international collective life' (Inglis and Robertson 2008: 19). In other words, he was open to the idea of a new moral universalism.

Liberal solidarity was not simply a French phenomenon, for it was implicit in the social liberalism developed in Britain and elsewhere. The dire social consequences of free-market economic liberalism made it clear to theorists such as John Stuart Mill (1806–73), T. H. Green (1836–82) and Henry Jones (1852–1922) that the state had a duty to intervene in order for the liberal ideal of individual development to become a substantive possibility for all citizens. Their influence on the activists who established the principles of what later became the welfare state was immense (Bellamy 1992; Boucher and Vincent 2000). Social liberalism involved an explicit reaching out to include the working class in a new form of harmonious citizenship, and many of the theorists involved placed special emphasis on the merits of education to achieve this. They were, more often than not, fired by a strong ethical commitment, and we can see in this an affinity with the ethico-inclusive model of working-class solidarity, in which socialism is regarded as a rational development and realisation of liberal principles.

National solidarity

The popular patriotic fervour which greeted the call to arms in August 1914 showed that in the face of perceived external threat, national solidarity trumped class solidarity. Few people had argued with conviction that international socialism was in any position to prevent war, even though that proposition had been discussed at every congress of the Second International, but the positive support given to the war effort by the leaders of the socialist parties of the principal protagonists proved to be a decisive moment in the unravelling of international socialist solidarity.

How can we understand the strength of patriotic feelings exhibited in 1914? Although there had been discussions about the idea of the nation throughout the nineteenth century, serious analysis of what constitutes a nation and what accounts for nationalist sentiment was a relatively late starter, dating back only to Ernest Renan's celebrated essay, 'What Is a Nation?', in 1882. Renan defines a nation as 'a large-scale solidarity', and comments that this is based on the constant expressed desire to continue a common life, a process he likened to a 'daily plebiscite' (Renan 2010: 19). In the twentieth and twenty-first centuries, explanations of the strength of national identity have wavered between those which stress the deep-rootedness of common bonds in ethnic or cultural terms, and those which stress its social construction in modernity through identifiable processes of socialisation. From the first perspective, the deep divisions in French society outlined in the previous section can be seen as differences within a culture in which, notwithstanding those differences, there is broad agreement on what constitutes its territory, commitment to a public education system stressing national ideals, and devotion to the French language (Smith 1991: 13). Nevertheless, even the agreement on French territory is revealed as fundamentally a nineteenth-century creation (Hobsbawm 1990: 91), while other binding myths, such as the Bastille Day national holiday, the cult of Joan of Arc and the acquisition of colonies, were all products of the late nineteenth century (Gildea 1996: 38–40, 121, 156–8). Throughout Europe, the extension of elementary education and the growth of popular newspapers and mass entertainment all contributed to the construction of strong national identities, in a variety of forms. In Britain, for example, there was a strong focus on the monarchy and empire (Stedman Jones 1983: 179–238).

The binding power of nationalism was manifested in the bloodletting of the two world wars of the twentieth century, extraordinary, as Benedict Anderson observed, 'for the colossal numbers persuaded to lay down their lives' (Anderson 1991: 144; cf. Hutchinson 2007). However, although national solidarity has often been invoked and displayed at times of war, in peacetime it has been used as a mobilising force in two distinct and antithetical forms: first in struggles for national liberation, second in fascism. One of the earliest uses of the term 'national solidarity' came in 1850 from Giuseppe Mazzini, when appealing to Italians to support the cause of a united independent state (Mazzini 1966: 175). Mazzini's vision always encompassed more than just his native Italy, and he was a consistent supporter of national democratic movements elsewhere in Europe. His ideal was a cooperative world of democratic republics (Recchia and Urbinati 2009: 16–22; Mazzini 2010: 132–40). He devoted most of his life to the cause of Italian unification, founding the Young Italy movement but also supporting similar organisations for Polish and German unity, and arguing for a United States of Europe. This form of liberal nationalism was an important feature of European politics in the nineteenth and early twentieth century, when the struggles for self-determination helped to secure cross-class support in countries that saw statehood as a prerequisite for social and political freedom (Smith 1991: 59–61). Outside Europe, the anti-colonial movements helped to create forms of nationalism that associated national independence with social liberation (Smith 1991: 106–22).

National solidarity has been invoked in the most aggressive way by anti-democratic movements, conventionally termed 'fascist' after Benito Mussolini's original party that seized power in Italy in 1922. According to our normative definition of solidarity, with its trajectory of ever-greater social inclusion, fascism's claim to national unity is illusory. Fascism is based on the exclusion of all political and social opposition to the regime, and, more seriously in the case of the Nazis in Germany, on the exclusion and elimination of whole groups defined in terms of race, sexual orientation and mental and physical health. However, if we adopt a purely descriptive meaning of solidarity to denote any form of strong group allegiance, then it is possible to speak in terms of a fascist model of solidarity, based on the subordination of all individuals to the state (Stjernø 2005: 278–83). The principal means for achieving this were the unchallenged authority of a mass ruling party and the transmission of policy through corporations of employers and employees that were fully under the control of the state. This appearance of inclusivity in the fascist model was achieved through coercion, giving the members of the ruling party a sense of power while reducing the mass of people to powerlessness. The corporatist language of fascism was a veneer on a totally authoritarian socio-political system and is therefore incompatible with any models of social solidarity based on democratic negotiation and consent.

Communism

The class struggle model of solidarity emphasised the development of socialist parties and other working-class organisations struggling to achieve state power in order to socialise the economy and trigger an international transformation. Solidarity was essential to the practice of class struggle, and the goal of international human emancipation lent this struggle a universal dimension. The damage done to this ideal by the decision of the European socialist and labour parties to support the war efforts of their states can be gauged by the judgement of Rosa Luxemburg (1871–1919), one of the leaders of the German socialists, expressed in 1916:

> The World War has destroyed the results of forty years' labour of European socialism by destroying the moral prestige of socialism and the significance of the revolutionary working class as a factor of political power, by breaking the proletarian International, leading its sections to mutual fratricide and chaining the wishes and hopes of the masses in the most important countries of capitalist development to the ship of imperialism. (Luxemburg 1971: 346–7)

Angered by what she perceived as a betrayal, Luxemburg called for the creation of a new workers' international based on the worldwide solidarity of workers, with executive authority over national sections on issues of foreign and trade policy; any national party that failed to submit to this authority was to be expelled (Luxemburg 1971: 350). This would mean an inevitable split in the international working-class movement between left-wing socialists and reformists, now branded by the Left as 'national liberals'. Such a schism would constitute a major blow to the class struggle model of solidarity, which had been built on the declaration in *The Communist Manifesto* that communists 'do not form a separate party as opposed to other working class parties', nor do they 'set up any sectarian principles of their own by which to shape and mould the proletarian movement' (Marx 2010a: 79). The schism, however, was assured once the Russian Bolsheviks, led by V. I. Lenin, seized power in November 1917 and held on to it against all the odds.

We shall never know how Luxemburg would have reacted to the creation of the Third International, for she was murdered during a revolutionary uprising led by the newly formed German Communist Party, against a government led by German Social Democrats, in January 1919 (Braunthal 1967b: 118–32). This armed conflict between revolutionary and reformist socialists marked the beginning of a split in world socialism that was to last for more than seventy years. When the new International convened, in Moscow in March of that year, it was clear from its programme that reformist socialists would not be welcome. The twenty-one points adopted at the second congress in 1920 demanded the removal of all reformers and centrists from all positions of responsibility, and accused the old official social democratic or socialist parties of having 'betrayed the banner of the working class' (Braunthal 1967b: 162–8, 537–42). The Bolsheviks, seeking to draw a clear line between revolutionaries and reformists, adopted the name 'communist', as favoured by Marx and Engels; they became the Communist Party of the Soviet Union, and communist parties developed throughout Europe and later throughout the world. They claimed to be the real inheritors of Marx's theories, although it is inconceivable that Marx could have thought it responsible to seize power in a country in which the urban working class formed a tiny minority. The mass of the peasantry had already declared their support for the Social Revolutionary Party in the election at the end of 1917 that produced the Constituent Assembly, in which the Bolsheviks won only a quarter of the seats. The Assembly was dissolved by the Bolsheviks after its first sitting in January 1918, and all other political parties were banned in 1921.

The theoretical arguments behind this calamitous split in world socialism can be found in the exchange between Lenin and the German socialist theoretician Karl Kautsky (1854–1938) (Townshend 1996: 82–92). In *The State and Revolution*, written in the summer of 1917, Lenin prepared the way for the Bolshevik seizure of power by arguing that the dictatorship of the proletariat 'cannot lead simply to an expansion of democracy' and that it would involve the suppression of the liberties of 'the oppressors, the exploiters, the capitalists'. Nevertheless, despite criticising the shortcomings of 'democracy for the rich' as practised under liberalism, he promised 'democracy for the gigantic majority of the people' (Lenin 1992: 79–80). Kautsky's criticisms of the authoritarianism of the Bolsheviks were published in 1918 as *The Dictatorship of the Proletariat*, in which he argued that without democracy 'socialism as a means towards the liberation of the proletariat is inconceivable' (Kautsky 1983: 99). Socialism, he claimed, presupposes numerous free economic and political organisations, and was incompatible with the organisation of labour 'modelled on a military barracks' (Kautsky 1983: 119). In his splenetic reply, *The Proletarian Revolution and the Renegade Kautsky*, Lenin claimed that soviet power was 'a million times more democratic than the most democratic bourgeois republic' (Lenin 1977: 33). In the soviet system, 'bourgeois democracy' was to be replaced by a 'higher form' of democracy based on workers' councils or 'soviets', but in practice their functions were quickly replaced by the dictatorship of the party-state.

When Stalin established unrivalled power in the late 1920s, democracy within the party was entirely destroyed, and an authoritarian model was swiftly imposed on all communist parties, under tight control from the leaders in Moscow. The authoritarianism was backed with terroristic methods, even against elements within the parties, to the extent that most of the original leaders of the Russian Revolution were executed by Stalin's regime. When communist power was forcibly installed in the states of eastern Europe after the Second World War, the model of the authoritarian party dictatorship was followed, accompanied by party purges that resulted in the execution of party leaders convicted of trumped-up charges.

Throughout the existence of Soviet communism the fiction that it represented 'true democracy' was maintained. It was trumpeted in the final constitution of the Soviet Union, adopted in 1977, and the states held under the tutelage of the communist parties in eastern Europe were named 'people's democracies', with no hint of irony. Most of the ruling parties in eastern Europe were termed 'socialist' because they had incorporated old social democratic parties, and the dictatorial system was often known as 'actually existing socialism' (Bahro 1984). This perversion of socialism, emptied of its democratic and humanistic content, did enormous damage to the reputation of a doctrine that had placed solidarity as its guiding principle.

As Steinar Stjernø has observed, 'discipline' and 'unity' were more frequently invoked terms than 'solidarity' under communism (Stjernø 2005: 266–7). The policies of the Third International changed in accordance with Soviet foreign policy, and the bizarre changes of position were imposed on all parties and party members, often with no explanation even attempted. Prior to the rise of Adolf Hitler, communists considered their principal enemy to be social democrats, denouncing them as 'social imperialists' and 'social fascists'. In Germany, the Communist Party (KPD) was jubilant at every setback for the SPD. In November 1932, at the last free election before Hitler's assumption of power, the two left-wing parties together attracted one-and-a-half million more votes than the Nazis, but both were swept away without serious resistance within months of the Hitler dictatorship (Braunthal 1967b: 364–90). It was not until 1935 that the Third International decided that it should cooperate with socialist and other democratic forces against the threat of fascism, even working with the Labour and Socialist International, which represented the social democratic parties (Braunthal 1967b: 470–1). Communist parties everywhere were suddenly at the forefront of anti-fascist politics, and agitated for preparation to defeat fascism in the war that seemed inevitable.

The moral hollowness of the Soviet leadership of the International became evident when Hitler invaded Poland and the war began, in September 1939. It was revealed within weeks that a friendship and non-aggression pact had been made between Nazi Germany and the Soviet Union, and the Soviets occupied the eastern parts of Poland. Communist parties everywhere were ordered to drop their anti-fascist position and denounce the war as an inter-imperialist conflict. The small Communist Party of Great Britain provides a good illustration of this amazing volte-face. Shortly after the invasion of Poland the party leader, Harry Pollitt, issued a pamphlet, *How to Win the War*, but the day it appeared a telegram arrived from Moscow issuing the order that the war must be opposed. Pollitt was forced to resign and a new pamphlet was issued denouncing the war (Beckett 1998: 90–101). Communists throughout the world, having encouraged war against fascism, now opposed it, until, in June 1941, Hitler attacked the Soviet Union. The communists were then able to throw all their energies into supporting the war effort, and Pollitt was restored to office. In fact, the energetic war efforts of the communists greatly increased their popular following, although only in Italy and France did they go on to attract more electoral support than the socialist parties in the post-war period.

The military victory of the Soviet Union and the implantation of communist regimes in eastern Europe appeared to secure a basis for developing the international battle with capitalism. The communist camp was enlarged by the victory of the Chinese communists in 1949, adding to this picture of a world movement based on the social ownership of the means of production that could offer an alternative model of development to newly industrialising states. There were, however, two profound and closely related problems that blocked the rise of communism as a world movement: economic efficiency and political paralysis.

In economic terms, the Soviet command economy, in which

the market was replaced by production planned and delivered by the state, succeeded in creating an industrialised society with enormous growth rates in the 1930s, at a time when market failures produced the Great Depression and mass unemployment in most parts of the capitalist world (Wilde 1994a: 121–6). The concentration on mass production of iron, steel and coal stood the Soviets in good stead in the military conflict with Germany, but the costs of the conflict were felt for many years after the war. Even then, the Soviets found it extremely difficult to improve the consumer sector of the economy. Economic reform became a recurring theme from the death of Stalin in 1953 until the disintegration of the Soviet Union in 1991 (Wilde 1994a: 127–37). The planned economy provided full employment, good levels of education and health care, and the provision of basic goods, but it could not compete with the market economies of the West in terms of the variety, volume and quality of consumer goods. Ironically, the disparity between the two systems grew to crisis proportions as a result of capitalism's response to the economic crisis that erupted in the late 1970s. The emergence of globalization, accompanied by the opening up of markets and the expansion of multinational corporations using computer technology, led to productivity gains in the capitalist world that the planned economies could not even begin to match. Right up to the end of the Gorbachev years the Soviet government sought in vain to make its currency, the rouble, convertible with the dollar. In China, since 1978 the ruling Communist Party has progressively introduced private ownership and a market economy without surrendering its monopoly of political power, producing sustained high economic growth and full integration into the world economy (Harvey 2009: 120–51).

Communist supporters in western Europe engaged in solidaristic activities in trade unions, community groupings and international campaigns, often supporting national liberation struggles. Before 1956, many denied the tyrannical nature of the Soviet regime, declaring criticisms of it to be no more than Cold War propaganda. Others acknowledged that there was no democracy within the system, but hoped that it would develop at some later date. The revelations made by the new Soviet leader, Nikita Khrushchev, at the twentieth congress of the KPSS in 1956, that Stalin had been responsible for the murder and imprisonment of tens of thousands of fellow party members, led many members in the West to reconsider their loyalty. Later in the year, when Hungary tried to leave the Soviet bloc and adopt democracy, its occupation by Soviet troops led to a mass exodus from the western European parties (Braunthal 1980: 428). It became even more difficult for democratic communists in the West to defend the Soviet system when the Soviet leadership ordered the military invasion of Czechoslovakia in 1968 to suppress a hugely popular reform movement initiated by the Communist Party and its leader, Alexander Dubček (Dawisha 1984). Most communist movements in the Western democracies felt the need to assert a distance between themselves and the Soviet Union, adopting 'Eurocommunism' in order to acknowledge the permanence of the institutions of representative democracy (Townshend 1996: 177–200; Simon 2007). In doing so they effectively renounced their uncritical association with the Soviet model of socialism, clinging to hopes that it would somehow democratise itself. Those hopes were revived in 1985 when Mikhail Gorbachev assumed power, but his reforms unleashed forces totally opposed to the communist system, leading to the collapse of communist rule in eastern Europe in 1989 and the disintegration of the Soviet Union in 1991 (Wilde 1994a: 132–9).

Ironically, given the importance of the concept of solidarity in the history of socialism, it was the spontaneous eruption of a Polish trade union movement calling itself Solidarity that played a pivotal role in the demise of the communist dictatorships in Europe (Kamiński 1991; Wilde 1994a: 155–62). Trade unions in all communist states were part of the party-state apparatus. After all, in the self-styled 'people's democracies' the working people theoretically controlled the state and the means of production and therefore had no class enemy to strike against. In practice, the Polish communist government felt powerless to control an economic crisis which involved high levels of international debt, and Solidarity expressed the overwhelming rejection of communist dictatorship by the Polish people. It originated in a strike in August 1980 in the Lenin shipyard in Gdańsk provoked by the victimisation of one of the workers. Lech Wałęsa, who had been dismissed four years earlier for his agitation for workers' rights, quickly became the leading figure, and the strikers formulated twenty-one demands, crucially including the right to form a union independent of the ruling communist party (the PZPR) and the state. Three weeks later the Solidarity trade union was formally launched and spread like wildfire throughout Poland, claiming ten million members by the time it was legally sanctioned by the Supreme Court in 1981 (Touraine *et al.* 1983: 196–201). Amazingly, one million members of the PZPR joined the union, reflecting the fundamentally socialist nature of many of the twenty-one demands. In addition to the demand for free trade unions there were also calls for open participation in a national reform programme, an end to privileges enjoyed by PZPR members, an end to political appointments in industry, the release of political prisoners, freedom of the press, reduced working hours, extended maternity leave, improvement of the health service and a lowering of the retirement age (Potel 1982: 219–20).

At the first Solidarity national congress in September and October 1981 there were more radical calls for free elections and workers' self-management of industry, but the leadership followed a more moderate line of self-limitation, choosing to act as a pressure group rather than threatening the communist grip on the state (Sanford 1990). This moderation was not enough to satisfy the PZPR, and the new party leader and Prime Minister, General Wojciech Jaruzelski, imposed martial law in December 1981, dissolving the union and jailing its leaders. Although martial law was lifted in 1983, the last of the political prisoners was not released until 1986, by which time the economic situation had deteriorated even further, and a wave of strikes in 1988 persuaded the regime to enter into 'round table' talks with Solidarity, leading to elections in 1989 that quickly produced the downfall of the communist regime and its replacement with a government dominated by prominent union members. Once it was established that Gorbachev's Soviet regime was not prepared to repeat the military interventions of Hungary in 1956 and Czechoslovakia in 1968, the majority of citizens in the other communist states of eastern Europe took their cue from Poland, overthrowing their communist governments and ushering in political democracy and market capitalism.

Although Solidarity played an important role in government in the early post-communist years, its popularity plummeted when the hardships produced by the sudden transition to a market economy became severe after Wałęsa's election to the presidency in December 1990. Sharp divisions within the movement quickly appeared and, amidst much acrimony, the movement disintegrated as a political force (Crow 2002: 102–5). The solidarity of Solidarity had come from two powerful sources, hatred of communist power and a vague but determined yearning for freedom, but once the 'enemy' had been removed, such a broad-based coalition could no longer be sustained. It served its purpose, and was by far the strongest civil society dissident movement to appear in any of the communist states.

One of the curious aspects of the movement was its adoption of the word 'solidarity' in a society in which the vocabulary of communism and socialism had exhausted its attraction. This may be explained by the strength of Catholicism in Poland, boosted by the election of the first Polish Pope, John Paul II, in 1978. His visit to Poland in 1979 gave encouragement to the Polish people, and he affirmed the importance of solidarity as a Catholic principle. In his encyclical in 1981, written when Solidarity was still legal, he emphasised the justice of solidarity among workers fighting exploitation and insecurity, and in later encyclicals in 1989 and 1991 he elevated it to the status of a key concept of Catholic thought (Stjernø 2005: 70–5).

The revolutions of 1989 and the disintegration of the Soviet Union in 1991 marked the end of communism as an effective political force in Europe. It is tempting to think that the anger that Lenin put into his denunciation of the 'renegade' Kautsky really expressed his own awareness of the impossible predicament he found himself in. He had ignored Marx's dictum that a social revolution could take place only when it was clear that a superior social system was readily available:

> No social order is ever destroyed before all the productive forces for which it is sufficient have been developed, and new superior relations of production never replace older ones before the material conditions for their existence have matured within the framework of the old society. (Marx 1975: 426)

Although the seizure of power by a workers' party excited enthusiasm throughout the world, without democracy the degeneration of the communist model into tyranny was inevitable, as Kautsky had foreseen. Millions of people around the world stayed loyal to the communist family for much of the twentieth century, for it seemed to represent the only feasible alternative to capitalism. This did not necessarily reflect support for the Soviet system, but rather a belief that in the global battle for supremacy between capitalism and communism, something good had to come out of the Russian Revolution or all was lost. In everyday struggles on behalf of working people and their communities, communists contributed to putting solidarity into practice, but they were never able to escape the suspicion that for communists, democracy was dispensable, and without democracy there can be no social solidarity.

The welfare state as social solidarity

Emile Durkheim's vision of social solidarity stood in stark contrast to the reality of social relations in all the leading industrial countries at the end of the nineteenth century. The 'pathologies' dividing society described in the final part of *The Division of Labour*, particularly the conflict between capital and labour, were rife, and Durkheim's conviction that solidarity was a 'natural' development appeared to be without foundation (Durkheim 1964: 353–409). However, within fifty years of his death in 1917 most of the countries of western Europe, North America and Australasia had developed welfare states, embracing social protection and free education, with civil societies vigorously populated with the sort of voluntary associations he had advocated (Durkheim 1964: 1–31). This raises the question as to whether the welfare state, at least in its most egalitarian form, is the embodiment of social solidarity, as commentators such as Gøsta Esping-Anderson (1990: 9–35) and Peter Baldwin (1999: 47–54) have argued. First, however, we must account for the social transformation achieved in these societies in the mid-twentieth century.

The pressure on the state to take a greater responsibility for the welfare of its citizens came both from the organised labour movement and from elements of the middle class adopting a social-liberal outlook. The end of the nineteenth century and the beginning of the twentieth saw a massive upsurge in working-class trade union and party-political activity that not only strengthened the bargaining power of labour in the economy but also began to threaten the domination of political power by the propertied classes. The organised labour movement was pressing simultaneously for political inclusion, in terms of voting rights for all men and women, and for social rights. Additionally, the specific discrimination against women generated a militant women's movement demanding the vote, and women secured voting rights in Britain, the United States and Germany after the First World War, and in France after the Second World War. The efforts of women during those conflicts created an irresistible pressure for political inclusion (Dubois 1991: 20–44). Writing during the establishment of a comprehensive welfare state in Britain after the Second World War, the academic sociologist T. H. Marshall depicted the achievement of social rights as part of a historical trajectory in the development of citizenship. It had begun in the sixteenth and seventeenth centuries with the establishment of civil rights, such as the right to a fair trial and the rights of association and free speech, then progressed to the achievement of political rights in the struggle for democracy in the nineteenth and early twentieth centuries, culminating in the establishment of social rights, as manifested in the welfare state (Marshall 1973: 65–123).

The demands from groups who considered themselves excluded politically and socially were accompanied by a growing consciousness of the enormity of social distress in the industrialised world. In Britain, for example, the first systematic studies of poverty, conducted by Charles Booth in London (1892) and Seebohm Rowntree in York (1901), revealed that about 30 per cent of the population were living in poverty (D. Fraser 2009: 163–5, 342–5). The Liberal government of 1905 introduced limited measures of social insurance and old-age pensions, a clear indication that the principle of the duty of the state to secure the welfare of all its citizens was eclipsing the traditional attachment to the principles of *laissez-faire* economic liberalism (D. Fraser 2009: 175–208). In the United States, Henry George's *Progress and Poverty* (1879) and Edward Bellamy's utopian novel *Looking Backward* (1888) created enormous controversy with their denunciations of the extremes of poverty and wealth, and this gave rise to the National Party movement, which helped put social reform on the political agenda (Bellamy 1982; George 2006). In Germany in the 1880s the authoritarian government of Otto von Bismarck adopted a dual approach of coercion and pacification. Between 1878 and 1890 it banned socialist parties, but also introduced the first national social insurance scheme for workers, albeit one that gave miserly benefits paid for by compulsory contributions from the workers themselves (Baldwin 1999: 96–9). The measures failed to halt the impressive electoral progress of the German Social Democrats, but they provide an early example of 'top down' welfarism, in contrast with the 'bottom up' gains extracted by strong social democratic movements in Scandinavia, based on universal benefits paid for out of progressive taxation (Baldwin 1999: 55–94; Stjernø 2005: 109–18). This solidaristic approach was the model for the comprehensive welfare state introduced in Britain by the Labour government after the Second World War, based on the Beveridge report, published in December 1942.

William Beveridge (1879–1963) was a social liberal who had worked on the welfare reforms introduced by the Liberal government before the First World War. The thirst for reform was clearly indicated by the enormous demand for the report, which sold 635,000 copies, and the commitment was not limited simply to social insurance but the whole range of social problems that required comprehensive state intervention. Derek Fraser rightly sees this as a radical shift in ideological outlook:

> A country whose history had been so much concerned with freedom, the freedom *to* speak, *to* write, *to* vote, was now being given a new lesson in liberty; true freedom lay in freedom *from* want, *from* disease, *from* ignorance, *from* squalor and *from* idleness. Here, in the totality of the vision, was the revolutionary element of the Beveridge Report. (D. Fraser 2009: 255, original emphasis)

The principle adopted was an equal and universal entitlement to benefits based on insurance contributions, rather than a means-tested system in which individuals were subjected to the humiliation of proving their helplessness. Adequate pensions, unemployment pay, family allowances, the National Health Service and a commitment to policies producing full employment were all part of the 'cradle to grave' security guarantee. Britain, along with Sweden, was in the vanguard of promoting the welfare state, and the model was adopted in various forms by all major democratic states by the 1970s (Pierson 1991: 111–40). The commitment to complete social responsibility for individual wellbeing was clearly weaker in liberal welfare systems, such as the United States and Canada, than those classified as interventionist social democratic ones, such as Sweden, Denmark and Norway (Esping-Anderson 1990: 26–33; Pierson 1991: 184–7; Jessop 2002: 61–8). However, even though these states were held up to be paragons of social solidarity, in the 'golden age' of social democracy in the 1960s and 1970s, it needs to be asked whether in fact they displayed genuine social solidarity, and why welfare state systems have come under so much pressure in the era of globalization.

One way of addressing these questions is to look at alternative explanations of how the welfare states emerged, whether as concessions from elites or the results of intensive struggles from the working class. Peter Baldwin terms the concessions-from-above approach 'Bonapartist', after the palliative reforms offered by Napoleon III during the French Second Empire and typified by the Bismarck policies mentioned above (Baldwin 1999: 39–40). In this view, welfare guarantees are introduced by ruling elites to placate the disaffected and dissuade them from pressing for more radical change. In contrast, it is possible to explain the emergence of the welfare state as the result of the power of organised labour to secure an egalitarian 'peace formula' from the class struggle (Offe 1984: 147). Baldwin terms this the 'social' explanation, whereby welfare reforms are forced out of the state through relentless pressure from below, through a combination of economic and political and industrial struggle (Baldwin 1999: 40–4). This interpretation would cite the triumphs of the Swedish Social Democrats (SAP) from the 1930s on, and the Labour government in Britain after the Second World War, as decisive moments.

As Baldwin points out, the success of social democracy would not account for the early establishment of welfarism in the Netherlands, with a small socialist presence, or its later development in France, where the Left was polarised and out of power during the period when the welfare state developed. It also ignores the fact that the first agreements on which the welfare state developed in states such as Sweden and Britain took place prior to the success of their labour parties. Neither of these explanations is adequate, and instead Baldwin sees the evolution of the welfare state in terms of complex inter-relationships between class interests in which, at different stages of historical development, competing interests identify mutual benefits in agreeing to widespread state provision (Baldwin 1999: 288–99). Key historical developments, such as the emergence of political democracy and the experience of war and economic depression, play an important role, but ultimately it was tough negotiation between self-interested actors that produced the 'few instances' of solidaristic welfare states. Baldwin regards solidarity as 'the outcome of a generalised and reciprocal self-interest' and concludes that 'not ethics but politics explain it' (Baldwin 1999: 299).

Baldwin's conclusion is both persuasive and also somewhat misleading. It is persuasive because it dispels any complacency that the welfare state is based on a resolute moral consensus. If the welfare state emerged from a process of complex negotiation and compromise, it can be strengthened or weakened according to the changing balance of class forces. This is precisely what has happened since the return of mass unemployment in the late 1970s. However, it is also misleading to consider that ethics plays no part in securing outcomes. 'Interests' are not simply structurally determined reflections of economic positions, and in practice the articulation of interests is extremely complex. Forging alliances and making compromises is facilitated by a variety of historical and cultural factors, often expressed in explicitly ethical terms, as, for example, in the religious contributions to debates about social solidarity (Stjernø 2005: 60–92). The processes of organising and expressing interests and formulating social goals are infused with values, so although ethics may not explain the emergence of solidaristic social arrangements, it is an indispensable part of the process. Ongoing struggles to secure changes in welfare systems, such as the passage of the Patient Protection and Affordable Care Act in the United States in 2010, are conducted explicitly in ethical terms concerning the limits of social and individual responsibility and the principles on which the society is based. As Durkheim said in the conclusion to *The Division of Labour*,

> everything which is a source of solidarity is moral, everything which forces man to take account of other men is moral, everything which forces him to regulate his conduct through something other than the striving of his ego is moral, and morality is as solid as these ties are numerous and strong. (Durkheim 1964: 398)

When put in these explicitly moral terms, which requires a high level of reflexive consciousness in constructing social solidarity, possibly only Sweden, Denmark and Norway qualified as strong solidaristic societies. In Sweden, for example, there was a clear commitment to solidarity, manifested in the most comprehensive welfare system seen anywhere, financed by high levels of taxation (Milner 1989: 186–212). Yet even in Sweden various social groups started to see themselves as competitors when the pressure to maintain growth rates began to undermine the system in the 1980s (Wilde 1994b: 196–9). In most states, however, welfare systems often coexisted with educational systems in which different social classes went to different schools, protecting class privilege and impeding equality of opportunity. Ralph Miliband's study *The State in Capitalist Society* argues convincingly that social hierarchies were being reproduced irrespective of social democratic advances (Miliband 1969).

Patriarchal assumptions were also built into the welfare state, particularly in benefit systems that preserved women's dependence within a family led by a male breadwinner (Lister 1997: 173–5). An array of discriminations faced women in post-war society, including lower pay for the same jobs as men, formal or informal prohibitions from entering an array of occupations, and, in some states, restrictions on the rights of married women to own property. As Ruth Lister points out, when T. H. Marshall drew his trajectory of citizens' rights from civil to political and then to social, his gender blindness prevented him from seeing that women achieved political rights before achieving full civil rights (Lister 1997: 68). So, even in societies marked by full employment and high levels of welfare, explicit and institutional discrimination was rife, not just on grounds of gender but also on the bases of race, age, disability, sexual orientation and religion. Traditional forms of solidarity based on occupation, class or community did not meet the requirement of our normative definition of solidarity to embrace full social inclusion, too often reproducing hierarchical social strata and remaining insensitive to the new needs of increasingly pluralist societies. Additionally, as Kurt Bayertz has argued, the principle of welfare provision by impersonal bureaucracies lacks the 'motivated care' associated with personal services. In turning care into a depersonalised, low-paid service, Bayertz suggests that aspects of welfare provision are prone to a form of de-moralisation (Bayertz 1999: 24).

It is possible that the welfare state could have responded creatively and solidaristically to the new identities and the needs they expressed, if full employment and economic growth had continued unabated. However, the re-emergence of mass unemployment against a background of high inflation saw the end of the 'Keynesian' model of economic management, named after the famous British economist John Maynard Keynes (1883–1946), which had previously shown the benefits of state borrowing and other interventions to secure prosperity. Since the 1980s, Keynesianism has been eclipsed by the free-market doctrine of neoliberalism, involving 'rolling back' the state and encouraging market forces in all walks of life. Naturally this has had important implications for social solidarity. Although the immediate pressure on the welfare state was for support for the unemployed, the accelerated global competition sparked by tariff reductions and expanding transnational corporations put immense pressure on governments to shape their economies so that they could attract inward investment and compete in the world market. This produced steep cuts in rates of taxation and tariffs and reduced funding for public expenditure on pensions, health care, education and social benefits. This transformation has been identified by Bob Jessop as a tendency to move from a 'welfare' state to a 'workfare' state, in which universal benefits are replaced by schemes that, for example, make benefits dependent on the applicants proving that they are actively seeking work, undertaking job preparation courses, or undergoing stringent tests to prove that they are incapable of paid employment. The workfare state sees public money as an investment in competitiveness by providing penalties and/or incentives to move people into productive work (Jessop 2002 152–71). In effect there has been a swing back to means-testing, accompanied by a rhetoric assailing welfare 'scroungers' and benefit fraudsters. Social policy is directed to pressuring people into finding some sort of work, even though high levels of unemployment reveal that there is precious little work available.

Perhaps the greatest blow to traditional forms of solidarity in the old industrialised countries under globalization has been dealt by the dramatic switch in economic activity from manufacturing to the service sector. The immediate result of this in the 1980s saw the closure of industries that had required skills from generations of workers and had provided the basis for strong communities. As coal, shipbuilding, steel and textiles closed down for good, so communities were devastated and assailed with a range of social problems that were beyond their dwindling solidaristic powers to control. Globalization has brought to the richest societies a major increase in inequality, with the effect of imposing social exclusion on the poorest section (Dorling 2010: 139–40; Bauman 2001: 92).

Zygmunt Bauman argues that the 'new poor' differ from the poor of other ages because they have no social role. In feudal societies, poverty was considered natural, but the existence of the poor at least demanded that the wealthy practised charity as the means of personal salvation. In capitalist society the poor became the reserve army of unemployed, a vital factor in the market economy, and although their lives were precarious, they were a part of the wider working-class community. The new poor, in contrast, are not groomed for future work, nor do they serve a function as useful consumers. They are 'now purely and simply a worry and a nuisance ... a black hole sucking in whatever comes near and spitting back nothing, except, perhaps, trouble' (Bauman 2001: 87–91). The new poor are seen as removed from mainstream society, the source of drug addiction, alcohol abuse and criminality. Often the 'problem' of the new poor is racialised, as is evident from the incarceration figures in the United States, where black men comprise approximately 40 per cent of the prison population compared with 12.6 per cent of the overall population; there are more black men in prison than there were slaves before emancipation (Alexander 2010). In France, the desperation of socially excluded young men of north African origin exploded in riots throughout the country in October and November 2005, leading to a three-month state of emergency and almost 3,000 arrests. In Britain, in the last three months of 2011, the rate of unemployment among young black people was 47.4 per cent, compared with 20.8 per cent for white youngsters. Over half of young black males were unemployed (Ball *et al.* 2012).

The 2008 financial crisis has increased the pressure on the welfare state. Cuts in welfare benefits and public services are justified by the need to reduce public deficits, and an ideological shift away from the principle of social responsibility for those in need of help has become noticeable in some parts of the affluent West. However, there is still a will to defend social inclusivity. Thomas Meyer's empirical analysis of institutional indicators of social inclusivity reveals six highly inclusive societies – Sweden, Denmark, Norway, Finland, the Netherlands and Austria – and five moderately inclusive – Switzerland, Germany, Japan, France and Belgium. The United Kingdom ranks lowest of the 'less inclusive' states, and the United States is classed as 'exclusive' or 'libertarian' (Meyer 2007: 213). There appears to be a determination to hold on to the commitment to social inclusion in continental Europe, as empirical studies have suggested (Alesina and Glaeser 2005; Pontusson 2005). The struggle against neoliberal attacks on welfarism in the UK and the USA takes on a pivotal importance, as without a supportive, enabling state, there is no hope for achieving social or global solidarity. Are there ways of reviving the principle of social responsibility for the welfare of all citizens? Although this issue will be dealt with in more detail in Chapter 7, at this stage it is important to assess what new forms of solidarity are in development that might open the way for a more caring society.

New forms of solidarity?

There can be no doubt that the restructuring of the world economy has not only produced a squeeze on welfare and the emergence of a swathe of 'new poor' in the affluent states, but has also increased the gap between the rich and poor throughout the world (see Chapter 7). Nevertheless, despite this alarming picture, the period in question has seen the rise of new forms of solidarity, in both the affluent societies and the developing world. In the West, radical new social movements have made enormous progress in demanding recognition of the rights of groups who have suffered prejudice and discrimination, and others that have demanded a new relationship between humanity and nature. The discriminations faced by women that persisted for decades after they had gained political rights were challenged with remarkable success by second-wave feminism, first striking down the legal impediments to equality, and then organising, more locally, to address the particular abuses faced by women in everyday life. In the sphere of sexual orientation, progress was made from a situation in which homosexuality was punishable by imprisonment in most countries in the Western world to one in which civil unions and same-sex marriage have become accepted. In confronting the scourge of racism, there has been progress from open segregation in the United States of the 1960s to the election of Barack Obama as the first black President in 2008, and, in South Africa, from apartheid in 1990s to the emergence of full political democracy. Within states, anti-racist organisations have exposed and challenged racism in all aspects of social life.

In dealing with the environment, from a position in the 1960s in which there was only marginal political interest in ecology, we have seen the explosion of green politics. The entry of the Greens into the German Bundestag in 1983 symbolised a significant shift in political priorities, bringing issues such as pollution, waste, deforestation and water supply to the forefront of policy debate (Dobson and Eckersley 2006; Carter 2007). Green politics has forced awareness of the danger that global warming holds for sustaining human life on earth, prompting radical new ways of thinking about alternative energy resources and putting pressure on governments to reach agreement on cutting greenhouse gas emissions. This reconsideration of human interaction with nature has led to new communities developing around issues of animal welfare groups, exposing the horrors of factory farming methods and experimentation with animals, and, in so doing, questioning the logic of an economics that puts profit above everything (Singer 1995, 2005; Francione and Garner 2010).

These struggles should not be categorised as either single-issue campaigns or expressions of narrow group self-interest, as Eric Hobsbawm once argued (Hobsbawm 1996: 38–47). He viewed collective identities as asserting themselves against others, and the proliferation of 'causes' as a sign of social fragmentation and a loss of the 'universalism' that was once embodied by the socialist movement. The problem with this perspective is that it denies in advance the possibility of articulating different struggles in the direction of ever-expanding social inclusion. The politics of new social movements can be seen as part of a wider movement for inclusivity and sustainability. Often these struggles go well beyond the defining aims of their group. For example, the women's peace camp outside the United States Air Force base at Greenham Common became a worldwide symbol of opposition to the deployment of nuclear weapons from 1981 until the removal of those weapons ten years later. Differences within new social movements have sometimes been fractious, but the sense of continuity in struggles for rights can generate a broad sense of solidarity among diverse groups. Ruth Lister has argued the case that shared exclusions experienced by all women should enable feminists to overcome factionalism through a 'politics of solidarity in difference' (Lister 1997: 200). This book suggests that this principle can be extended to all humanity.

One of the striking aspects of the politics of new social movements is that it quickly embraced a global dimension. The UN World Conference on Women in Beijing in 1995 brought together more than 4,000 representatives of women's groups around the world and it has been claimed that by the twenty-first century transnational campaigning had become the predominant form of feminist activism (Desai 2005: 319). International campaigns around a range of issues have developed, including legal and domestic violence against women, denial of human rights, and poor levels of health care and education, and often these campaigns are conducted with other progressive groups from outside the feminist 'family' (Dufour *et al.* 2010). In environmentalism, groups that started within nation states quickly developed into international organisations. For example, Greenpeace was founded in Canada in 1971 and has grown to almost three million members in forty states at the time of writing, while Friends of the Earth was founded in the United States in 1969 but became international within two years and now has over two million members and groups in seventy-six states (Greenpeace 2010; Friends of the Earth 2012). Obviously, many environmental problems are not confined to particular states, and the most compelling threat of all, global warming, cries out for coordinated international action. In this case, green activists have been at the forefront of what limited progress has been made at the UN summits at Kyoto, Copenhagen, Cancun and Durban.

Economic globalization has generated global resistance to the policies produced by the neoliberal consensus among economic elites and administered through the WTO, the IMF and the World Bank. The 'battle of Seattle' at the WTO summit in December 1999 quickly became the symbol of the global resistance to neoliberalism and sparked similar protests at various meetings dealing with global economic governance throughout the world. More significantly, the protesters created the World Social Forum (WSF), which has grown into a global networking hub since its inaugural meeting at Porto Alegre in Brazil in 2001 (Mertes 2004; Pleyers 2010). It is significant that the annual meetings of the WSF have been based in the 'global south' rather than the affluent north, although the WSF also meets on a continental basis. This loose network of anti-capitalist movements offers a rich resource in generating the normative commitment to global solidarity, epitomised in its slogan, 'Another world is possible'.

In a more focused way, civil society movements played an important part in securing agreement on debt cancellation and increased levels of aid at the Gleneagles summit of the G8 in

2005. In Britain, the driving force was a coalition of global justice movements around the inspiring slogan of 'make poverty history', while in the United States the ONE advocacy group, which now has more than two million members worldwide, played a leading role. In a relatively short time period a global civil society has begun to emerge, with the development of movements of activists focused on global issues and effectively practising global citizenship (Schattle 2008), as discussed in Chapter 1. Much of this activity has been directed at fulfilling or surpassing the targets set by the UN Millennium Development Goals for 2015 (Hanhimäki 2008: 101–3), but most activists recognise that aid alone is not the answer to development problems. Only when a more humane form of global governance is established will it be possible to see a way forward to global solidarity.

In the area of human rights, despite the nominal commitment to upholding them made by all UN member states, in practice the principle of state sovereignty has meant that little could be done to prevent human rights abuses. However, global pressure has been exerted in an effective way by human rights groups. Amnesty International is an excellent example. Founded in Britain in 1961 it now has over two million members active in 150 states, in many of which being an Amnesty activist involves severe risks (Amnesty International 2012). Through persistent casework and country reports, a normative power has developed to help break down the barriers protecting the abusers.

The new forms of solidarity outlined above have developed in the affluent societies, but new forms have also developed in poorer parts of the world, in response to the astonishing social changes that have taken place in the past three decades. David McNally provides a good example in analysing how, in Bolivia, the development of privatisation policies in the 1980s broke the strength of the established miners' trade union, but in the late 1990s mass movements developed in opposition to the privatisation of water and gas. This quickly gave rise to a political movement involving new solidarities between a range of social groups representing peasants, workers, the unemployed, women and indigenous peoples (McNally 2011:152–61). This was crowned by the decisive election victory of Evo Morales in 2005, and the adoption of redistributive policies and links with other left-wing Latin American governments that offer a regional resistance to neoliberalism (Crabtree 2009). Resistance to privatisation measures throughout the less developed world has featured local and national non-governmental organisations that have succeeded in networking internationally to bring attention to injustices involved in, for example, water supply to the poorest (Sultana and Loftus 2011).

These activities reflect both new forms of solidarity at local and national level and a growing awareness of global issues that need to be addressed through coordinated international action. When the global financial crisis of 2008 exposed the recklessness of the neoliberal insistence on deregulation and the rule of free-market forces, many commentators and politicians thought that a change of direction to some form of global Keynesianism must follow, but it did not. The new forms of solidarity outlined above are vitally important if such a change of direction is to be achieved. They also form an important part of the content of the new theories of solidarity that have developed in recent years, and it is to those theories that we must now turn our attention.

3 Theories of Solidarity

Following an extended period of neglect in social and political theory, the concept of solidarity eventually began to receive the theoretical attention it deserved towards the end of the twentieth century. This chapter looks critically at a selection of approaches and relates them to the broader normative goal of global solidarity. It is fitting to begin with Richard Rorty (1931–2007), for the publication of *Contingency, Irony and Solidarity* in 1989 brought the concept back in from the theoretical cold. It did so in a rather startling way, for Rorty's postmodernist approach denied the possibility that philosophy could provide the grounds for justifying beliefs. Resolutely anti-essentialist, Rorty's commitment to furthering human solidarity was deliberately free from 'metaphysical' claims about a common human nature or the unfolding of reason. The next theorist considered is Axel Honneth (b. 1949), whose *Struggle for Recognition*, first published in German in 1992, places special emphasis on solidarity as the highest form of recognition, and presents a theorisation of the politics of recognition quite distinctive from the class struggle approach discussed in the previous chapter. Indeed it has triggered an extended debate about the centrality of recognition as opposed to redistribution in social justice, with important implications for the consideration of global solidarity (Fraser and Honneth 2003). The third theorist to be considered is Jürgen Habermas (b. 1929), Honneth's predecessor as head of the Frankfurt School, and one who shares an 'intersubjectivist' philosophy, whereby only free and equal discourse between people can justify moral claims. Although Habermas has not engaged in a sustained analysis of the concept of solidarity, it is a recurring theme in both his philosophical and political work (Pensky 2008). Because of this willingness to venture into the territory of how global solidarity might be developed, Habermas's contribution receives extended attention. The fourth section is devoted to Alain Touraine (b. 1925), and in particular his book *Can We Live Together?*, which first appeared in French in 1997. His work raises important questions about the possibility of a multiculturalism that can draw people together rather than keeping them apart, and also demands an ethical turn in politics to promote solidarity. The final section deals with the contribution of Carol C. Gould, particularly her 2004 book, *Globalizing Democracy and Human Rights*. She is a leading advocate of 'transnational solidarity', and her idea of 'concrete universality' as a basis for global solidarity challenges the notion of a more abstract universalism favoured by radical humanism.

Richard Rorty

Richard Rorty's commitment to human solidarity, allied to a traditional liberal attachment to tolerance and individual liberty, has exerted a strong attraction for those who share his scepticism towards the professed certainties of traditional metaphysics and epistemology. Not only does he favour progressing towards greater solidarity among the peoples of the world, but he asserts that there is such a thing as moral progress and that it is 'in the direction of greater human solidarity' (Rorty 1996: 192). However, Rorty is at pains to point out that his commitment does not involve an acceptance of some recognition of a core self, the human essence, in all human beings. Beliefs of that sort are, for him, remnants of an outdated, metaphysical way of thinking. Rorty sees the idea of an intrinsic nature as a vestige of the idea that the world is a divine creation, and he commends instead an attitude whereby nothing is worshipped or treated as a quasi-divinity, and everything is seen to be a product of time and chance

(Rorty 1996: 21–2). It is an illusion to conceive of solidarity as something pre-existing which can be realised once we shed our prejudices, for solidarity is something that needs to be created by the 'imaginative ability to see strange people as fellow sufferers' (Rorty 1996: xvi). He contrasts his own pragmatism with the traditional metaphysical reliance on ideas of a 'larger shared power' such as God, truth or rationality which has to be invoked in order to demonstrate that we all share something in common (Rorty 1996: 91). Rorty is convinced that although we can adhere to beliefs and even think of them as worth dying for, such beliefs are caused 'by nothing deeper than contingent historical circumstance' (Rorty 1996: 189). Awareness of the contingency of beliefs is part of the radical doubt required by Rorty's ideal type figure, the liberal ironist, but what would persuade the liberal ironist to further the cause of human solidarity?

The liberal ironist does not offer a reason to care about suffering, but she will recognise that what unites her with the rest of humanity is simply a susceptibility to pain, and in particular the special pain meted out only by humans – humiliation (Rorty 1996: 92–3). Rorty argues that the moral progress towards greater human solidarity comes when the traditional differences between people, such as religion and ethnicity, are perceived as unimportant 'when compared with similarities with respect to pain and humiliation' (Rorty 1996: 192). The fear of humiliation is shared by us all, and this recognition of our common susceptibility to humiliation is the only social bond that is needed to widen human solidarity.

For Rorty, moral obligation to one's fellow human beings derives from the fact that they are considered to be 'one of us', the 'us' referring always to membership of a specific group. He argues that an appeal to 'one of us human beings' will never possess the same force as an appeal to the 'us' which refers to a smaller and more local group. As an example he selects the plight of young urban black men in the United States, arguing that an appeal to help them will be both morally and politically more persuasive if they are described as fellow Americans rather than as fellow human beings (Rorty 1996: 190–1). Progress in the direction of human solidarity is achieved by widening the scope of those who are considered to be included as 'one of us'.

The task of encouraging this perception belongs not to the philosopher but rather to the journalists or creative writers who reveal the tribulations of others in wholly unfamiliar situations. Through this act of *description* we learn more about others and become more sensitive to their pain; in the process we learn more about ourselves, an act of *redescription* through which we are obliged to reinvestigate ourselves. Although this can be accomplished through a variety of media, the novel is accorded particular significance (Rorty 1996: xvi), and in his book he devotes chapters to the impact of George Orwell's *1984* and the novels of Vladimir Nabokov, which, he argues, share a concern with getting on the 'inside' of cruelty (Rorty 1996: 146). This focus on cruelty and humiliation as quintessentially human expressions of power is extremely negative, and, as Diane Rothleder has pointed out, is unlikely to inspire a political response to injustice (Rothleder 1999: 64–71). Furthermore, the prospects of increasing our sensitivity to humiliation and cruelty are made more difficult by the tendency of so much popular culture today to make entertainment out of these destructive proclivities. Nevertheless, at least Rorty has identified the positive potential of shared cultural experiences in an increasingly globalized communicative culture.

Through a combination of Friedrich Nietzsche's rejection of all philosophical certainties and John Dewey's commitment to democracy and self-improvement, Rorty advocates the building of a utopia of human solidarity as an 'endless, proliferating realisation of Freedom, rather than a convergence towards an already existing truth' (Rorty 1996: xvi). It should be added that his emphasis on developing empathy fits well with some of the other ethical arguments for solidarity, and points to the efficacy of promoting human rights arguments in an increasingly interactive world. This point is made forcefully in his 1993 Oxford Amnesty Lecture, 'Human Rights, Rationality, and Sentimentality' (Rorty 1998: 167–85), but again it must be stressed that in arguing for a culture of human rights he eschews any possibility of grounding them in notions of essential human needs. He rejects all appeals to human rights based on anything that attaches to humans by nature of their humanity. Human rights should be viewed only as positive rights that are struggled for and created, not based on any inherent entitlement that needs to be 'realised'. In this account, philosophical attempts from Plato onwards to establish a foundation for morality, including Kant's claim to an inherent sense of moral obligation, are outmoded and irrelevant (Rorty 1996: 169–70, 183).

Rorty proposes that we argue, in whatever ways are appropriate, in favour of widening the circle of those who are included as 'people like us', without recourse to appeals to common humanity (Rorty 1996: 175–6). Furthermore, he reiterates his conviction that moral progress has been discernible since the French Revolution, with the widening acceptance of equality and the progressive elimination of legal discriminations on the basis of economic status, race, gender or sexual orientation (Rorty 1996: 175, 185). For Rorty, moral progress has nothing to do with getting closer to the truth, but rather reflects 'an increase in imaginative power' (Rorty 1999: 87). The important thing is to create openness to worthy goals even when there is no compelling reason to accept the principles which might justify them. In a posthumously published speech on the contrast between religious and secular ethics, he rejects the idea of spirituality as 'yearning for the infinite' but is perfectly receptive to it as 'an exalted sense of possibilities opening up for finite beings' (Rorty 2011: 14). On this basis he rejects the vision of 'vertical ascent toward something greater than the merely human' in favour of 'horizontal progress toward a planetwide cooperative commonwealth' (Rorty 2011: 17).

There are a number of problems raised by Rorty's antifoundationalist support for human solidarity, and the most important one centres on his rejection of human essence as a philosophical ground for solidarity. We note that he concedes the need to invoke a common feeling, albeit a negative one, to extend the scope of our mutual understanding. As Rothleder points out, it is theoretically necessary in Rorty's account for the appeal to solidarity to be couched in negative terms in order to avoid the notion of a 'positive shared project' (Rothleder 1999: 45). Rorty avoids the risk of providing something that might inspire a quasi-religious sense of devotion, such as love or caring, but we are obliged to question his selection of the susceptibility to humiliation as the crucial aspect of our humanity and to query why this does not amount to simply another form of essentialism. However, setting aside the questionable choice of 'humiliation' as the central experience, it is surely the case that Rorty *is* offering an alternative form of essentialism. This has been persuasively argued by Norman Geras, who points out that Rorty is ultimately falling back on the fact that human beings have a nature, one which may be repressed or violated (Geras 1995: 89–90). He suggests that it is implausible to insist on the communal sources of strong solidarity, and at the same time deny the relevance of the idea of a common humanity 'to the goal of more expansive solidaristic relations' (Geras 1995: 90). Geras points out that in the Oxford Amnesty Lecture Rorty supplies a number of examples of atrocities being justified by the perpetrators on the grounds that their victims were not properly human, and Rorty's acknowledgement of this need to dehumanise the victim undermines his claim that the appeal to common humanity is weak and unconvincing (Geras 1995: 97, cf. Rorty 1998: 178). Rorty also fails to acknowledge that his own argument for greater solidarity assumes a human potential to reach understanding and achieve cooperation, or even consider the possibility of invoking the idea of human nature without appealing to something that is 'ahistorical' or somehow antecedent to lived experience. Despite Rorty's claim that there is nothing in human nature to appeal to 'because humans don't have a nature' (Rorty 2011: 24), I will argue in Chapter 4 that it is possible to build a coherent normative theory on the basis of a strong conception of human nature.

There is an important tension between Rorty's appeal to patriotism and his cosmopolitan support for human solidarity. As a cosmopolitan, he recognises that there is a global overclass that makes the major economic decisions that maintain existing inequalities, and suggests that the best that people in his position can do is argue for a global polity that can act as a countervailing power against the rich, through some sort of revitalisation of the UN, however slim the chances (Rorty 1999: 233–4). However, as a pragmatist he feels there is a much greater chance of appealing to people's sense of patriotism than to some more generalised notion of common humanity. He is bitterly critical of the Left in America for turning its back on patriotic appeal, and condemns the burning of flags in the protests against the Vietnam War as the kind of act that broke the link between left-wing ideas and their potential working-class base (Rorty 1999: 260). The problem with this patriotic tactic is that it ignores a major cause of the rupture that he mourns between left-wing ideas and the working class, namely the 'patriotic' attacks on all things left wing by Senator Joseph McCarthy and his followers in the era of the 'un-American activities' witch-hunts of the early 1950s. The power of patriotic sentiment is such that politicians of all major parties routinely play the patriotic card (Billig 1995), and Rorty should have considered why patriotism is invariably used as a substitute for solidarity rather than a path to it. Fierce patriotism rarely extends to redressing social injustices within the patria, but more often leads to uncritical endorsements of aggressive foreign policy, viewing the rest of the world in purely instrumental 'friend or foe' terms.

Rorty's aversion to developing a theoretical understanding of how solidarity might be advanced is evident in an essay titled 'The End of Leninism', where he opposes the master narratives that have been pushed on us by philosophers like Plato and Marx (Rorty 1998: 228–9). Rorty rejects the idea of a 'large theoretical way of finding out how to end injustice', favouring a more banal and untheoretical political vocabulary. He suggests dropping the terms 'capitalism' and 'socialism' and urges the Left to eschew the rhetoric of 'the anti-capitalist struggle'. In his view, progressives should give up trying to grasp the course of 'history', favouring instead whatever egalitarian reforms may be struggled for in any given situation. There is something superficially attractive in this stance, which is almost certainly a response to a certain type of left-wing argumentation that explains all injustices in terms of capitalism and rejects all attempts to overcome them within capitalism, thereby trusting in some revolutionary transformation for which there is no longer any popular support. However, the sheer scale of global injustice, and the power of the vested interests which reproduce it, surely cries out for systemic analysis of the driving forces of the world economy, identification of possible alternatives, and assessment of the political forces that bring forward the solidarity he desires. This does not amount to what Rorty dismisses as 'amiable exercises in nostalgia', but is rather the sort of forward-thinking radicalism favoured by his intellectual hero, John Dewey (Rorty 1998: 239).

Axel Honneth

Axel Honneth theorises the preconditions for the achievement of human solidarity in *The Struggle for Recognition*, first published in German in 1992. He sets out to meet a challenge posed by the young Hegel, to present a philosophical reconstruction of an ethical community as the culmination of a sequence of stages involving the struggle for recognition of various groups (Honneth 1996: 67). Honneth also deploys the work of the social psychologist George Herbert Mead to provide a materialistic and naturalistic exposition of the crucial role of inter-subjective recognition in the formation of identity, arguing that for both Mead and the early Hegel the reproduction of social life is governed by the imperative of mutual recognition, because 'one can develop a practical relation-to-self only when one has learned to view oneself from the normative perspective of one's partners in interaction' (Honneth 1996: 92–3). This imperative produces the normative pressure to remove constraints on the meaning of mutual recognition, so that, as individualisation develops historically, so too should the relations of mutual recognition. What Honneth finds lacking in Hegel and Mead is an explanation of the social experiences that would generate the pressure through which the demands for recognition are transformed into social movements, and to find such an explanation he suggests that we need to study the specific forms of disrespect through which actors realise their oppression (Honneth 1996: 93).

Honneth identifies three patterns of recognition. First, there is the love and friendship developed in intimate relations, which gives us self-confidence. Then there is the recognition which we achieve through the acquisition of rights, a form of recognition which, he contends, produces self-respect. With regard to the development of rights claims he endorses T. H. Marshall's broad description of the widening of civil rights as belonging to the eighteenth century, political rights to the nineteenth century and social rights to the twentieth century (Honneth 1996: 116). Finally, solidarity occurs in groups when each individual understands that she or he is 'esteemed' by all citizens to the same degree. Solidarity is understood as 'an interactive relationship in which subjects mutually sympathise with their various different ways of life because, among themselves, they esteem each other symmetrically', while societal solidarity is achieved when 'every member of a society is in a position to esteem himself or herself' (Honneth 1996: 128–9). Honneth thus describes a trajectory in which self-confidence flows from love, self-respect emerges with the acquisition of rights and, ultimately, self-esteem flows from the development of solidarity. When speaking of people esteeming each other 'symmetrically' Honneth refers to a situation in which we view each other in the light of values that allow the abilities and traits of the other to appear significant for shared practice, thereby inspiring a genuine concern for the other person rather than simply exercising a passive tolerance. The essential point here is that every subject is free from being collectively disparaged, and competition for social esteem acquires a form free from pain, or 'not marred by experiences of disrespect' (Honneth 1996: 130). The significance of this is that unlike in some messianic or utopian constructions of human solidarity there are still significant differences between people, as well as competing claims.

A central claim of Honneth's theory is that there is a strong moral force inherent in the expectation of recognition involved in struggling for rights and forging solidarity. It is moral feelings of indignation against various forms of disrespect that act as an important motive force for members of movements in struggle. Honneth rightly complains that social science has tended to reduce motives for rebellion, protest and resistance to categories of 'interest', with the interests emerging out of objective inequalities in the distribution of opportunities (Honneth 1996: 161). For Honneth, this 'fixation' on interests has obscured the significance of moral feelings (Honneth 1996: 166). This raises the key question of what sort of moral claims may be justified, or, on what grounds may some claims to recognition be regarded as regressive. He accepts that the significance of particular struggles has to be measured in terms of the positive or negative contribution that each makes to the realisation of 'undistorted forms of recognition' (Honneth 1996: 170), which points to a strong link with Jürgen Habermas's discourse ethics. In a short final chapter he takes some tentative steps towards fleshing out the goal of a solidaristic society, while taking care to avoid a particular vision of the good life. The chapter opens by accepting that if the struggle for recognition is to be viewed as a critical framework for interpreting the processes by which societies develop, in order to complete the model there needs to be a 'theoretical justification for the normative point of view from which these processes can be guided' (Honneth 1996: 171). However, what follows does not meet this promise.

Honneth reiterates the point that unless a certain degree of self-confidence and legally guaranteed autonomy is presupposed, it is impossible to imagine successful self-realisation, and the freedom to acquire this self-realisation can be realised only in interaction with others (Honneth 1996: 174). However, despite the emphasis on inter-subjectivity, the conditions for recognition outlined here clearly give priority to the individual over the community, as Andreas Kalyvas has pointed out (Kalyvas 1999: 104). Indeed, remarkably little is said about concrete social goals or preconditions for social harmony, and the analysis remains abstract and formal. Honneth considers that outlining the patterns of recognition in this abstract and formal manner is preferable to a more substantive approach to social justice because it avoids falling into the utopian trap of specifying particular forms. In addition, he claims that the explication of the conditions for recognition offers more detail about the structures of a successful life than a more general appeal to individual self-determination (Honneth 1996: 174). He comments that Hegel and Mead had failed to achieve their aim of defining a horizon of ethical values that would admit to a plurality of life goals without losing the collective identity through which solidarity is generated (Honneth 1996: 179). This may be true, but does the recognition of moral claims inherent in some (unspecified) struggles bring us any closer to resolving that problem? Honneth claims that only a transformation of culture can meet those demands in expanded relations of solidarity, but he is reluctant to specify what forms this might take. As possible candidates he mentions political republicanism, ecologically based asceticism, and collective existentialism, but he is unwilling to say whether human solidarity is compatible with capitalism, for questions of that sort are 'no longer a matter for theory but rather for the future of social struggles' (Honneth 1996: 176). This self-denying ordinance evades the tricky question of the extent to which the demands of certain social movements are consonant with the broader goal of human solidarity.

As Kalyvas has argued, Honneth's concept of recognition does not provide the means to distinguish between progressive and reactionary movements or identities (Kalyvas 1999: 103). In his response to this criticism, Honneth denies that he had ever intended to provide such an evaluative criterion from which to judge demands for recognition, and also denies trying to provide a 'social-theoretical sketch which is able to grasp the social reality of recognition relations' (Honneth 1999: 252). What he claims the book is really about is no more and no less than highlighting the type of morality at work in the form of the expectations raised in the struggles for recognition. The severe limitations of the inter-subjective approach here become apparent, for even though Honneth acknowledges the need to appeal hypothetically to a provisional end-state and agrees that social solidarity can grow only out of collectively shared goals (Honneth 1996: 171, 178), he is unable to say anything about these substantive issues. This point has been seized upon by Nancy Fraser when she claims that Honneth's view of human flourishing as 'intact identity' effectively denies any substantive content to human flourishing, 'for if he were to supply content to that notion, it would effectively become one concrete ethical ideal among others'. The result is that his theory of justice 'lacks sufficient determinacy to adjudicate conflicting claims' (Fraser 2003b: 224–6).

The strength of Honneth's approach is that it gives an alternative framework for recognising the moral content of social struggles that enables us to understand the shift in Western societies from the sort of solidarity struggles that developed in the nineteenth century to contemporary struggles against oppression based on ethnicity, gender, sexuality and religion. However, it does not seem to be as helpful in understanding movements focusing on peace, environmentalism, human rights and world poverty, which do not revolve around 'identity'. Indeed Honneth is very clear about the differences between identity politics and other social movements in his response to Fraser's criticisms (Honneth 2003: 117–25). He argues that all these struggles can be viewed through a single framework of recognition 'that locates the core of all experiences of injustice in the withdrawal of social recognition, in the phenomena of humiliation and disrespect' (Honneth 2003: 134). Fraser accepts the strength of the recognition framework in understanding the 'new' social struggles, while insisting that no account of social justice can do without an insistence on redistribution (Fraser 1997: 11–40; Fraser 2003a: 88–94).

Honneth gives scant consideration to more robust conceptions of human flourishing. He claims that an orientation towards the moral perspective of solidarity is built into every practical discourse, in the act of reaching out to achieve understanding. In *Disrespect*, he defines solidarity as 'the moral principle of reciprocal concern' (Honneth 2007: 123), and insists on the necessity of the numerous particular experiences of community interaction as the only possible grounding for solidarity. He is sceptical of broader claims to human solidarity, caricaturing this view as resting on an assumption that 'all human beings share a common goal beyond their equal cultural differences' and dismissing the notion of a solidarity that encompasses all humanity as 'abstractly utopian' (Honneth 2007: 124). I use 'caricature' because 'common goal' implies reaching agreement on objectives on a scale that is unthinkable. 'Common needs', however, need not be so abstract (I. Fraser 1998: 123–64). As for the charge of abstract utopianism, the argument of this book is that exploring the prospects for human solidarity clarifies both the causes of social division and the steps required to overcome them. This is an appropriate task for political theory.

A final problem with Honneth's conception of solidarity is its scope. Besides the observation that his requirements for societal solidarity are most certainly both abstract and utopian, they require a level of communal interaction that makes it difficult to see how such solidarity might operate outside a traditional republican ideal of a homogenous deliberative democracy. Honneth's idea of solidarity is very much tied in with notions of community, and he is less than convincing in arguing that 'post-traditional' communities can avoid the exclusionary practices of the traditional ones (Honneth 2007: 254–62). In order to offer a convincing argument that exclusionary practices could be overcome it would have to be made clear how the divisive processes of the economic system can be overcome, but that is a path Honneth is unwilling to go down. The monist conception of justice as recognition is clearly inadequate for conceiving solidarity at the global level.

Jürgen Habermas

Writing in 1986, Jürgen Habermas declared solidarity to be the 'reverse side' of justice. Whereas justice concerns itself with the equal freedoms of individuals, solidarity concerns itself with the welfare of citizens who are 'intimately linked in an intersubjectively shared form of life' (Habermas 1990: 244). In emphasising this indispensable reciprocity, Habermas goes beyond a simple meaning of solidarity as a binding force within groups, insisting that his ideal solidarity is transformed in the process of achieving democracy, as a realisation of 'the idea of a general will formation'. Justice and solidarity emerge from the mutual recognition of citizens seeking to justify their actions (Habermas 1990: 245). This identification of the significance of solidarity as the communicative force that secures the subjective grounding of principles and processes of justice has great theoretical potential.

Solidarity is, therefore, an important element of Habermas's conception of social justice, even though he has not provided a systematic analysis of the concept (Pensky 2008: 18). One of the problems with his conception of solidarity is his close association of it with the evolution of the modern state, as this institutional context is not available in an increasingly 'post-national' world. The 'intimate linking' specified by Habermas in the early formulation of solidarity sits somewhat uneasily with his later commitment to the idea of 'solidarity among strangers', first set down in *Between Facts and Norms* (1992) and reiterated in more recent political writings such as *The Divided West* (Habermas 2006: 78). Habermas conceives the idea of solidarity among strangers as a situation arising out of the gradual development of democratic societies, overcoming bitter class and religious divisions and eventually learning to deal with their social complexity. In this situation, overcoming these conflicts constitutes the sole source of solidarity among strangers, 'strangers who renounce violence and, in the cooperative regulation of their common life, also concede one another the right to *remain* strangers' (Habermas 1996: 308, original emphasis). This is an attractive appeal to a form of solidarity in which different identities are drawn together while their differences are respected, anticipating a society that has thrown off the shackles of social stratification and exploitation. Significantly, the 'society' he has in mind need not be confined to the nation state, for in the same work he argues that a 'world citizenship' is already taking shape and that the 'cosmopolitan condition is no longer merely a mirage' (Habermas 1996: 514–15).

Habermas argues that within nation states there is a common political culture in which the various actors engaged in negotiations operate with 'common value orientations and shared conceptions of justice' that enable agreements to be made beyond the limits of instrumental rationality. In other words citizens can agree to make some sacrifice of their narrowly defined self-interest in order to strengthen society, as, for example, when assenting to economic redistribution through progressive taxation. This sort of 'thick communicative embeddedness' is what is missing at the international level (Habermas 2001: 108–9). But what is the nature of this thick embeddedness that Habermas attributes to the nation state? First, he makes an important conceptual distinction between national consciousness and civic solidarity. National consciousness develops when the idea of the nation becomes the principal source of collective identity, but civic solidarity develops only in a democracy in which people recognise themselves as free and equal citizens. National consciousness replaces pre-modern forms of solidarity and enables social divisions to be contained, but it also develops in pre-democratic political contexts in which the state is exalted as that which must be obeyed and indeed venerated. Civic solidarity develops in a democratic community of free and equal citizens, and the preservation of the liberal order within the society becomes more important than the assertion of the state against and above others. 'Identification with the state mutates into an orientation to the constitution,' writes Habermas, enabling solidarity among strangers within states, and 'meets a transnational extension of national solidarity halfway' (Habermas 2006: 78). According to this perspective, the high value placed on our liberties and democratic processes expressed in civic solidarity can have a universalistic content beyond national boundaries.

Since the late 1980s Habermas has identified this gradual uncoupling of democratic identity from nationalism as 'constitutional patriotism' (Habermas 2006: 78–9), a term originally developed by Dolf Sternberger in 1979 as a contribution to the debates among German historians about the moral legitimacy of patriotism in a state in which extreme nationalism had culminated in catastrophe. Habermas adopted the concept to emphasise the importance of an enriched public sphere in the development of a healthy democracy (Habermas 1999: 224–6; Müller 2007: 26–38). In the case of Germany, the importance of building on the hard lessons of history can be seen in the passing of the 1985 law criminalising Holocaust denial, a notable example of the legal application of the principle of constitutional patriotism. The emphasis on the power of democracy to bind a society together by providing the means through which conflicts can be successfully mediated moves us away from the idea that citizenship needs to be rooted in shared ethnic or cultural origins. 'Constitutional patriotism' enables Habermas to reject one aspect of the 'Janus face' of national consciousness, blind obedience to the 'fatherland', while defending the other, the feeling of social responsibility in the political public sphere (Habermas 2001: 101–2). Nevertheless, however attractive the concepts of civic solidarity and constitutional patriotism might be, they remain problematic.

In his earlier work, Habermas was far more critical of the state and the way in which the public sphere is manipulated by powerful economic and administrative elites (Habermas 1992: 244–50), and is fundamentally 'depoliticised' through a process of 'civic privatism' (Habermas 1988: 36–7). Habermas has not formally rejected the earlier work, but he had basically dropped his criticisms of the weakness of democratic life by the time he came to write the more optimistic and abstract *Beyond Facts and Norms* in 1992 (Cooke 2001: 142). Yet even in *The Divided West*, first published in 2004, he admits that civic solidarity at the national level is 'relatively thin' (Habermas 2006: 55). It is paid for 'in small change', in the sense that citizens pay their taxes but are no longer prepared to die for their country, and he comments that neither the US nor Britain could sustain the war in Iraq if they had to rely on conscription (Habermas 2006: 77). Within the nation state, the commitment to a strong civic solidarity favoured by communitarian and republican theorists appears to be swimming against the tide of increasingly individualised societies in which inequalities are actually growing. 'Civic' implies a republican commitment to the political community reflecting an ultimate sense of togetherness, but this is not, nor ever was in most states, widespread, for the good reason that inequalities in both wealth and power have been simply too great to permit it. As for constitutional patriotism, even if it is understood in a broad sense to mean commitment to the democratic process, in many states there is considerable disquiet at the way that process operates. It is surely misleading to portray solidaristic action a within a highly contested civil society as some sort of celebration of democratic principles embodied in the state.

Despite his claims to 'go beyond' Durkheim (Habermas 1989: 47–59), Habermas encounters the same sort of problem in visualising social solidarity as a normal development in modern society provided that certain 'abnormalities' could be overcome. Social stratification and economic exploitation obstruct the development of social solidarity and leave the question of social justice unresolved. Far from being abnormalities, they are endemic to the social system, and in so far as solidaristic action is needed to mitigate them it is likely to see existing state apparatuses as part of the problem rather than part of the solution. Although Habermas's commitment to an 'egalitarian public of citizens' (Habermas 1996: 308) specifies a post-exploitative society, the thrust of his work assumes that this will emerge as part of a 'normal' development of the Enlightenment ideals of liberty, equality and fraternity. This tendency is also evident in Hauke Brunkhorst's *Solidarity*, in which the goal of a global legal community is depicted as the rational development of the constitutionalism projected by the French Revolution. 'Constitutional patriotism' is again invoked as a rallying cry for driving this outcome, but Brunkhorst is also obliged to admit that the bond of solidarity is becoming 'frayed and brittle' (Brunkhorst 2005: 170–2). The danger in urging support for the construction of civic solidarity and constitutional patriotism in stratified and exploitative societies is that the old deceptions of nationalism are revisited, only with a less chauvinistic veneer. We are invited to identify with a civic community of formally equal citizens, but the equals are not really equal at all. The systemic causes of social fragmentation are set to one side while various schemes for democratic renewal and civic education become the order of the day. Habermas's reverence for the discursive ideal found in constitutionalism causes him to elide real social tensions. The sources of solidarity are to be found not in a commitment to the constitution or the state, but rather in the motivating force of overcoming perceived injustices in a range of arenas. Respect for democratic processes is necessary for the development of a public sphere, but it is not sufficient to constitute social solidarity, or social justice as its 'reverse side'.

Habermas places great importance on the emergence of the European Union (EU) in overcoming national enmities and establishing solidarity in a 'post-national' arena. In *The Postnational Constellation*, first published in 1998, he expresses the desire to see a federal Europe emerge, not simply through new common procedures of legislation but also through the formation of an active European public sphere. He insists that a European identity is a precondition for a cosmopolitan Europe, and that means that forms of civic solidarity previously limited to the nation state would have to be expanded to the European level (Habermas 2001: 99). He accepts that we cannot, at present, speak of the existence of a European identity, but the real question ought to be whether we can realistically conceive of the conditions whereby citizens are able to extend their civic solidarity beyond national borders 'with the goal of achieving mutual inclusion' (Habermas 2006: 76). It is important to note that Habermas uses the words 'expansion' and 'extension' in relation to civic solidarity (Habermas 2001: 99; Habermas 2006: 63, 78), implying a trajectory from a solidarity-building civic consciousness developed at the national level to some sort of equivalent at the European level, minus the negative aspects of nationalism. According to Habermas, solidarity within the EU would require a widespread sense of belonging if Europe were to speak with one voice in foreign affairs and execute an active domestic policy (Habermas 2006: 80). However, whereas this sense of belonging at national level draws on notions of a shared national history and therefore appears to be some sort of natural evolution, at the European level such an allegiance would have to rely on an *explicitly* constructed collective identity.

Habermas considers the shared experiences that may be mobilised to foster such an identity. He outlines these building blocks for European identity in an essay of 2003, co-signed by the French philosopher Jacques Derrida, entitled 'February 15 or: What Binds Europeans', prompted by mass demonstrations across Europe against the impending invasion of Iraq (Habermas 2006: 46–8). He invokes seven experiences as likely candidates for 'conscious appropriation', as a necessary step in the development of a progressive European mentality. In other words there would need to be an explicit acknowledgement of these common experiences by a considerable part of European citizenry if a solidaristic identity were to emerge. These experiences include the secularisation of the state, confidence in the state to compensate for market failures, a 'solidary' ethos of struggle for greater social justice, revulsion towards violence, a commitment to reciprocal restriction of the scope of sovereignty, and a determination to learn from the past and understand the experience of others. This new European identity is not intended to replace national identities, but rather to supplement them and help to marginalise their chauvinistic elements. What is on offer here is a prescriptive list of positive, identity-building apprehensions of experiences common to Europeans. They reflect a consciousness of different aspects of a conflict-ridden past from which Europeans ought to derive hard lessons and, in the process of acknowledging their ability to overcome deep conflicts, create a European Union that is more than an administrative fix. From the negatives of the past may emerge the positives of reconciliation, inclusion and cooperation.

These principles can be regarded as appropriate for a European constitutional patriotism, an idea that has been positively embraced by a number of scholars as the basis of a solidaristic European identity (Lacroix 2002; Cronin 2003; Müller 2007). However, it must be doubted whether any feeling of support for such an identity is widely held outside academic and EU administrative circles. In recent years the rejection of the European Constitution and the confused and divided response to the financial crisis in the eurozone indicate a rather weak sense of European identity. Is it not reasonable for European citizens to accept the Union for what it is, a functional arrangement that provides mutual benefit, without being persuaded of the need to create a new state accompanied by an ersatz identity? Perhaps those who see the development of the EU as progressive should be satisfied that it has punctured the myths of reactionary nationalism more effectively by the guaranteed free movement of citizens than by the creation of a strong European identity. The successful assimilation of large numbers of workers from the new member states of eastern Europe, despite dire warnings from the reactionary press, is an encouraging indication that the exclusionary nationalisms of the past are being eclipsed.

Habermas does not consider the possibility that a strong European identity may actually hinder the development of a cosmopolitan consciousness rather than promote it. Such an identity may unwittingly reinforce the old imperialist myth of civilisational superiority. As Robert Fine and Will Smith have pointed out, rather than turning Europe into a 'vehicle for cosmopolitan ideas and solidarity', the idea of a strong European identity risks turning it into one for a 'new form of transnational chauvinism', an outcome that would contradict everything Habermas is trying to do (Fine and Smith 2003: 483; Heins 2005: 447). It may well be better for the development of global solidarity if we move away from all political identities based on territorial political units at all levels. This would open the way for the emergence of multiple forms of political affiliation, along the lines developed by advocates of cosmopolitan democracy (Held 1995; Archibugi 2008). In place of state-centred political identity, other forms of solidarity develop in movement politics that engage with issues such as global warming, social exclusion, human rights abuses and poverty. From this perspective it is possible to view a weak European identity not as an arrested development but rather as a signal for the development of post-national consciousness. Activists developing new forms of solidarity will acknowledge the importance of working with the EU because it is a significant player in global politics. This functional connection may help to democratise the EU without necessarily developing a form of identity that looks like an extended version of the nation state. If a cosmopolitan consciousness is to emerge it is better that the attachment of Europeans to Europe remains emotionally weak. To embrace the world at large it would be better to put down the flags and silence the anthems, rather than create new ones.

Since *Between Facts and Norms* Habermas has increasingly turned his attention to the possibility of the development of the 'solidarity of world citizens' (Habermas 2001: 108). He situates his cosmopolitan project in the normative framework of Kant, but in his discussion of Kant's *Perpetual Peace* he expresses dissatisfaction with the latter's insistence on the inviolability of national sovereignty (Habermas 1999: 179–80). Perhaps more significantly, for Habermas, Kant's approach does not adequately address the problem of how conflicting moral judgements can be reconciled, whereas the discourse ethics approach insists that the moral point of view can be justified only through the processes of open discussion and agreement (Habermas 1999: 40–6; Rehg 2007: 17–18). Essentially Habermas wants to see the emergence of real mediating discourses capable of overcoming the disintegrating forces at work in the world (Habermas 1999: 183–4). However, he recognises the lack of effective supranational agencies and questions whether democratic opinion and will formation at the global level could ever exert a 'binding force' (Habermas 1999: 127). In the absence of these institutions, agencies and civic movements, the idea of cosmopolitan solidarity 'has to support itself on the moral universalism of human rights alone' rather than being rooted in particular collective identities (Habermas 2001: 108). Moral outrage over violations of human rights provides a sufficient basis for solidarity among activists engaged in global politics, but this activism takes place in a 'weakly integrated' cosmopolitan society. What is lacking at the global level, according to Habermas, is a 'common ethical-political dimension' to sustain a collective identity.

Habermas's stress on constitutionalism causes him to look in the wrong place for solidarity, but there are at least two insights flowing from his communicative theory that offer hope for the development of wider solidarity and, from that, progress towards global justice. The first insight comes in the shape of the success of social movements in contributing to a process he describes as 'normative framing' (Habermas 2001: 109–10). In discussing the possibility of resisting global neoliberalism he invokes the normative goal of the reregulation of world society and insists that this goal has been placed on the agenda by citizens and citizens' movements rather than governments or political parties (Habermas 2001: 111). He points out that discourse and communication are powerful forces for the development of a new form of collective identity. Although common-value orientations are lacking at the international level, the processes of global negotiations produce this normative framing. The process of normative framing flows from the reality of a global discourse on a range of issues. So, for example, international non-governmental organisations can help to shape the agendas of UN summits by bringing key issues to the attention of citizens across the world and by using institutionally established forms of lobbying. This in turn helps to produce agreements on concrete targets and action plans to achieve them. The adoption of the UN's Millennium Development Goals is a good example of this. As Habermas rightly argues, in this way apparently weak forms of legitimation in global politics 'appear in another light' as this ability of citizens to shape agendas is taken into account.

Habermas's other insight concerns the politically disempowering effects of economic globalization and the possibility of politics 'catching up' with global markets (Habermas 2001: 81, 109). He recognises that at some stage political parties will need to take decisive action to move beyond the mere management of the status quo, and he argues that this is likely to happen only when global issues become part of domestic political agendas (Habermas 2006: 81–2). In the years since the appearance of *The Divided West* this has happened in a number of areas, for example in the debates about greenhouse gas emissions, the conduct of the war on terror, debt relief and aid, and, more recently, the management of the global financial system in the light of the financial crash of 2008. Nevertheless, even though the gap between domestic interests and global interests may be bridged, what is missing at the global level, according to Habermas, is a 'common ethical-political' dimension and a 'thick communicative embeddedness' allegedly on offer within states (Habermas 2001: 108–9). This means that cosmopolitan solidarity is difficult to conceive within a Habermasian framework, and this in turn leaves the idea of global justice somewhat marooned. Habermas's claim that 'only those norms can claim validity that could meet with the agreement of all those concerned in their capacity as participants in a practical discourse' is extremely demanding (Habermas 1999: 33–4). If the discursive process is the *only* possible source of norm validation, as he claims, we are left with a very thin appeal to global solidarity and its reverse side, global justice.

One answer to these difficulties in Habermas's approach is to question the commitment to a unified public sphere as the precondition for solidarity. This was done in relation to his earlier work on the public sphere by Nancy Fraser in a critique made in 1991, when she argued for the need to confront social inequality, promote a multiplicity of publics rather than a single public sphere, and admit both weak and strong publics in a more inclusive notion of the 'public' (Fraser 1997: 92–3). However, as Fraser herself acknowledges, all participants in the public sphere debates at that time operated within a 'Westphalian' analytical framework, assuming the more-or-less autonomous nation state as the only realistic arena in which public spheres could operate (Fraser 2008: 82–5). The blinkers have now been removed, and Habermas is surely right to suggest that cosmopolitanism is no longer a mirage. Citizens are mobilised around global issues, operating through INGOs, networking through social forums and supporting UN action plans. Many of these initiatives are emerging from within the less developed countries, as, for example, in the struggles against the privatisation of water and energy supplies. Through the process of normative framing, the global issues begin to emerge on domestic agendas and create more globally orientated citizens. What we now have to look for are the conditions in which the various solidarities orientated to a more humane global society articulate their goals, reconcile competing claims and link old and new politics in ways which transform them both. As Fraser says, we need not only to create transnational public powers but to make them accountable to new, transnational public spheres (Fraser 2008: 98).

However, even if we adjust Habermasian notions of the public sphere and civic solidarity to make them more flexible and responsive to cultural plurality, I would still argue that appeals to global solidarity require a stronger philosophical commitment to shared human needs and potentials. Habermas has consistently rejected what he has termed, at various times, 'expressivist' or 'neo-Aristotelian' approaches that strive to clarify what is common to human beings and what is required for human flourishing. In his essay 'Genealogical Analysis' he argues that notions of the common good on which the solidarity of all human beings could be grounded will necessarily fall between two stools – substantive conceptions will be intolerably paternalistic, while conceptions abstracted from local contexts undermine the concept of the good (Habermas 1999: 28). Neither here nor elsewhere is this standard 'too thick or too thin' objection thoroughly argued, with careful consideration of the positions adopted by those who have formulated virtue or character ethics. Instead he simply dismisses a number of candidates for a 'postmetaphysical level of justification' for moral philosophy as too implausible to merit further discussion (Habermas 1999: 11). He has been similarly evasive when it comes to dealing with humanist approaches associated with the Marxist tradition that have focused on alienation from human essence (Wilde 1998: 78–91).

In Habermas's recent work there are signs that after decades of dismissing the humanist position, he may now be revising his opinion, particularly in his championing of the idea of a 'species ethic'. This has arisen in the course of his discussion of the ethical implications of genetic interventions. His concern is that the application of 'liberal eugenics', in striving to correct perceived faults, would vitiate the human capacity to 'be oneself' and open the danger of the species denying its own spontaneity. If we are to make decisions about what constitutes a transgression of what it is to be properly human, we need to develop 'an ethical self-understanding of the species' which is shared by all moral persons (Habermas 2003: 40). As Pensky has recognised in his study of Habermas, *The Ends of Solidarity*, Habermas's 'species ethics' appears to reach out to the philosophical anthropology he 'repeatedly rejects yet seems unable to break from entirely' (Pensky 2008: 211). There is much to commend Pensky's conclusion that the humanist and inter-subjectivist approaches could supplement one another, with conceptions of human nature providing the anthropological context for mutual recognition (Pensky 2008: 236–8). Habermas's softening towards the radical humanist tradition is to be welcomed. It is an opening that moves us closer to considerations of our shared fate and the possibility of developing human solidarity across cultural and political borders, thereby promoting a better understanding of the conditions necessary for the construction of global justice.

Alain Touraine

Alain Touraine, in *Can We Live Together?*, first published in French in 1997, examines the problem of the increasing fragmentation of societies in the face of unfettered market forces. His analysis of the human condition and his normative commitment to a 'politics of the subject' is refreshing because its central thrust is the subject, conceived as the individual attempt to transform lived experience into the construction of the self as an actor. It is an assertion of freedom against the seemingly overwhelming constraints imposed by market forces on the one hand and the confinement of strong communitarianism on the other (Touraine 2000: 13–14 and 57). Although the subject is the starting point it needs for its realisation a social movement and a social goal. Thus democracy is its goal and the achievement of the subject is deemed to be inseparable from the development of inter-cultural communication and human solidarity. Such a goal involves the realisation of three inseparable and inter-related themes, namely the subject, communication and solidarity (Touraine 2000: 301). Touraine displays a hard-headed awareness of the obstacles to achieving the old revolutionary principles of liberty, equality and fraternity, and he translates these principles for the age of globalization into the imperatives of recognising cultural diversity, rejecting exclusion, and 'the right of every individual to have a life story in which he or she can realise, at least to some extent, a personal and collective project' (Touraine 2000: 252).

Touraine argues that the economy and culture have become divorced or 'dissociated' (Touraine 2000: 9). The emergence of economic globalization has destroyed old forms of social and political association and left politics in a state of decay, reducing the ambition of 'government' to the administration of economic and social organisation in order to maintain competitiveness in the global economy. While politicians look to the world market, voters look to their private lives (Touraine 2000: 5). The space between the realities of the economic system and the desocialised mass culture is often taken up by increasingly conservative appeals to values and institutions that are no longer fit for purpose. One response to this crisis of modernity is to revive social models of the past which stress unity and emphasise the 'us', but this call for community, even if it is infused with liberal sentiments, is inevitably exclusionary and therefore authoritarian. Another is the postmodernist view that we should embrace the rupture that is desocialisation and celebrate the new diversity, emphasising the 'me', but the problem here is that the regulation of social life is left to the market and leaves us defenceless against its consequences such as violence and racism (Touraine 2000: 6–7). A more promising alternative is the liberal commitment to procedural democracy with rules guaranteeing respect for personal and collective freedoms. However, this is a minimalist solution which safeguards coexistence but does not ensure communication – Touraine likens it to recognising Chinese as a cultured language but not being able to converse with the Chinese because we haven't learned to speak it (Touraine 2000: 8).

Touraine asks what power 'can bring together and reconcile a transnational economy and infra-national identities' (Touraine 2000: 11). The answer he proposes to fill this space between instrumentality and identity is a personal life project which implies a refusal to allow our experience to be reduced to a 'discontinuous set of responses to the stimuli of the social environment' (Touraine 2000: 13). The subject is formed in the attempt to transform lived experience into the construction of the self as a social actor, and, as such, it is the 'only possible' source of social movements that can oppose the masters of economic change or communitarian dictators. The second part of Touraine's book deals with how the apparently non-social principle of the subject can be used to reconstruct social life, or to defend an ideal of solidarity, as he expresses it in the conclusion (Touraine 2000: 299). The first principle is one of reciprocity, whereby the subject can develop only if others are recognised as subjects striving to reconcile a cultural memory and an instrumental project, as in multiculturalism, the topic of Chapter 5 of his book. The second is that the subject requires institutional safeguards that allow development, as, for example, an alternative educational system (Touraine 2000: 265–87). Touraine argues that there is a central conflict being waged, by a subject 'struggling against the triumph of the market and technologies, on the one hand, and communitarian authoritarian powers, on the other' (Touraine 2000: 89). This cultural conflict is as pivotal in the twenty-first century as the political conflict between liberals and monarchists was at the outset of modernity, and the economic conflict between labour and capital was in industrial society.

The idea of a central conflict erupting at the level of individual experience leads Touraine to recognise the importance of ethics in the development of solidarity, and leads him to call for a double move, from politics to ethics and then from ethics back to politics (Touraine 2000: 294–305). Unfortunately, this suggestion of bringing ethical values to the forefront of political contestation is not accompanied by any specificity concerning the content of such a liberational ethics. When he poses the problem of the nature of this ethics he leaves the answer frustratingly elusive, concluding that neither liberalism nor communitarianism can explain how inter-cultural communication is possible, 'or how we can live together with our differences' (Touraine 2000: 138). The universality of liberalism is so far removed from the reality of social life that it offers no more than procedural safeguards for tolerance and cannot provide a principle for social integration or inter-cultural communication. Communitarians emphasise shared values but, argues Touraine, the logic of their standpoint privileges homogeneity over diversity. Even when communitarians attempt to overcome this problem by emphasising tolerance they fall back into a position similar to that of the liberals. What Touraine seems to be getting at here is that for both perspectives the 'other' is recognised, after a fashion, but remains estranged from either the individual or the group. In order to light the way for a genuine inter-cultural communication, he opts for a principle of mediation which is more concrete than the liberal universalist principle or the appeal to cultural communities. It is found in the individual action that allows us all to reconcile instrumental action and cultural loyalties in our personal lives, in the process of which we become truly individual. When society recognises and safeguards every individual's attempt to become a subject, and encourages every individual to succeed in reconciling instrumentality and identity, inter-cultural communication becomes possible.

Touraine accepts that there can be no communication unless those communicating have a common unitary principle, but only the *attempt* at reconciling instrumental action and identity can supply that principle, and that is the definition of the subject.

Crucially, he adds that the individual cannot recognise her or his own desire to be an actor without recognising that others also have the right to be actors in their own lives, something which he regards as akin to a 'natural right or an ethical law' (Touraine 2000: 138). Touraine clearly feels that invoking the subject in this way is preferable to an appeal to shared communitarian values, which, he feels, implies a form of homogenising power which is bound to provoke resistance. This sort of resistance, he argues, has been under-estimated by Habermas and John Rawls in their attempts to provide general principles and procedures which, if followed, would promote social harmony.

According to Touraine, the pain of not being a subject gives rise to the 'tragic power' of a social movement. We are divided and fragmented, but what can allow us to live together is the 'kinship' between our attempts to harmonise our interests and our cultural identities (Touraine 2000: 139). It is interesting that he chooses to use 'kinship' in this respect, because it implies a natural basis for the development of this ethic of self-realisation, but clearly this is not a path that he wants to go down. His approach implies that any invocation of such 'thick' universal principles as 'common humanity' would lead to the negative outcomes he attributes to communitarian logic. However, without a consideration of common human needs it becomes difficult to argue *why* people should choose to move away from either egoism or the determination to live in gated communities. Touraine asserts that the starting point for the universalism of the subject has to involve placing restrictions on the powers of markets on the one hand and communities on the other (Touraine 2000: 140), but it is hard to imagine how support for such a radical turn could be generated on the basis of an appeal to his very 'thin' ethical rule of reciprocal freedom. Radical humanism tries to address these issues by considering the questions of human nature and human flourishing. It aims to draw out from people's own experience an awareness of the deep inadequacy of both egoism and tribalism and an awareness of the possibility of richer ways of self-realisation and inter-cultural communication.

There is less emphasis on the concept of solidarity in Touraine's subsequent writings, although he continues to promote his normative goal of reaching reciprocal understanding through the development of socially responsible subjects. In *A New Paradigm for Understanding Today's World* he reiterates the view that the new 'central conflict' is the struggle between the non-social forces driven by global market mechanisms and the subject, striving for new institutional forms promoting freedom and creativity. He continues to give a prominent role to new social movements, and particularly the contributions of women's and 'alter-globalization' movements, in this struggle (Touraine 2007: 208–10). However, this is premised on a broader perspective that assumes a shift in our understanding of present-day society whereby the economic and social paradigm is replaced by a cultural paradigm, with less emphasis on social struggles for control of the state and more on cultural issues. As Touraine admits, there is a superficial similarity here with Honneth's stress on recognition, but he argues that, *contra* Honneth, the role of new social movements is vital, and their strivings cannot be confined to particular social entities that somehow fulfil the conditions for justice (Touraine 2007: 149–56). Here we glimpse why 'solidarity' may no longer appear to be the appropriate concept for this new form of individualised reciprocity, as the Durkheimian idea is so rooted in the institutions of a tightly bonded society. This paradigm of classical sociology has, in Touraine's view, 'finally been destroyed' (Touraine 2007: 52–3).

Solidarity, of course, need not be restricted to this dependence on formal social institutions, and in *Thinking Differently* Touraine makes it clear that it is a vital ingredient in the value orientation of the new progressive subject. Again he is concerned to dispel the legitimacy of a succession of 'dominant interpretative discourses' which explain social reality as the outcome of structural factors over which the individual citizen has no control, effectively 'eliminating' the actor as an active subject in what he calls a 'blind society' (Touraine 2009: 36). Touraine declares his 'permanent battle' against this tendency to negate the subject, but reminds readers that for the subject to assert its own subjective power it must recognise within experience 'the pulsation of friendship, of love, self-sacrifice, of solidarity and the call to arms to defend freedom and drive out the enemy' (Touraine 2009: 146). Interestingly, he avers that his own approach amounts to 'humanism' but he is reluctant to announce that because it is a term that has been 'worn out' by so many different and often contradictory uses. In the next chapter I will try to rescue a form of radical humanism from the rhetorical mire, in pursuit of goals which are broadly sympathetic to Touraine's approach.

Also in *Thinking Differently*, Touraine returns to the issue of solidarity, when considering how the social bond might be reconstructed. He identifies two major ways, the first of which involves a reinvigoration of local social bonds in a way which does not resort to the aggressive exclusionism of some forms of communitarianism. He finds this new communitarianism too defensive to be significant, although this conclusion may be rather too hasty. However, he also rightly warns against the emergence of new 'tribes' based on a variety of identities that are always defined against other groups and militate against a broader solidarity (Touraine 2009: 184). This danger prompts him to bemoan the 'monster of identity' and warn against the 'obsession' with identity, which he regards as a regressive trend (Touraine 2009: 48 and 89). The other way of recreating the social bond is through voluntary organisations, intervening in civil society, guided by humanitarian goals but also operating in militant ways to defend the vulnerable. He sees them as progressive in so far as they are not driven by the promotion of sectional interest, and as long as they prioritise the principles of 'freedom, justice or solidarity' (Touraine 2009: 184–5).

Carol Gould

Carol Gould approaches the concept of solidarity from her work on democracy. In *Rethinking Democracy* (1988) she argues for the extension of democratic rights from the political sphere into economic and social life, while recognising that the achievement of democracy alone will not guarantee justice for all. It is conceivable that democratic decisions could violate the rights of some citizens, and there should be some way of arguing that such an outcome is 'unjust'. As we shall see, in *Globalizing Democracy and Human Rights* (2004), she elaborates a theory of human rights to resolve that problem based on a principle of equal positive freedom, and feelings of care, empathy and solidarity are accorded great significance. In order to do this, however, Gould has to make clear her dissatisfaction with philosophical accounts of justice in which the only validation for justice is to be found in ideal democratic procedures, and in this respect she cites the contributions of John Rawls, Robert Dahl, Iris Marion Young and Jürgen Habermas (Gould 2004: 14–31). Even in those accounts which somehow hold justice to be a condition for democracy, the principle of justice is ultimately grounded in some ideal form of deliberation.

In her alternative account Gould holds freedom to be the 'common foundation that normatively grounds the conceptions of both justice and democracy', where freedom involves both a capacity for choice and the exercise of that choice in long-term projects and the development of potentials (Gould 2004: 33). The self-development of individuals entails social interaction, involving joint activities and shared goals, so the individual is always the social individual. Furthermore, self-transforming activity requires the ability to make effective choices, involving means of subsistence, activity, freedom from domination and the reciprocal recognition of each other's freedom. Since this freedom characterises all human beings, Gould argues that there is an equal and valid right to the conditions of self-development of each human being. We recognise others as human beings primarily because of their capacity to act freely, and we recognise that if they are denied the means to do so this capacity is 'abstract and empty'. This acknowledgement of the right of people to exercise self-transforming activity, individually and socially, is termed 'equal positive freedom', and constitutes Gould's principle of justice (Gould 2004: 33–4). It is important to note that this claim for human rights is based on a social ontology, a conception of being in the world in which we recognise from the everyday observation of social interaction that we are all making claims to the conditions for our self-development (Gould 2004: 41). Gould's emphasis on reciprocity between individuals also takes on a socio-political significance, in the mutual recognition of common rights to participate in setting common goals and the processes of achieving them.

In relation to the idea of reciprocity Gould introduces notions of care and empathy associated with Carol Gilligan's ethics of care approach. This will be discussed more fully in Chapter 4, but in essence Gilligan argues that on moral issues women place greater emphasis on caring and empathy than men, and she takes this to be the foundation for an ethics of justice and care in which human relationship is central (Gilligan 2000: 62–3). Gould uses the ethics of care model to bolster the claim for respect to the right to equal positive freedom, and she identifies three aspects that can be generalised at the level of democratic communities. First, respect for the specific individuality of the other encourages an empathy that will distinguish social and political deliberations from 'mere compliance' with democratic rules of the game. Second, it encourages a sense of responsibility in the way cooperation takes place in the process of making decisions and achieving the goal. Third, it helps to focus concern on those most vulnerable in society, providing security with the aim of eliminating the conditions of dependence (Gould 2004: 42–6). In many respects, as we shall see in Chapter 5, the struggle by women in Western societies for equal rights and equality of esteem exemplifies this demand for social inclusion (Gould 2004: 139–58).

Gould sees solidarity as a 'social correlate' of care and empathy that needs to be brought back into political philosophy. She argues that feeling solidarity with others 'normally applies between people in different social groups and is a sort of standing with others based on an empathic understanding of their concrete situation' (Gould 2004: 66). She acknowledges the historical link between solidarity and socialist movements but argues that there is no reason why this cannot be carried forward into other contexts, such as transnational support for oppressed groups. She also offers a distinction between solidarity with others on the grounds of shared interest and a more general human solidarity that can be shared with everyone. This becomes part of Gould's normative ideal of 'intersociative democracy', involving care, empathy and solidarity, which can extend internationally as a form of 'cosmopolitical democracy' (Gould 2004: 181–2). In general she is supportive of the ideas on cosmopolitan democracy advocated by David Held and Daniele Archibugi, who propose the extension of democratic accountability to all decision-making at all appropriate levels, from the local through to the global (Held 1995, 2004; Archibugi 2008). Like them, however, Gould resists the idea of a world government, which would centralise power and authority on a global scale at the expense of the plurality of modes of self-determination (Gould 2004: 182).

At the global level, Gould identifies two major deficits: a global justice deficit, manifested in the millions of people forced to live in impoverished conditions, and a global democratic deficit, whereby institutions such as the WTO and the IMF – as well as global corporations – make decisions impacting on the welfare of millions without being properly accountable (Gould 2004: 200–1). She acknowledges the work of INGOs in bringing some of the more controversial aspects of global economic governance and corporate malpractice to the gaze of public inquiry. She also recognises the gulf between the limited success achieved by global solidarity activists and the radical institutional reforms advocated by the theorists of cosmopolitan democracy. Nevertheless, she identifies progress in establishing human rights claims through these struggles (Gould 2004: 214–16). Although Gould grounds her conceptualisation of solidarity in concrete social interaction, she envisages the development from empathy through personal interaction to a broader feeling of solidarity:

> Although it is unreasonable to suppose that people will feel a solidarity with all the interests of other individuals or groups, particularly

inasmuch as some of these conflict with their own, nonetheless a sort of human solidarity is certainly possible and necessary, where this suggests an empathic understanding of the common needs and interests of others and a standing with them in view of these. (Gould 2004: 254)

She goes on to argue that it is also possible to feel solidarity through differences in which we empathically understand the distinctive situation of others. This would involve acknowledging their unique challenges and conflicts and recognising the growing inter-dependence with these different groups. However, note the tentativeness of her commitment to the idea of human solidarity, stemming, I will argue, from her resistance to essentialist accounts of universal human needs.

In 2007 Gould coedited with Sally Scholz a special edition of the *Journal of Social Philosophy* on the concept of solidarity. In her own contribution, 'Transnational Solidarity', she develops an idea of 'overlapping solidarity networks', without invoking an all-embracing idea of solidarity of the whole universe of human beings. In saying this she wants to avoid a formulation that would fall foul of Richard Rorty's criticisms of purely abstract concepts of human solidarity (Gould 2007: 149). The idea of 'network solidarity' acknowledges that it would be impossible to apply a norm that required people to express solidarity with every human being, so the norm relies on our relations to particular 'others'. However, this need not be limited to individuals but can apply to associations that can be remote, and solidarity can therefore be extended across borders. Gould argues that the shared values invoked in such solidarity relationships consist in 'a shared commitment to justice, or perhaps also, in more consequentialist terms, to the elimination of suffering'. The stress here is on feelings for others, so that what is known as the affective element is central, and importance is placed on the disposition to act towards others who are in a different situation from ourselves. As examples she cites the tremendous responses to the plights of people involved in the Boxing Day tsunami of 2004 or Hurricane Katrina in 2005 (Gould 2007: 155–7). Although this solidarity is

Theories of Solidarity

expressed in concrete ways, it points to a more general development of feelings of openness and receptivity, and in that sense Gould accepts that there is some utility in retaining a notion of 'general human solidarity' as what she terms a 'limit notion'. It also involves an ethical disposition that supplements the political commitment to human rights and democracy across the world (Gould 2007: 160).

Gould notes three problems in moving from theory to practice (Gould 2007: 160–3). In the first instance, it appears to require altruistic behaviour, depending on a high level of moral motivation that is unlikely to be extended in a transnational way. Within smaller groups, solidaristic behaviour can be shown to deliver mutual benefits, and Gould cites Michael Hechter's *Principles of Group Solidarity* in this respect (Hechter 1987), but at the global level this is more difficult to establish. Gould claims that recognition of the equal right of all to the fulfilment of human rights, combined with the role of empathy in specific social contexts, can sustain the motivation required for solidaristic action. To this it might be added that the growing awareness of the significance of the impact of global decision-making on issues such as debt, poverty and global warming makes these issues less remote. The second problem she identifies is the episodic nature of some solidaristic action, which is over-dependent on selective media coverage of particular 'stories'. She offers no easy solution to this problem, but it may be possible to develop solidaristic work beyond the short-term attention generated by media coverage. An event that occurred after the publication of Gould's article that illustrates this problem was the rescue of the Chilean miners stranded underground for several weeks in 2010. It was a great global good news story, and a tremendous example of human resilience and solidarity. Nevertheless, global activists were quick to point out how many such accidents occur across the world, often because of lax safety regulations. Gould's final problem is a more theoretical one, concerning the link between the particularity of solidaristic relations and the universality of appeals to human rights. Here the point is that principles of human rights do not emerge from pure rationality but rather from the range of solidaristic relations, and they express universal claims that we make on each other for 'the positive fulfilment of the basic conditions of human activity'. This issue of the basic conditions for human activity brings to mind the capabilities approach adopted by Martha Nussbaum, and this is specifically raised by Gould in *Globalizing Democracy*.

Gould considers Nussbaum's approach to be a form of 'abstract universalism' that she wants to avoid. Nussbaum adopts an openly essentialist philosophy that identifies ten capabilities which need to be available to all human beings if they are to lead a fulfilled existence. This form of eudaemonistic ethics is grounded in Aristotle's goal of developing human potentials to fulfil human essence and achieve flourishing, and also in the commitment to human flourishing contained in the early writings of Karl Marx. Gould's objections reflect a more general unease with essentialist approaches, in particular that they always reflect a particular cultural viewpoint that will be imposed on all others as universal, that they exclude people from the human community by nature of their specification of human powers, that they ignore negative potentials, and that they imply fixed qualities that detract from the deep plurality of human nature (Gould 2004: 51–73). She judges quite reasonably that the particular version offered by Nussbaum tends to shy away from the issue of what sort of social power prevents the emergence of human fulfilment (Gould 2004: 58). However, her other criticisms of the essentialist approach are far less convincing, and fall into the category of standard criticisms of essentialism that I will deal with in the next chapter. It will become clear that I think the aversion to identifying common human needs undermines appeals to global solidarity, and this may account for what looks like a retreat from her earlier position in an article published in 2009. Here she concludes that solidarity 'need not take the form of general human solidarity' and then pushes even further away by saying that it 'perhaps' *cannot* take this form (Gould 2009: 210).

Conclusion

The theorists of solidarity have contributed in different ways to bringing this important concept to prominence. From Rorty there is an uplifting commitment to an ongoing project to widen the reach of human solidarity, combined with the important insight that the processes of redescription necessary to move us in that direction are located in the cultural sphere. From Honneth we can understand modern social struggles not simply as the claims of 'interests', but as struggles for recognition containing an immanent moral dimension, with solidarity as an ultimate normative ideal. From Habermas it is possible to take a critical but hopeful view of a socio-political trajectory that transcends the nation state and contributes to the development of post-national solidarity. Touraine's conception of the subject encourages the view that the development of individualism need not lead to social disintegration, but to new forms of multicultural solidarity. From Gould, we see an important link between the historical achievements of democracy and the need to extend it to the recently developed decision-making processes that structure our modern globalized world. However, all these theorists, in various ways, resist the idea that we can support the appeal to global solidarity on the basis of a strong view of human essence and its realisation. The next chapter will offer a radical humanist position based on such a view, identifying key human potentials that would need to be developed in order to bring global solidarity into sight.

4 Radical Humanism

The appeal to a sense of common humanity is frequently heard as a rhetorical ploy, but within social theory there is a widespread scepticism that such an appeal can be philosophically justified. For example, Margaret Canovan has described the invocation to common humanity as 'the grandest but flimsiest of contemporary imagined communities' (Canovan 2001: 212). In general, there is a resistance to the idea of theorising about human freedom on the basis of a common human essence, not least because such 'essentialism' appears to be incompatible with human plurality. Iris Marion Young expressed this succinctly when she wrote that 'any definition of a human nature is dangerous because it threatens to devalue or exclude some acceptable individual desires, cultural characteristics, or ways of life' (Young 1990: 36). On this view, any account of what is good for all humans on account of their humanity is bound to be historically contingent and culturally specific, leading to the sort of exclusions or excommunications that reproduce oppression. On the other hand, Young admits that normative theory can hardly avoid making assumptions about human nature, and her suggestion that an 'image' of human nature could be employed rather than an explicit theory seems to me to be evasive and unhelpful (Young 1990: 137).

In this chapter I argue that it is possible to make meaningful generalisations about what humans need to live a truly human life, without denying the legitimate aspirations of groups and individuals. In so doing I offer a form of virtue ethics, which has enjoyed a notable revival in recent years (Slote 1992; MacIntyre

1994; Statman 1997; Hursthouse 1999; Crisp and Slote 2002; Foot 2003). Such an approach is often labelled 'neo-Aristotelian', in honour of Aristotle as the first to argue for the goal of human flourishing – *eudaemonia* – as the fulfilment of human essence by practice of the virtues. The prefix 'neo' simply indicates that while Aristotle's framework is broadly accepted, his specific opinions about who could and could not achieve *eudaemonia* are regarded as no longer relevant (Hursthouse 1999: 8–16). The radical humanism advocated here also draws on the philosophy of the young Marx and the social psychology of Erich Fromm. This humanism is radical because it directly addresses the structural causes of oppression and exploitation and demands systemic change as a precondition for global solidarity. First, however, the chapter will outline what is meant by virtue ethics and counter some common objections to it. The second part will focus on the ideas of Marx and Fromm on human essence and its realisation. The third part will look at the human potentials that would need to be developed by individuals and societies if the goal of global solidarity were to be advanced. This will take into account a number of important objections to radical humanism, such as the claims that it is unreasonably optimistic, anthropocentric and/or inherently opposed to social pluralism. Finally, some comparisons will be made between the radical humanism advocated here and the work of Martha Nussbaum, whose capabilities approach to global justice shares important similarities.

Virtue ethics

As Alasdair MacIntyre points out in *After Virtue*, the moral scheme analysed by Aristotle in the *Nichomachean Ethics* involves three elements: the idea of an untutored human nature, the goal of a fully realised life in which that nature is perfected, and a set of moral precepts that can enable people 'to understand how they make the transition from the former state to the latter' (MacIntyre 1994: 52–3). This framework, with its account of the human *telos* or final end, is a teleological theory. As MacIntyre argues, each of the elements requires reference to the other two to make sense. This ethical viewpoint prevailed in the ancient world and was introduced into European universities in the twelfth and thirteenth centuries, following the rediscovery of ancient Greek texts via Arabic and Hebrew translations (Kenny 2000: 126–50). The eudaemonistic ethical framework was embraced by theistic scholars and brought into alignment with Islam by Averroes (1126–98), Judaism by Maimonides (1135–1204) and Christianity by Thomas Aquinas (1225–74). This revival of classical scholarship and its reconciliation with religious beliefs was at the heart of the humanist movement of the European Renaissance from the fourteenth to the sixteenth centuries (Burckhardt 2004: 129–84). It should be noted that only in the twentieth century did humanism became associated primarily with opposition to religion (Norman 2004: 8–15), a variation that plays no significant part of the radical humanist perspective outlined in this chapter.

MacIntyre argues that in dropping the teleological element of a human essence striving for realisation, the great moral philosophers of the Enlightenment such as Immanuel Kant (1724–84) and David Hume (1711–76) left themselves the impossible task of reconciling a view of 'untutored' human nature with a set of moral precepts that could not be deduced from that nature. Indeed, the various moral precepts the Enlightenment philosophers developed were implicitly operating to correct and discipline human impulses, so that that the precepts and human nature are 'expressly designed to be discrepant with each other' (MacIntyre 1994: 55). The serious consequence of this is that morality came to be viewed as a corrective to human nature rather than an expression of its development, reflecting a deeply suspicious view of our own nature. The emphasis in Kantian ethics was on duty, or obedience to an inner conviction of what is right. The external source of moral authority, God, is replaced by an internal authority. In utilitarian ethics, what is morally right and wrong is decided by a calculation of the consequences of actions. In both cases the emphasis is on right and wrong actions and the formulation of rules and principles to guide those actions. In contrast, virtue ethics emphasises the character of moral agents, asking the question 'What sort of person should I be?' rather than 'What sort of action should I do?' (Hursthouse 1999: 17). If people develop their positive potentials and act in good conscience, then good actions will follow.

At this early point in the discussion it is necessary to deal with the standard philosophical objection to eudaemonistic approaches, namely the naturalistic fallacy, which argues that it is impermissible to derive a prescriptive 'ought' from a descriptive 'is'. The objection was originally made by Hume in his *Treatise of Human Nature* in 1739 and then developed as a philosophical truism following the publication of G. E. Moore's (1873–1958) *Principia Ethica* of 1903 (Graham 2006: 8–10). In twentieth-century academic philosophy it was routinely invoked to reject the sort of essentialism put forward by Aristotle. However, as Philip Kain has argued, even if we accept that it is illegitimate to deduce moral conclusions from non-moral premises, real-world facts already have values embedded in them, in which case we can derive values from these facts. The human essence is not just factually given but constituted by social and cultural activity, and as values and needs play a part in constituting that culture, our essence is formed by these values and needs. Values are therefore embedded in our essence so that when we derive morality from a view of the human essence we are not deducing moral conclusions from non-moral premises (Kain 1991: 30–2). The misunderstanding arises from what is meant by the 'fact' of what constitutes our human essence. As MacIntyre comments, if the naturalistic fallacy was to hold good, it would have to exclude functional concepts from its scope, but for the whole Aristotelian tradition, including its medieval versions, humanity was conceived in terms of its purpose and function (MacIntyre 1994: 56–9). The formulations of human essence were functional, and they cry out for the full realisation of that defining function. If we are defined as rational and social beings it follows that we ought to act to perfect that rationality and sociability, just as holders of certain functions should perform them well. If a person develops a talent and chooses to pursue it, the person negates her essence if she neglects to hone that talent and succumbs instead to complacency or greed.

Human essence: Aristotle, Marx and Fromm

Aristotle argues that humans are by nature rational and social beings. In Book One of the *Nichomachean Ethics* he contends that the human being 'is, by nature, a social being', possessing the 'rational principle' which is demonstrated functionally, by pursuing the good in accordance with virtue, just as the function of a good harpist is to play the harp well (Aristotle 1976: 74–6). Similarly, in the *Politics*, he denotes the 'rational principle within us' as the capacity that makes humans unique (Aristotle 1969: 314). In his view, it is the 'peculiarity' of human beings that they alone possess 'a perception of good and evil, of the just and the unjust' (Aristotle 1969: 6). Furthermore, humans are essentially social beings, living in political association, causing Aristotle to add that although the human being, 'when perfected', is the best of animals, 'if he be isolated from law and justice he is the worst of all' (Aristotle 1969: 7). In other words, although his account of human flourishing is directed towards the individual, it is clear that the individual can achieve a good life only within a well-ordered community. For both the individual and for society, Aristotle advocated, via the doctrine of the mean, a balanced life that avoided extremes. The idea that humans are essentially rational and sociable has enduring appeal, although in making this abstraction from Aristotle's philosophy we are setting to one side his acceptance of the inequalities of his time in which slaves, women and workers were simply not considered as candidates for *eudaemonia*. His ideal of the fully realised human life was one of learned contemplation, the 'highest' and 'most continuous' form of activity (Aristotle 1976: 328–9).

Marx shares with Aristotle the view that humans are rational and social beings, but unlike Aristotle he emphasises the centrality of productive activity in establishing human uniqueness. In considering what distinguishes humans from other animals, he focuses on the unique way in which humans produce. His discussion of human nature in *Economic and Philosophic Manuscripts of 1844* is best understood as one aspect of a philosophical attempt to conceptualise the human costs that flowed inevitably from the spread of commodity production. He bemoans the fact that work is experienced as deadening compulsion, with the worker feeling free only in functions such as eating, drinking and copulating, which, taken abstractly, are animal functions (Marx 1975: 327). The fact that these functions are shared with animals does not mean that they are not also human needs which are being met, but clearly Marx feels there are specifically human needs are not being met. The theme of alienation is the leitmotif of the *Manuscripts*, and although Marx begins by talking about alienation arising from the process of production itself, he also talks of alienation from 'species-being', a term adopted by Ludwig Feuerbach (1804–72) to refer to human essence. In order to explain how humans under capitalism become alienated from their human essence he is obliged to discuss what is unique to humans by comparing them with other animals. According to Marx, 'conscious life activity' distinguishes humans from animals, for whereas animals are 'immediately one' with their life activity, humans make their life activity the object of their will and consciousness. This emphasis on rational planning of our 'activity' is followed by a sharper focus on the human capacity for social production, designing and making products for social consumption.

Marx's argument is that by creating a world of objects, humans prove themselves to be conscious species-beings, or, in other words, they demonstrate their essence. Animals too produce, but only for what they or their young immediately need; they produce only to meet their immediate physical need, while humans produce even when they are free from physical need. Indeed truly free production occurs only when immediate needs are taken care of, and humans gain knowledge of how to produce in accordance with the standard of every species, and how to produce according to ideas of beauty (Marx 1975: 328–9). In other words, although animals can adapt to their environment by changing themselves, only humans can radically change their environment and evaluate their actions.

In the development of modern industry Marx saw both an objective demonstration of the human essence of conscious social life activity and its simultaneous contradiction in the subjective experience of the mass of producers, for whom alienated labour was nothing more than compulsion in order to survive. The development of industry reveals the 'open book' of humanity's 'essential powers', even though its immediate effect is the 'dehumanisation of man' (Marx 1975: 354–5). This conception of dehumanisation is present throughout Marx's works, as a deprivation that can be remedied only in the process of the struggle to take production out of the hands of private capitalists and into social control. The task of communists was to lead society away from this alienation, so that our essential human potentials could be realised. At this stage, still in philosophical mode, Marx defines communism as the 'true appropriation of the human essence' by and for human beings, the 'return' of humans to themselves as social beings (Marx 1975: 348). In other words, the young Marx sees communism as a struggle for the rehumanisation of the world. This conception of the young Marx is fundamentally eudaemonistic, and I would argue that it is implicit in his later work in political economy, even though he dropped explicitly philosophical and moral discourse after 1846 (Wilde 1998: 10–50).

Marx chose not to develop this moral critique of capitalism in his later works for strategic reasons that were understandable at that time. His chief concern was to offer a structural explanation of exploitation and oppression as a reliable guide to social and political action rather than to resort to the moral appeals that were commonly adopted by socialists at that time. To Marx and his later followers, moralising discourse was considered a digression from the task of analysing the capitalist mode of production and exposing its contradictions. However, it can be argued that he abandoned only the discourse of an ethics of freedom as self-realisation rather than its substance, because his analysis of capitalism involved strong rhetorical denunciations of the sufferings it inflicted, and he maintained a commitment to the achievement of the 'true realm of freedom' (Marx 1981: 959). Indeed Marx offers some insightful comments about the need for theorising human nature in ethics in *Capital* in a footnote upbraiding the English utilitarian philosopher Jeremy Bentham (1748–1832) for failing to deal with the issue:

> To know what is useful for a dog, one must investigate the nature of dogs. This nature is not itself deducible from the principle of utility. Applying this to man, he that would judge all human acts, movements, relations, etc., according to the principle of utility would first have to deal with human nature in general, and then with human nature as historically modified in each epoch. Bentham does not trouble himself with this. (Marx 1990: 758–9n)

Unfortunately, Marx himself did not delve further into human nature in general and its historical modifications, and his proscription on moral discourse was adhered to by his followers in the Marxist tradition. Only a small number of Marxists, usually standing apart from party politics, tried to introduce ethical considerations into what was, after all, a theory of human liberation (Wilde 2001). In terms of developing ethical theory in line with Marx's philosophy of human nature, the most explicit attempt has come from Erich Fromm.

Fromm's major presentation of humanistic ethics occurs in *Man for Himself* (1947) (Fromm 2003: 27–87), reiterated with different emphases in *The Sane Society* (1955) (Fromm 1990: 22–66) and *The Heart of Man* (Fromm 1964: 115–50). Although he locates himself in a tradition including Aristotle, Spinoza and Marx, Fromm's background in psychoanalysis and social psychology leads to a distinctively psychological account of character traits. He argues that the proper purpose of human life is the fulfilment of our essential human potential, with the emphasis on the virtuous character and the nature of the good society. The task of ethics is to work out how the human essence can achieve its *telos* or purpose through the exercise of the virtues. Fromm is concerned with the kind of society in which wellbeing and integrity can be realised by all people, through the development of the potentials which are innate to us as human beings. For Fromm, loving one's neighbour does not involve transcending human nature but something that radiates from it. Humans find fulfilment and happiness 'only in relatedness and solidarity' with their fellow humans. Humanistic ethics affirms life through the unfolding of human powers, provided that this empowerment is not at the expense of others, for this would be tantamount to 'evil'. In this conception, virtue is regarded as self-responsibility and vice as irresponsibility (Fromm 2003: 5–14).

What is it that makes us essentially human? Like Aristotle and Marx, Fromm asks what distinguishes us from other animals. He regards the human essence not as a given quality or substance but as 'a contradiction inherent in human existence' (Fromm 1964: 116–17). Unlike other animals, the instinctual apparatus of humans is very poorly developed, but this weakness is compensated for by the development of quintessential human qualities (Fromm 2003: 28). Human beings develop self-awareness, becoming aware of the past and the inevitability of death, of our own smallness and powerlessness, and of our relationship to others as friends, enemies or strangers. This self-awareness disrupts the oneness experienced by other animals and turns us into anomalous, contradictory beings, at once subject to the laws of nature and at the same time transcending nature. Human existence is in a 'state of constant and unavoidable disequilibrium', but this condition generates needs which transcend those of animal origin and result in an 'imperative drive to restore a unity and equilibrium' between humanity and the rest of nature (Fromm 2003: 33).

Fromm insists that it makes sense to talk about essential human qualities or potentials only within the framework of a more general view of human essence, that singular form of life which is aware of itself:

Man is confronted with the frightening conflict of being the prisoner of nature, yet being free in his thoughts; being a part of nature, and yet to be as it were a freak of nature: being neither here nor there. Human self-awareness has made man a stranger in the world, separate, lonely, and frightened. (Fromm 1964: 117)

The working through of the contradiction leads either to the final goal of human solidarity or, if the regressive path is taken, to 'complete dehumanisation which is the equivalent of madness' (Fromm 1964: 121). The progressive solution involves the development of authentically human qualities towards the goal of human solidarity, a condition in which all human beings feel sympathy for each other and are determined to resolve problems peacefully through cooperation. The regressive responses are manifested, according to Fromm, as neuroses in individuals and a 'socially patterned defect' at the social level (Fromm 2003: 166).

Framing human nature in terms of an existential contradiction dispels a common criticism of accounts of human flourishing, namely that only positive potentials are stressed rather than negative ones. To the contrary, Fromm's discussion of the contradiction emphasises the daunting nature of the challenge of being in the world as the only creatures that are aware of the inevitability of death. He is also quite clear that it is likely that this challenge prompts negative reactions, either through submission to authority or through communalistic intolerance and xenophobia. This idea of existential dilemma as the heart of human essence also avoids the trap of conceiving a philosophy of human flourishing as a form of 'perfectionism', implying a utopian state of pure harmony, with all predicaments resolved (Lukes 1985: 142). The goal of human solidarity is not seen as a path to perfection, but rather as something that can be worked for in the conviction that it is possible to overcome major antagonisms that produce war and social injustice. Even though Fromm considered the chances of such a radical turn towards solidarity as slight, he argued that it was all the more imperative to work for a new ethic of human solidarity (Fromm 2002: 195–6). Accordingly, he places great emphasis on reforms that move society in the right direction, rather than following the conventional Marxist path of declaring the impossibility of significant change as long as capitalism exists (Wilde 2004: 75–130).

As a psychoanalyst and social psychologist, much of Fromm's work deals with the development of non-productive character orientations, most of which are similar to those identified by Sigmund Freud (1856–1939). However, Fromm's distinctive contribution to these negative orientations, the modern 'marketing character', provides the basis for his argument that affluent alienation is a widespread phenomenon in liberal capitalist societies. The marketing character involves the replacement of authentic self-development and the achievement of happiness by a constant readjustment of the self in response to the market (Fromm 2002: 147–54; Fromm 2003: 49–60). This 'automatisation' of the individual is conceived as a loss of self, reproduced in a social condition of alienation, an extension of Marx's theory of alienation from the sphere of production to the sphere of consumption, a theme also developed by Herbert Marcuse in his influential *One-dimensional Man*, published in 1964 (Fromm 1990: 120–51; Fromm 2002: 154–60; cf. Marcuse 2002: 1–20). However, what is crucial for the possibility of solidarity is the idea of a progressive response to the human dilemma, encapsulated in *Man for Himself* as the development of the productive character (Fromm 2003: 60–79) and later, in *To Have or to Be?*, as the 'being mode' (Fromm 2002: 87–107). The productive character displays the independent, rational realisation of human potentials, in a general 'mode of relatedness' in all realms of human experience. Through productiveness we resolve the paradox of human existence by simultaneously expressing our oneness with others *and* our uniqueness. At one point Fromm specifies the necessity of achieving happiness by the full realisation of the quintessentially human qualities of reason, love and productive work (Fromm 2003: 32). However, the list of these qualities should not be taken as definitive. Across a range of books Fromm discusses other virtues such as faith, responsibility and joy, and delves further into the complexities of reason, productiveness and love.

Core potentials

One of the problems with virtue ethics is that the virtues which are commended as of universal value are invariably culturally specific and often frustratingly ambiguous (MacIntyre 1994: 181–203; Foot 2002). If potentials are described in abstract terms, then they may simply be too vague to act as criteria for evaluating action in practical ethics. On the other hand, if the virtues are specified more stringently, their claim to universality will be rejected by those who think their cultural practices are offended or undervalued. As mentioned in Chapter 3, Jürgen Habermas considered this problem insuperable:

> For any attempt to project a universally binding collective good on which the solidarity of all human beings – including future generations – could be founded runs up against a dilemma: a substantive conception that is still sufficiently informative entails an intolerable form of paternalism ... but an empty conception that abstracts from all local contexts undermines the concept of the good. (Habermas 1999: 28)

The difficulty is clear enough, but not so daunting that we should abandon the possibility of offering a neo-Aristotelian grounding for human solidarity that escapes this 'too thick or too thin' trap.

As a first step it is useful to point to the anthropological evidence to support the idea that human beings from all cultures share a range of characteristics that can be thought of as universal attributes. This version of essentialism was resisted for many years in anthropology, just as essentialism was shunned in the wider social sciences, but it has been argued that the immense variability of human customs should be understood as different ways of expressing traits and capabilities that are common across the species (Brown 1991: 1–7). Donald Brown has drawn on the range of studies of 'human universals', including his own work, to compile a picture of what he terms 'the 'universal people'. The list covers the use of language and gesture, the development of a complex culture, and the ability to use varied and complex tools, including tools to make tools, as well as sociability, socialisation and reciprocity. It also includes psychological factors such as emotions, prestige, morality, religion and aesthetic sensibility (Brown 1991: 130–41). Interestingly, Brown considers that this acknowledgement of human universals contradicts the Marxist view of the variability of human nature, although he concedes that Marx himself may have had different views (Brown 1991: 60). In fact the empirical findings on which Brown bases his work confirm the observations on human essence of both Marx and Fromm, as outlined above. However, in order to develop a humanistic ethics it is necessary to emphasise key positive potentials that would need to be nurtured, individually and socially, to achieve the sort of human flourishing required for global solidarity. In what follows I will argue that the positive development of the core potentials of rationality, compassion, productiveness (not 'productivity', for reasons explained below) and cooperation can be seen as ethical preconditions of global solidarity. These potentials are intended to be sufficiently general so that they can be realised in a wide variety of cultural forms, but at the same time clear enough to serve as criteria for judging progress towards the normative goal of human solidarity as ever-widening inclusion. It follows that in so far as individuals realise these potentials they do so as *social* individuals, and this is important when considering what such a realisation would look like, particularly in the categories of rationality and productiveness, which can be practised in egoistic ways that are inimical to human solidarity.

Rationality

As we have seen, from Aristotle onwards the capacity to exercise reason has been regarded as a quintessentially human ability. Even though Marx switched the emphasis to production, he conceived it as the material evidence of the human ability to act in accordance with intentions, fulfilling often complex plans. However, individuals can apply reason in ways which are successful for them but may be detrimental to others. The radical humanist conception of rationality as a progressive potential takes into account not only the logical achievement of individual goals but also the consideration of what is good for humanity as a whole. This conception of reason comes closer to Max Weber's idea of 'substantive rationality', whereby actions are calculated according to their efficiency in achieving 'ultimate ends', which inevitably involve some sort of ethical commitment (Weber 1978: 85–6). In a valuable discussion of Weber's typology of rationality, Immanuel Wallerstein points out that Weber draws two pairs of distinctions, between 'instrumental' and 'value' rationality in the sphere of social action, and between 'formal' and 'substantive' in the sphere of economic action. 'Value rationality' refers to action informed by ethical considerations which is undertaken irrespective of its prospects for success, and Weber is clearly sceptical of its prospects in the face of the seductive power of instrumental rationality. However, he is far more receptive to the possibility of achieving substantive rationality, and this opens up the possibility of subordinating the pursuit of short-term individual gain to long-term social goals (Wallerstein 1999: 141–4).

The unfettered pursuit of formal economic rationality in the nineteenth and early twentieth centuries led to vast inequalities in the distribution of resources, but this was rectified to some extent within the industrialised countries by the assertion of substantive rationality through the commitment to full employment and the provision of high standards of social welfare. The emergence of economic globalization can be seen as a triumph of formal economic rationality. Substantive rationality would involve regulating the economy to serve human needs, rather than the situation existing under neoliberalism, in which human needs are subordinated to economic imperatives. Weber was careful not to specify what the 'ultimate ends' ought to be, but for radical humanism the goal is global solidarity. The aim would be to strive for a situation in which individuals are free to develop their potentials, provided that this freedom complements the freedom of all others to do likewise. This is similar to Alain Touraine's goal of the reconciliation of instrumental reason with cultural identity as the defining feature of the subject (Touraine 2000: 292), as discussed in Chapter 3.

The difficulties in moving from instrumental to substantive rationality are immense, but it is important to challenge the fatalistic view that it is simply impossible for such a transformation to occur. This fatalism flows from assumptions about human nature that are deeply embedded in Western culture, recalling religious conceptions of unworthiness and self-renunciation dating back to St Augustine. It is not difficult to show that the dismal account of human nature given by Thomas Hobbes (1588–1679) in *Leviathan* contradicts all that we know anthropologically about human historical development, but the idea of the war of each against all in a ruthless state of nature has a strong resonance in modern competitive societies (Hobbes 1991: 86–90). The response of radical humanism is not to see that human beings are really naturally good, but that they have within their nature the potential to be good. In this way it rejects the false dichotomy that we are condemned to live either in destructive mayhem or servile abjection, or some combination of the two. The baleful and all too common acceptance of the unavoidable reproduction of social injustice, on the grounds that 'human nature' is infused with an irresistible power of myopic greed, leaves no grounds for hope, even though it rarely takes into consideration the anthropological evidence. The recurrence of wars, genocide and unprovoked brutality throughout human history fuels the intuition that a destructive urge innate to humans will always prevent the achievement of the sort of substantive rationality mentioned above, but the evidence advanced in favour of this view has always been circumstantial and unconvincing.

In *The Ego and the Id* (1923), Sigmund Freud first postulates a death instinct that will be directed as destructiveness towards the outside world and other life forms, a formula he repeats in

Civilization and its Discontents (1930) (Freud 2001, 2004). Thus the death instinct runs in tandem with the conflicting instinct of Eros, or the preservation of life. Prior to that, Freud operated with a different pairing of instincts, between the ego and the sexual instinct. Although Freud presents his switch as a logical development, Erich Fromm surmises that Freud's death instinct resulted from his shocked response to the horrors of the First World War after many years of peace, and also from his tendency to theory-building at the expense of basing his theoretical findings on clinical findings (Fromm 1997: 619–20). Ultimately, the death instinct is pure speculation, and Fromm notes many more examples, in *The Anatomy of Human Destructiveness* (1974), of similar unjustifiable inferences that imply either that destructiveness is an essential human drive, or that humans can easily be socially conditioned into cruelty (for example, Fromm 1997: 77–86). In particular the experiments that purport to show the latter consistently underplay the immense distress that is shown by the subjects, just as, in reality, soldiers who have been trained to kill often find killing almost impossible to deal with (Grossman 2009). A harrowing example of this is the fact that more British soldiers involved in the Falklands War of 1982 committed suicide in the years that followed than died in combat (Bignell 2007).

Fromm's overall conclusion is compelling, namely that 'malignant aggression' is not innate but essentially a response to socio-economic conditions that turn human beings into 'psychic cripples', but it is easier for people to resort to the lazy assumption that human nature is evil, for it gives them an 'alibi' for their own sins (Fromm 1997: 575–9). All too often the possibility of achieving substantive rationality is denied by invoking the negative power of destructive human nature, the shoddiest of defences for an indefensible status quo. The important conclusion is that there is nothing to prevent humanity from learning from the past and fashioning a world in which substantive reality prevails. In emphasising this 'species potential', David Harvey rightly concludes that 'we have worked ourselves into a position in which the future of all evolution, including our own, is as much a function of conscious political and social choices as it is of random events to which we respond' (Harvey 2000: 212).

Compassion
Mary Clark, in her magisterial study *In Search of Human Nature*, describes compassion as 'the primary characteristic of human kind' (Clark 2002: 342). The literal meaning of 'compassion' is 'suffering with', and this may appear to be somewhat negative, but in the broader sense of 'feeling with' it means that the undeserved pain experienced by others becomes our pain too. It is close in meaning to 'empathy', which involves the 'imaginative reconstruction of the experience of the sufferer' (Nussbaum 2001: 327–35), and empathy is an important component of 'care' and the ethics of care mentioned in Chapter 3. Martha Nussbaum, following Aristotle, defines compassion as 'a painful emotion occasioned by the awareness of another person's undeserved misfortune' (Nussbaum 2001: 301), but the reference to pain misses the positive experience of the emotion arising from the feeling of solidarity that is evinced. Thomas More (1478–1535) recognised this positive affective force of compassion 500 years ago in his *Utopia*, when he declared it to be the finest sentiment of which our human nature is capable (More 1991: 57).

A commitment to the development of compassion as a human potential affirms the importance of emotion in morality, and also avoids some of the problems associated with related virtues such as love, friendship and charity. The intimacy inherent in love and friendship creates difficulties in attempting to apply those feelings to wider social relationships. Despite impressive attempts to do so, as, for example, in the case of Fromm's work on love (Fromm 2003, 1995) and Jacques Derrida's on friendship (Derrida 1997), there remains a problem in relating intimate emotional bonds to a wider social and political commitment to solidarity. In the case of charity, although Rosalind Hursthouse points out that most virtue ethicists assume that charity is on the list of virtues and would provide the motivating force for helping those in distress (Hursthouse 1999: 6–8), we are reminded of the reasons why Pierre Leroux originally argued a preference for solidarity over charity (Leroux 1985: 163). It is conceivable that a society of charitable people could be blind to social arrangements that reproduce distress. For most of human history poverty was regarded as natural, and the function of charity was to respond to that misfortune. To respond to distress from a developed sense of compassion, however, would be to demand that the causes of distress are confronted and resolved.

Compassion is central to the ethics of care referred to in Chapter 3. Carol Gilligan's *In a Different Voice* (1982) is based on the findings of three psychological studies, and she argues that the women participants showed a different view of moral issues than the men. The women focused on concern for others arising from a sense of close inter-connectedness, whereas the men's ideas focused on abstract rules and principles applicable to all moral problems. Gilligan suggests that this different voice expressed by women arises from experiences of inequality and inter-connection, inherent in the relation of mother and child, leading to a distinctive ethics of care. The ideals of human relationship involve a vision that self and other will be treated as of equal worth, and that, despite differences in power, things will be fair. It is a vision that 'everyone will be responded to and included, that no one will be left alone or hurt' (Gilligan 2000: 62–3). Gilligan concludes that in the different voice of women 'lies the truth of an ethic of care, the tie between relationship and responsibility, and the origins of aggression in the failure of connection' (Gilligan 2000: 173). To paraphrase the distinction, the idea of justice, based on impartial rules arrived at through reason, is contrasted with care, based on feelings of empathy with our fellow beings, derived from emotion. However, at this stage it should be noted that while care ethics might flow from emotion, it is applied through reason (Slote 2007: 119–21). Nussbaum has mounted an impressive defence of compassion against the philosophical tradition that thinks that its emotional nature must detract from reason (Nussbaum 2001: 354–400).

Two important questions arise from the argument for a

distinctive ethics of care that have important philosophical and political implications. The first relates to the source of this caring faculty – whether it lies in biology, pure and simple, or in processes of socialisation developed throughout history. The second is the scope of the ethics of care, that is to say, whether it is a sufficient principle to guide all moral judgement, or whether it requires supplementation by other forms of ethics. In relation to the first question, it can be argued that dispositions could develop from biological roles practised over millennia, without any implication that they are permanent or non-transferable. Although this appears to flout the Darwinian rejection of the inheritability of acquired characteristics, it involves only the recognition of a form of Lamarckian development specific to human cultural relations, as has been argued by the biologist Stephen Jay Gould and the historian Eric Hobsbawm (Gould 2001: 103–5; Hobsbawm 2004). An important implication of this is the extent to which we can hope, as a species, to learn from our mistakes and develop a disposition to peaceful cooperation and mutual respect.

Gilligan, although developing the idea of an ethics of care from empirical analysis of the experiences of women, thinks that the different voice of the ethics of care does not have to be female, but can be developed by both sexes – 'the different voice I describe is characterized not by gender but theme' (Gilligan 2000: 20). The basis of care ethics may be located in the historical role of motherhood, but the ethics of care is not confined to mothers or potential mothers; it is available to all humankind. Michael Slote, in his affirmation of an ethics of care and empathy as a full-blown ethical alternative to conventional approaches to justice, points to the moral sentimentalism of past male philosophers such as David Hume, Francis Hutcheson and Adam Smith, and also to Christian ethics, to suggest that there is nothing to prevent men from achieving this outlook. He argues that we should be encouraged to think of a fully developed ethics of care as 'nothing less than a total or systematic *human* morality, one that may be able to give us a better understanding of the whole range of moral issues that concern both men and women than anything to be found in traditional ethical theories' (Slote 2007: 3, original emphasis).

Does an ethics based on compassion or care contradict or complement conventional approaches to justice? Joan Tronto supports the ethics of care approach and argues that the care-versus-justice dichotomy is false (Tronto 1994: 166–7). The care approach is needed to rectify the one-sidedness of justice approaches, but a care approach can be dangerous if it does not accept that the political context in which care operates needs to be regulated by conventional justice principles. In general this places less strenuous demands on notions of care and compassion and is more open to dialogue with alternative ethical systems which seek to highlight our natural concerns for others. Interestingly, Slote is careful to declare his 'neutrality' on whether care ethics should be conceived as a form of virtue ethics (Slote 2007: 7), but it would appear to be a very thin form of virtue ethics that relied on a single virtue.

Finally, one of the strengths of emphasising the potential for compassion is to bring the discussion of the relationship between humans and other animals back into the frame. Humanism, by definition, is anthropocentric, but anthropocentrism does not necessarily produce a dismissive view of animals. As we have seen, ethical outlooks based on definitions of human nature invariably begin with a comparison with animals, and all too often this can imply superiority in the human and a deficiency in the animal. A humanism that emphasises compassion, however, recognises other animals as fellow sentient beings whose nature demands respect. Thomas More's compassion, as declared in *Utopia*, led him to deplore hunting, saying that it was plain wrong to 'want to see a living creature torn apart under your eyes', something that was 'unworthy of free men' (More 1991: 73). And although Karl Marx has been accused of disrespecting animals (Benton 1993: 40–5), in fact he recognised distinctive animal needs that ought to be met, specifying the needs to hunt, to roam and to have companionship, precisely the needs that are denied to animals in modern factory farming (Marx 1975: 360; Wilde 2000). We can extend this principle of respect for nature to the whole environment, which involves a commitment to generational solidarity. Marx insists that people do not own the earth but merely look after it with the obligation 'to bequeath it in an improved state to succeeding generations' (Marx 1981: 911), while Erich Fromm comments that 'caring means caring not only for our fellow beings on this earth but also for our descendants' (Fromm 2002: 189). What is envisaged in the radical humanist commitment to compassion is nothing less than a revolution in the relationship between humanity and nature.

Despite the ruthless competitiveness of contemporary social and economic life, inter-personal relations are rarely dominated by pure instrumentality. More often they are respectful and supportive, despite the antagonistic structures within which they are obliged to operate. This caring impulse often flows from resentment of and resistance to those structures and the disciplining processes inflicted by them. It is precisely in this 'space' that compassion can become expressed and embedded in social struggles aimed at resisting oppressions of various sorts, such as racism, sexism, the exploitation of the less developed world and the destruction of our environment (Nussbaum 2001: 401–54). Such struggles open up the issue of respect for persons and demand a reprioritisation of values so that the needs of life are no longer subordinated to the demands of economic competitiveness.

Productiveness
Philosophical attempts to prescribe the good life have often followed Aristotle in favouring contemplative activity above practical and productive activity (Aristotle 1976: 333–4). In this conception, work appears as a necessity to be performed as a lower-order activity. It is perhaps one of the most significant aspects of Thomas More's *Utopia* that it challenges this view, providing a more holistic account of human flourishing by explaining our dependence on, and collective responsibility for, the production and reproduction of our material life. In Utopia all men and women are obliged to participate in agricultural production as well as engaging in specialist crafts, while only a small minority

of officials, priests and scholars are exempted from physical work (More 1991: 50–5). Crucially, work is limited to six hours a day so that people do not have to exhaust themselves with 'endless toil', like 'beasts of burden' (More 1991: 51). More simultaneously values work for the satisfaction it gives to society and individuals, while warning against the dangers of over-work. Furthermore, the republican system adopted by the Utopians means that all the people are responsible for the structures adopted.

Marx, as we have seen, makes the capacity to produce central to his view of what it is to be human, with the implication that producers should control and benefit fully from the productive processes. However, Marx's analysis is concerned chiefly with explaining how and why the producers are denied control of the productive process. A stark contrast is drawn between the grim experience of those forced to work in horrendous conditions in order to survive, and the magnificence and potential of the products of that work. In other words, in abstraction work can be regarded as the human interaction with nature through which the species develops its powers, but in concrete terms it is experienced by the majority of workers as enforced, routine and stultifying (Sennett 1998; Beck 2000). Marx's prescription for overcoming this alienation is for society as a whole to take control of the productive system, replacing the privately owned market economy with collective control of production conducted in a rational way, with 'the least expenditure of energy and in conditions most worthy and appropriate for their human nature' (Marx 1981: 959).

Productiveness as a core potential, then, has nothing to do with 'productivity', or measurable economic efficiency, and everything to do with the freely chosen development of individual abilities that contributes to the public good. Erich Fromm is surely correct when he argues that there is a deeply rooted desire in human beings 'to express our faculties, to be active, to be related to others, to escape the prison cell of selfishness', and that most people would prefer to be active even without monetary reward (Fromm 2002: 101–2). However, he is less convincing when he holds up the artist as the epitome of productiveness, for two reasons. First, doing so sets a standard for excellence which implies that the majority of amateurs who engage in artistic or other recreational activities are somehow less productive than the professionals, when in fact the difficulties they face in striving to express themselves creatively may well mean that they are more productive, or productive in more varied ways. Second, professional artists, in abstracting themselves from the mundane aspects of the world of work and focusing entirely on intensive individual expression, place themselves in a difficult position when it comes to developing other positive potentials, such as cooperation. Indeed artists are often excused when their intense individualism seems to dull their sense of compassion and willingness to cooperate. The creativity involved in productiveness can just as easily operate in the commonplace practices of everyday life. The focus on productiveness acknowledges the crucial role of labour in human development, and also draws attention to the myriad ways through which people learn and reflect on the value of learning, whether it be in the daily processes of parenting and caring, or the development of particular skills, talents and interests. It is a continual and inventive process of transformation and self-transformation that is central to being human (Smith 2007: 243–59). Although productiveness is theoretically available to all human beings, it can flourish only when a sense of desperation is absent from people's lives, and when there is reason to be hopeful.

Cooperation
Cooperation can be defined as 'engaging with others in a mutually beneficial activity' (Bowles and Gintis 2011: 2). Cooperative action within and between groups has been a decisive factor in the successful evolution of the human species. Indeed, as Mark Pagel points out, ensuring that cooperation works on a social scale requires a level of psychological sophistication that is unique to the human species (Pagel 2012: 180–1). Despite the popular anthropological attempts to demonstrate that humans have been naturally murderous or war-like, from such writers as Robert

Ardrey (*The Territorial Imperative*, 1966), Konrad Lorenz (*On Aggression*, 1966) and Robert Edgerton (*Sick Societies*, 1992), there is no compelling evidence to support such a thesis. On the contrary, the survival of *Homo sapiens* through the fourth ice age, 50,000 years ago, depended on the human ability 'to stay in closely supportive, cooperating bands without too much internal strife', as Mary Clark has argued (Clark 2002: 115). She concludes that 'both culturally and genetically, there must have been natural selection for highly bonded and coordinated social groups'. Furthermore, she contends, 'it cannot be emphasized too strongly that a large brain *co-evolved* with an increasingly interdependent social life'. The propensities to communicate effectively and to share meanings with other group members became 'biologically grounded in the physical connections in the human brain between the emotional centres of the limbic system and the various cognitive centres in the expanding human cortex' (Clark 2002: 124–5). In evolutionary terms, then, the idea of group selection trumps the views of those who take the unjustified speculative leap of suggesting that gene competition must manifest itself in selfish behaviour, let alone justify the inevitability of violent conflict.

Samuel Bowles and Herbert Gintis argue that early human societies flourished because 'altruistic social preferences supporting cooperation out-competed unmitigated and amoral self-interest' (Bowles and Gintis 2011: 4). Cooperation was consolidated in a number of ways, such as the exclusion of free-riders or others whose behaviour threatened the cooperative norms. Processes of socialisation were developed that helped to turn those norms into assumptions, leading people to think in terms of what was good for the group. Additionally, the competition with other groups for scarce resources meant that the most cooperative groups were best placed to survive and reproduce. This last point is important because it challenges the simplistic dichotomy between competition and cooperation. Competition is a great creative urge, but only in a social framework that is essentially cooperative. Richard Sennett speaks of a 'fragile balance' between competition and cooperation, and in the second part of his book *Together* he discusses at length the ways in which cooperation has been weakened as a result of the social processes of modern societies (Sennett 2012: 133–95).

The managerial principles that govern the way we interact in workplaces and schools tend to discourage the sort of voluntary cooperation essential to developing solidarity. This is no accident, given the hegemony of the neoliberal outlook. Although this way of thinking is directly related to the principles of *laissez-faire* economic liberalism that prevailed in the nineteenth century, the newness of neoliberalism is found in its scope, extending competition into the processes of everyday life, in both production and consumption. One of the ideological founders of neoliberalism, Milton Friedman (1912–2006), encapsulated this as early as 1951, when he commented that, unlike the old liberal idea of *laissez-faire*, the state should have an important role to play in actively establishing the 'conditions favourable to competition' (in Peck 2010: 3–4). What neoliberalism has succeeded in doing is to impose competition throughout economic life and beyond, with targets set for all those in work, and systems of team work through which employees internalise the competitive ethos (Sennett 1998: 106–17). Neoliberalism has done something that nineteenth-century economic liberalism could not do: it has infused accelerated competitiveness into the practices of everyday life.

Is it possible, somehow, to revive voluntary cooperation in these inauspicious circumstances? The early socialist response looked towards workers' self-management as a way to resolve the disjuncture within production that involved sophisticated levels of imposed cooperation but denied control of those processes to the producers themselves. Marx observed in *Capital* that when workers cooperate in a planned way with others they develop the capabilities of the whole species (Marx 1990: 447). If workers were to realise this power as a liberating force they would have to take control over the productive process, and he advocated cooperative factories run by workers themselves as a transitional form in the replacement of capitalism by what he termed the 'associated' mode of production (Marx 1981: 571–2). In fact workers' self-management was tried on an extended scale only in Yugoslavia (Horvat 1976), but it was not accompanied by political democracy. In other states, both capitalist and communist, state-controlled industries reproduced the hierarchical organisation of production. With modern production increasingly dominated by transnational corporations, the idea of cooperative control of work appears to be a distant dream. Similarly, increased levels of inequality have effectively created ghettos of social deprivation that militate against cooperation. However, there are ways in which cooperation reasserts itself in daily life, and ways in which it could be encouraged if neoliberal practices are superseded.

In the workplace, resistance to imposed forms of cooperation can lead to the development of genuine cooperation among employees who recognise the ruthless expression of power behind modern work processes. It is possible to repair the failures of authoritarian management by more cooperative planning and delivery, and genuine rather than gestural consultation. In general terms, cooperation can be promoted better through social-partnership forms of management. Economic globalization has transformed the pattern of work in affluent economies, with a switch from the 'Fordism' associated with large-scale factory production to a 'post-Fordism' of short-term and part-time contracts and flexible hours in the service and information sectors. Although these new forms of labour can be regarded as inimical to the development of strong cooperation (Sennett 2012: 179), some theorists have suggested that they can open up new possibilities for autonomous cooperation. André Gorz has argued that within post-Fordism the development of multi-activity working and the pressure for shorter working hours can open up more cooperative and flexible labour processes, although he relies heavily on the adoption of a strong measure of security supplied by a basic guaranteed income (Gorz 1999: 32, 72–111). Similarly, Michael Hardt and Antonio Negri talk optimistically about the emergence of 'cooperative and communicative networks of social labor' as new forms of 'immaterial' labour become widespread. In their view, the new conditions of labour in all sectors place 'new importance on knowledge, information, affective relations, cooperation and communication' (Hardt and Negri 2000: 349–50, 113). There is, then, a potential for cooperation, but it is difficult to accomplish as long as the discipline of the labour process is strong, as it invariably is at times of high unemployment. In practice, the persistence of insecurity presents a major obstacle to developing new forms of cooperation in the world of work, and what we have instead is a site of struggle to establish the substantive rationality of more solidaristic practices.

In the wider social sphere, cooperation is expressed through voluntary activities in which people assist their groups and communities in a range of social and cultural settings. The social capital thesis developed by Robert Putnam stresses the importance of group association in building flourishing communities, but in *Bowling Alone* he argues that such community cooperation is decreasing in the United States (Putnam 2000). However, other researchers have questioned the over-simplicity of that approach and suggest that new forms of place-based community cooperation are still strong, both in the United States and in Europe (Keller 2005; Field 2008; Fine 2010). Perhaps more significantly, there are other forms of cooperation that engender what Liz Spencer and Ray Pahl have described as 'hidden solidarities'. Their work has focused on the development of cooperativeness at the level of informal personal relationships that are outward looking and open (Spencer and Pahl 2006: 190–212). This is an important reminder that the spirit of cooperation can still assert itself in market societies in which we might have expected it to be marginalised by rampant individualism and competitiveness.

Even when old forms have been threatened, new forms emerge by taking advantage of the opportunities arising from the revolution in communications technology. This helps to overcome the problem that cooperation depends on close and frequent contact, which tends to fall away in large groups (Pagel 2012: 364). The extensive use of the internet and the growth of social media provide the opportunity to develop cooperation that is not so territorially bounded, and, as we shall see in Chapter 7, this has been important for the development of alter-globalization politics. Joss Hands has argued that these networks should not be seen as the equivalents of the public sphere venerated by Jürgen Habermas, but as something fundamentally different because of 'the absence of hierarchical structure, fluidity of memberships, a multiplicity of hubs, and non-formal ties'. He conceptualises this coming together as a 'quasi-autonomous recognition network', which can bring different communities of interest into cooperative action on specific issues or causes (Hands 2011: 105–10).

In the radical humanist approach adopted here the argument is that cooperation is a core human potential that reasserts itself and implicitly or explicitly protests against the atomising tendencies of accelerated competition. However, there remains the objection that cooperation relies excessively on trust, and that the pursuit of egoistic self-interest will always be more productive for the wider group or society. In this respect a number of experiments have demonstrated theoretically that mutual cooperation can lead to optimum results for each individual. One of the best known of these is Robert Axelrod's prisoner's dilemma computer tournament, in which well-known games theorists competed and the clear winner adopted a cooperative strategy known as 'tit for tat' (Axelrod 2006: 27–54). Although all such experiments are inevitably abstract and artificial (Argyle 1991: 44), taken together they counter the view that altruistic behaviour rarely extends beyond family groups (Bowles and Gintis 2011: 19–45).

The successful cooperation strategies adopted in these experiments have also been suggested for conflict resolution and other forms of cooperation between states in international relations. In particular the mutual benefits of cooperation are at the heart of the liberal institutionalist paradigm in international relations theory (Lamy 2011: 121–2). The willingness of European states to cede sovereignty within the EU, after centuries of wars between them, is perhaps the clearest example that this form of cooperation can work. The instability of market globalism and the threat from global warming presses the need for more such effective forms of international cooperation, prompting Jean-Marc Coicaud to conclude that despite the discrepancy between the values of international solidarity and of international reality, the 'values of international solidarity are already a large enough part of reality to not be ignored' (Coicaud 2008: 293).

Capabilities

This section discusses the contribution of Martha Nussbaum, for her capabilities approach to human development and global justice shares many of the assumptions of radical humanism and also draws for philosophical support on the generalisations about human nature in Aristotle and the young Marx. Her first account of the basic human functions appeared in an extended article published in *Political Theory* in 1992 defending 'Aristotelian essentialism', a vigorously argued commitment to human universals. She introduces her argument by recounting experiences at conferences at which papers by postmodernists defended a variety of traditional cultural practices that would be intuitively deplored by defenders of human rights. The postmodernist view maintained that we should respect the traditions of others, having no right to impose Western values or make essentialist judgements about those traditions. Nussbaum objects that these anti-essentialist postmodernists are 'people who think of themselves as progressive and feminist and antiracists', but 'are taking up positions that converge with the positions of reaction, oppression and sexism' (Nussbaum 1992: 204). She adds that in her own essentialist way she commits to life over death, freedom over slavery, nutrition over starvation and knowledge over ignorance.

Nussbaum claims that the capabilities approach 'takes its start from the Aristotelian/Marxian conception of the human being as a social and political being, who finds fulfilment in relation with others' (Nussbaum 2006: 85). She endorses Aristotle's and

Marx's commitment to the idea of truly human functioning, involving a wide range of human life activities (Nussbaum 2006: 74). As essentially rational beings we need to exercise our human potentials, and a life reduced to survival is stripped of its humanity. Like Aristotle and Marx, she considers it a tragic waste when people are not enabled to develop (Nussbaum 2006: 346–7). In specifying core potentials or capabilities that are needed by all the peoples of the world, care has to be taken to be sensitive to the rich plurality of cultural differences, and Nussbaum does this in two ways. First, she has developed a worldwide network of contacts, not simply in academic circles but among those involved in one way or another in development issues. In this way, particularly through her work with the Human Development and Capabilities Association, she has been able to 'test' her capabilities against the real experiences of a wide variety of cultures, particularly the experiences of women (Nussbaum 2011: 1–16, 101–12). Second, she has drawn from a range of artistic and philosophical sources from ancient to modern times to emphasise the universality of emotions (Nussbaum 2001).

Capabilities are regarded as what people are able to 'do' and to 'be' (Nussbaum 2000: 71; Nussbaum 2006: 70), or a 'set of opportunities to choose and to act' (Nussbaum 2011: 20). Nussbaum's purpose is to identify the most important human functions so that we can make demands on our social and political institutions to provide a minimum threshold for all people (Nussbaum 1992: 214). She lists ten 'functional capabilities' in the 1992 article that are substantially retained in her later works, in particular *Women and Human Development* (Nussbaum 2000: 78–80), *Frontiers of Justice* (Nussbaum 2006: 71–6) and *Creating Capabilities* (Nussbaum 2011: 32–6). In broad outline, the ten capabilities are:

- *Life*, in the sense of being able to lead a full life;
- *Bodily health*;
- *Bodily integrity*, in terms of being able to have physical security, sexual satisfaction and choice about reproduction;

- *Senses, imagination and thought,* in terms of being able to use the senses in a truly human way through education and guarantees of free expression;
- *Emotions,* in terms of being able to develop our emotions of love, grieving, longing and gratitude;
- *Practical reason,* in terms of being able to form a conception of the good and to plan one's own life;
- *Affiliation,* in the sense of being able to live with and for others, and being free from discrimination on the basis of race, sex, sexual orientation, ethnicity, caste, religion or national origin;
- *Other species,* in the sense of being able to live with concern for animals, plants and the world of nature;
- *Play,* in terms of being able to laugh and participate in recreational activities; and finally,
- *Control over one's environment,* including being able to participate politically, being able to hold property on an equal basis with others, and being able to work with meaningful relationships of recognition with other workers.

It should be noted that two of the capabilities, practical reason and affiliation, are held to play a special, architectonic, role, holding the project together and making it human. The list's abstract and general nature allows for a wide variety of applications of the same principles, but Nussbaum gives the major liberties of speech, association and conscience 'a central and non-negotiable place' (Nussbaum 2006: 80).

Nussbaum favours the capabilities approach over that of contract theory for two major reasons. In the first place she is trying to take care of issues which John Rawls himself admitted are not dealt with adequately by his approach, namely what is owed to people with disabilities, what is owed to animals, the problem of justice across national boundaries, and the problem of saving for future generations (Nussbaum 2006: 23, cf. Rawls 1999: 21). These problems flow from the setting up of the framing of the contract, whereby the framers are considered to be more or less equal abstract individuals within a nation state who are also going to be the recipients of the justice outcome. The second reason is her unease with the contractarian presupposition that the pursuit of mutual advantage is the justification for social cooperation. Supporters of contractarianism would view this is a strength because it provides rational grounds to support whatever agreements are reached, where rationality is assumed to equate with narrowly conceived self-interest. In other words, it dispenses with altruism, which is intuitively taken to be irrational and simply too demanding. Although versions of the contractarian approach try to build in consideration of others to avoid egoism, the ghost of Hobbes continues to haunt all contractarianism. Nussbaum comments that the pursuit of mutual advantage is not 'less' than a compassionate commitment to the wellbeing of others, 'it is just different', and she considers that adopting the 'parsimonious' starting point of mutual advantage is likely to lead in a different direction from an 'other-committed' starting point (Nussbaum 2006: 35). Nussbaum's intuition here is that this ruling out of sociability and benevolence as a part of what it is to be human leads rather too easily to an acceptance that humans are by nature egoistic utility maximisers.

On the specific issues of global justice, Nussbaum describes the gross inequalities between the peoples of rich and poor countries (Nussbaum 2006: 224–5). The capabilities approach endeavours to identify human needs that must be available to all above a certain threshold, if we are to meet the requirements of global justice. In terms of advancing the development of her capabilities to a minimum threshold, Nussbaum specifies ten principles to guide the pursuit of global justice, the spirit of which is redistributive, appealing for greater fairness for the poor and developing countries (Nussbaum 2006: 315–24). So for example, all nations have a responsibility to promote human capabilities, and the prosperous nations have a responsibility to a give a 'substantial' portion of their GDP to poorer nations. Multinational corporations are expected to take responsibility for promoting capabilities in the regions where they operate. Nussbaum demands that the structures of the global economy should be designed to be fair to the poor countries, with a focus on helping the disadvantaged, the ill, the elderly, children and the disabled, and she is critical of the past record of the IMF. She favours a 'thin' global public sphere with limited coercive powers for global governance. She suggests that the family should be respected as precious but not private, and that all institutions and individuals should support education as a key to the empowerment of the disadvantaged.

Nussbaum regards her contribution as complementary to contractarian and human-rights arguments for global justice (Nussbaum 2006: 7) and she supports Rawls's suspicions about comprehensive doctrines that claim that they hold the only key to the way forward, thereby disrespecting the followers of other doctrines (Nussbaum 2011: 89–90). On the basis of the toleration of other points of view, substantive agreement may be reached on the political judgements that can promote capabilities (or indeed other principles of justice), from different conceptions of justice, in what Rawls describes as an 'overlapping consensus' (Rawls 1999: 340). Nussbaum is therefore anxious to distance herself from 'comprehensive guides to life', even arguing that she has been misread as offering a form of cosmopolitanism, on the basis that it does not require commitment to a primary loyalty to all mankind (Nussbaum 2011: 92–3). This clarifies the lines that she carefully draws around her use of Marx in *Frontiers of Justice*, for although she shares Marx's commitment to the fulfilment of human potentials, she eschews reliance on any 'deep metaphysics of human nature', which she regards as incompatible with political liberalism (Nussbaum 2006: 86). She insists that she uses the Marxian idea of truly human functioning 'for political purposes only, not as the source of a comprehensive doctrine of human life', adding that Marx made no such distinction (Nussbaum 2006: 74).

Nussbaum is clearly concerned about the dangers posed by the imposition of doctrinaire recipes for social redemption, but so too was Marx, who explicitly rejected them (Marx 2010a: 79; Marx 2010c: 213). Nor is Marx's view that exploitation and oppression are endemic to capitalism incompatible with a strong commitment to democracy. In effect, what Nussbaum has done is extract the positive side of Marx's philosophy of a fulfilled life from the theory of alienation of which it is an integral part. This leads her to adopt a much 'thinner' view of human nature than the spirited defence of essentialism contained in Nussbaum (1992). Moreover, her commitment to liberalism, rather than democracy, raises an unanswered question about the role of property in her principles of global justice, or, more specifically, whether the principles pay sufficient attention to the structural causes of global deprivation. The radical humanist perspective outlined above would place greater emphasis on the structural obstacles to the fulfilment of human potentials. This need not mean, as it does for some Marxists, that no social progress is possible as long as capitalism survives, but that reforms and regulation should restrain the unfettered nature of markets and point to substantively rational alternatives. In ethical terms, the elucidation of core potentials and the demand for the conditions that can maximise their realisation can be seen as a clarion call for global solidarity.

Looking at how these critical remarks relate to Nussbaum's principles of global justice, we can see that, although they are clearly designed to redress world poverty and oppression, some of the principles indicate an unwillingness to confront the structural causes of that poverty. For example, the principle that asserts the need for prosperous nations to give money to the poor (Nussbaum 2006: 316–17) does not make the point that the wealth of the rich states has accrued from the exploitation of the poor. It reads like a moral appeal to charity rather than a 'payback' demand that emphasises human solidarity. It is not aid that is needed but systematic redistribution. The principle calling for multinational corporations to take responsibility for promoting human capabilities in the regions where they operate under-estimates the nature of the problem (Nussbaum 2006: 317–19). While it is true that consumers can exert meaningful pressure on corporations, and that corporations are acutely aware of this and respond by drawing up codes of practice and resourcing their business ethics departments, in practice this response is totally inadequate (Fisher and Lovell 2008:

508–36). The demands of profit maximisation in a global market will always outweigh ethical considerations, and self-regulation has not prevented exploitation and environmental destruction. Progress will not flow from a change of heart in the boardroom, but from more effective global regulation. The principle should not be to ask corporations to accept responsibility, but to insist on it through regulation and enforcement. The principle calling for the main structures of the world economy to be designed to be fair to poor and developing countries gets closer to the heart of the problem, but it does not mention how the power relations in the institutions of global economic governance might be transformed. The 'fairness' demanded would require a level of regulation much more authoritative than that envisaged in the 'thin' global sphere Nussbaum prescribes (Nussbaum 2006: 319–21).

There is much to commend Nussbaum's capabilities approach, not least her criticisms of the parsimonious view of human nature implicit in the contractarian reliance on 'mutual advantage' (Nussbaum 2006: 414). However, what remains problematic is the relationship between political liberalism and economic liberalism. Nussbaum, in common with most liberal political theorists, tends to conflate liberalism and democracy, using liberalism in a purely political sense without delving too deeply into its intimate attachment to private property. In doing so she avoids the big questions about how a democratic political culture can emerge to promote human potentials when to do so runs against the perceived interests of global corporate capital.

Conclusion

Radical humanist ethics offers a philosophical grounding for an appeal for human solidarity. As well as identifying the key individual and social potentials that need to be developed, it recognises the structural obstacles that stand in the way of their development. In particular it points up the catastrophic destructiveness that accompanies neoliberalism, the whispered ideology of global economic elites (Harvey 2009: 152–206; Carroll 2010: 204–5; Peck 2010: 1–38). The pursuit of the core potentials of rationality, compassion, productiveness and cooperation opens to view the distant horizon of global solidarity. At every level of social and political activity the extent to which these potentials are promoted can act as a guide for solidaristic practice. In its substantive concerns the radical humanist approach to global solidarity works for the subordination of economic and technological rationality to the essential human needs of people everywhere, supporting a radical political 'catch-up' to remedy the democratic deficit created by economic globalization.

Finally, let us return to the widely stated suspicion that a normative view of human essence and its fulfilment necessarily invites authoritarian or exclusionary views of the good life. There are, of course, many dangers attending to strong theories of human nature, as will be clear in the discussions of race and gender in Chapter 5, and these examples of 'bad' essentialism have deterred most modern social and political theorists from going down that path. In the radical humanist perspective adopted here, the potentials outlined can be fulfilled only through the achievement of ever-widening social inclusion, involving processes of democratic negotiation at all levels of social activity, from the local up to the global, with the most careful consideration for individual and group rights. In the multiculturalism which has developed with globalization there are signs that this may be developing, despite the divisive consequence of neoliberal policies. However, in the absence of a radical humanist transformation of social conditions we are also witnessing the entrenchment of numerous fundamentalisms which constitute the greatest obstacle to the ideal of human solidarity. The radical humanist approach to global solidarity argues that these crippling ideological divisions require an *explicitly* ethical response to generate a powerful momentum for concerted political action. To develop this sort of reconciliatory politics it is essential to understand the nature of the social divisions that have marred human history, and also the attempts to overcome them, and this is the focus of the next chapter.

5 Social Division and Reconciliation

In Jonathan Swift's biting satirical novel *Gulliver's Travels* (1726), the eponymous hero finds himself marooned on Lilliput, a land of diminutive people at war with its neighbour, Blefuscu. The conflict had been triggered by a decree from one of the emperors that eggs must be broken only at the little end, which proved an intolerable provocation to those in the habit of breaking their eggs at the big end (Swift 1997: 51). This can be understood either as a condemnation of ineffable human stupidity or a more targeted attack on the capricious and irresponsible nature of monarchical power. Indeed Swift's praise of the idea of the 'government of reason' on the concluding page of the book indicates that he did hold out some hope that humanity could solve the problems it sets itself, provided that the causes of those problems are addressed. This chapter looks at the multiple causes and manifestations of social division throughout the world and invariably, in the process of classifying them, their enormity will seem forbidding. It may appear as though these antagonisms have recurred so persistently and with such destructiveness that this recurrence points to a congenital inadequacy to achieve reconciliation. However, I will argue that under each of the categories considered it is possible to discern at least the possibility of progress towards global solidarity. No false optimism is offered here, but rather an alternative to the fatalism and quietism that so often denies *a priori* the possibility of solidaristic self-realisation. The categories are not exhaustive but cover the major sources of social division. Of course new sources may be bubbling under and unforeseen antagonisms may yet emerge, but if we can identify the processes through which potentially conflicting interests can be accommodated, then it may be possible to envisage a solidaristic future in which the little-enders and big-enders of tomorrow can at least agree to differ.

As the initial theorisation of solidarity flowed from a problematic of exclusion based on social class, it is appropriate that this should be the first category to be considered. This will be followed by other sources of identity that have historically given rise to oppression and often horrendous violence – nation, race, religion and gender.

Class

The idea that class struggle is the driving force behind historical development will always be associated with Karl Marx. *The Communist Manifesto* famously declares that 'the history of all hitherto existing society is the history of class struggles' (Marx 2010a: 67), and Marx consistently warned socialists not to lose sight of the centrality of the class struggle to be fought by the workers against the bourgeoisie (Marx 2010c: 339–75). However, there is an important distinction evident in Marx's work between class struggle as political antagonism between self-conscious class subjects and class struggle as an objective process in the development of the structural contradictions of capitalism. Indeed, in his most succinct description of his theory of history, the 1859 preface to *A Contribution to the Critique of Political Economy*, the class struggle is not mentioned at all. Instead, he offers a structural account of historical development in which a key role is given to the development of a contradiction between the relations of production and the forces of production in causing social revolution (Marx 1975: 425–6). Not for the first time, Marx emphasises that people often act politically without awareness of the real interests they are defending, reminding the reader that people should be judged by what they do rather than what they say about themselves. So, despite the assertion in the *Manifesto* that modern society is splitting up into two great classes facing each other, the bourgeoisie and the proletariat (Marx 2010a: 68), throughout his political analyses Marx depicts a much more complex reality. The bourgeoisie is often divided into factions representing different forms of property, and therefore unable to act in unity, while divisions within the working class along national, religious and racial lines are frequently observed. In addition Marx also sees that political and industrial compromises may cause the workers to lose sight of the need to transform the system of ownership, and he explicitly warns the trade unions against exclusively pursuing 'narrow and selfish' gains (Marx 2010c: 91–2).

The development of mass labour and socialist parties and the spread of trade unionism to unskilled workers took place in the decades following Marx's death in 1883, but, as we saw in Chapter 2, the outcomes did not meet Marx's expectations. Even at the height of unified working-class action during the Second International (1889–1914), with the expansion of union membership and massive waves of strikes, the movements across Europe continued to be beset with differences over strategy, regionalism, ethnicity, religion, gender, skills and status (Geary 1992a: 1–10). The split in the international working-class movement following the Russian Revolution had far-reaching consequences for class solidarity, and in particular for the universalist aspiration for a solidaristic world free of class divisions. The sclerosis of the communist dictatorships meant the death of the political ideal of democracy that had been an essential element of the original conception of solidarity. In western Europe, the electoral advance of social democratic parties helped to secure the 'peace formula' of the welfare state, but, against a background of full employment and rapid economic growth, the goal of a qualitatively different socialist society was dropped. Social democrats, convinced that Keynesian economic management had consigned economic crises and mass unemployment to the past, viewed the mixed economy as a permanent settlement.

When the post-war boom came to a close in the 1970s, the effects of the response to the crisis were to transform class composition in the old industrial centres and, indeed, the world as a whole. The emergence of economic globalization, marked by free trade and the domination of the world economy by transnational corporations, placed enormous pressure on the governments of all states to make their economies attractive to inward investment and competitive in the world market. One of the features of economic globalization has been the rapid expansion of manufacturing in developing countries and the accompanying shift from manufacturing to services in the old heartlands of capitalism (Held and McGrew 2007: 73–116). The implications for class struggle are drawn out in an intriguing fashion by Paul Mason in *Live Working or Die Fighting: How the Working Class Went Global* (2007). Mason juxtaposes a series of contemporary labour struggles in the developing world with some of the great political and industrial struggles in European and American history. For example, the hardships suffered by sweatshop workers in Shenzhen in China in the twenty-first century are compared to the fate of the spinners and weavers who fell victim to the massacre of demonstrators at St Peter's Field (the Peterloo Massacre) in Manchester in 1819. The occupation of a tile factory in Argentina in the present century is discussed alongside a consideration of the factory occupations in Turin in 1920.

The conditions of contemporary struggle are viewed not simply as replications of old battles or as stages that must be passed through before modernity is achieved. Rather, Mason seeks to combat the 'amnesia' that exists concerning the social antagonisms that have always been part of the desperate scramble for profitability and the 'order' required to produce it. He is well aware of the major differences between the old and the new struggles, with economic life now dominated by transnational corporations and a global consumer culture that has swept away traditional working-class communities. Mason comments that although 'there is, for the first time, a truly global working class', it has not yet begun to organise itself in the way that the mass labour movement developed in Europe at the end of the nineteenth century (Mason 2007: 280). He goes on to identify three obstacles to the development of coordinated resistance to neo-liberalism: first, greater stratification of the workforce, which militates against the kind of self-organisation that created the old labour and socialist movements; second, a culture of individualism fostered by technological progress; third, the absence of influential advocates of a new social reformism. He sees the possibility of such a movement emerging from the anti-capitalist movement that has developed since the Seattle demonstration against the WTO in December 1999 (Mason 2007: 280–2).

Mason may be right that the working class has gone global, but this cannot be taken to mean that billions of workers around the world share a consciousness of their common position in the structure of the world economy. The dream of international working-class consciousness propounded by Marx and his followers has not materialised. Certainly the stereotypical image of the class-conscious worker developed in the Marxist tradition, that of the male factory worker in a privileged position compared with other types of worker, has long since run its course, as Michael Hardt and Antonio Negri have argued in *Empire* (Hardt and Negri 2000: 52–3). Their alternative concept is the multitude, a category referring to the broad plurality of 'productive, creative subjectivities of globalization' (Hardt and Negri 2000: 60). In the face of the ubiquitous power of globalized capital that they conceptualise as 'Empire', Hardt and Negri see the emergence of a multitude with the potential to take advantage of new forms of labour, involving deep networking and cooperation, in order to challenge existing power relations. The multitude is seen to be the social force presenting as its first political demand the realisation of global citizenship (Hardt and Negri 2000: 393–411).

However promising this sounds from the normative perspective of global solidarity, neither in *Empire* nor in the subsequent *Multitude* (2005) do Hardt and Negri advance beyond stating the need for a 'new science of democracy for the multitude', and their discussion of potential reforms is unsystematic and inchoate. The concept of the multitude is also inadequate to the task of understanding one of the most startling social developments in the affluent state, the detachment from the 'working' working class of the 'new poor'. In *Commonwealth* (2009) they note the spread of poverty into the heartlands of capitalism as signalling the 'multitude of the poor' emerging at the centre of the 'project for revolutionary transformation', but they do not explain why or how this has come about (Hardt and Negri 2009: 55). In reality, the new poor are detached, often in criminalised sink estates, occasionally exploding in apolitical riots, as in Britain in the summer of 2011. Sometimes, as in the French riots of 2005, the issue is racialised. As Ghassan Hage has noted, this form of social breakdown has been accompanied by a public backlash against social explanations of crime, so that attempts to explain the social causes are angrily dismissed as 'excuses' (Hage 2003: 140). The social exclusion suffered by the new poor is incompatible with any hope for social solidarity, and their social inclusion must be the primary goal of solidaristic politics.

If it is difficult to identify a global working class as a collective subject for solidaristic progress, it is somewhat easier to discern the emergence of a nascent global capitalist class that benefits from the growing inequalities that flow from the application of neoliberal principles. Leslie Sklair's pioneering work in this field centres on his primary proposition that 'a transnational capitalist class based on the transnational corporations is emerging that is more or less in control of the processes of globalization' (Sklair 2003: 5). Sklair describes four 'fractions' of this class, beginning with transnational corporation executives, then globalizing bureaucrats and politicians, then globalizing professionals and, finally, merchants and the media. Although his empirical work refers back to the 1990s, Sklair makes a case for the emergence of a well-networked class with a distinctive neoliberal ideology translated into concrete business strategies, including 'charm offensive' publicity. He also shows, via an analysis of annual reports, how corporations have quite explicitly moved away from national orientations to configure themselves as truly transnational (Sklair 2003: 276–82).

Elsewhere, William Carroll describes complex transnational

networks of economic elites through such policy groups as the International Chamber of Commerce, the Trilateral Commission and the World Economic Forum (WEF), and shows how this transnational networking has developed in the current century (Carroll 2010: 38–56, 105–31). However, he is rightly cautious about the extent to which the development of transnational networks constitutes a class, pointing out the continued significance of national networks and the fact that many of the transnational networks continue to be dominated by an Atlanticist (American and European) elite (Carroll 2010: 224–9). Focusing on North America, Jeff Faux delivers a powerful polemic exposing the extent to which policies once directed by democratically elected governments have become determined administratively through the enforcement of decisions made by bodies such as the North America Free Trade Association (NAFTA) and the WTO. Faux calls the new capitalist class the 'party of Davos' (Faux 2006: 163–6), after the resort in Switzerland where leading business, financial and political elites have been meeting to discuss the direction of the world economy at the annual meeting of the WEF since 1982. The financial crisis of 2008 has clearly exposed the blind faith in unregulated markets that has been a feature of neoliberalism, and it has also exposed the unaccountable privileges of the beneficiaries.

Marx was correct to see that the way in which profit is extracted determines the relationship of domination and servitude in any given society (Marx 1981: 927), but class consciousness did not develop as the central motivation for the creation of a solidaristic society, as he had expected, or at least hoped. Class is but one element of identity, and often not the decisive one in motivating political action. However, we should not lose sight of the persistence of the existential pain of class oppression. Throughout the world people are discriminated against because they bear the marks of class in the ways they speak, appear and gesture, while others receive privileged access to power and wealth because of their class background. At national level, many of the social gains associated with the 'golden age' of social democracy have been

Social Division and Reconciliation

eroded, while at the level of global economic governance there is a serious democracy deficit. Only when those issues are addressed and economic relations are steered primarily to meet human needs rather than corporate profits can progress towards global solidarity be made.

Nation

In his famous essay *What Is a Nation?* (1882), Ernest Renan (1823–92) defines the nation as a 'large scale solidarity, constituted by the feeling of the sacrifices that one has made in the past and of those that one is prepared to make in the future' (Renan 2010: 19). National allegiance, then, is a solidaristic force, but as this force is generated in the course of struggles against other nations, it would seem that it must preclude the emergence of solidarity on a global scale. In contrast to this orientation towards the nation is the cosmopolitan perspective, defined by Stan van Hooft as 'the view that the moral standing of all peoples and of each individual person around the globe is equal'. Van Hooft goes on to say that individuals 'should not give moral preference to their compatriots, their co-religionists or fellow members of their demographic identity groups' (Van Hooft 2009: 4). It follows that cosmopolitans cannot give moral preference to their fellow nationals, but are there other ways in which the cosmopolitan commitment to global solidarity can be reconciled with nationalism? This section is concerned with exploring possible mediations between the two apparently antithetical positions. The first part will look briefly at strong anti-nationalist positions, in order to see if any allowance can be made for a more benign form of national identity. The second part will discuss the reasons for the strength of national identity and its significance for community-building. In particular it considers the development of political and social rights within the framework of the nation state, frequently overcoming potential social divisions based on religion, ethnicity and language. It also takes account of the role of national consciousness in helping to establish liberation from colonial domination. Finally, we will discuss some ways in which national attachment may be modified in order to open it up for the wider solidarity of all humankind.

In *The Sane Society*, Erich Fromm condemns nationalism as being akin to incest, idolatry and insanity, and also decries patriotism as its 'cult', specifying that form of patriotism which puts nation above humanity and above the principles of truth and justice (Fromm 1990: 58). He points to the extreme emotional power of nationalism and the 'furious indignation' displayed towards those who dare to question their state's involvement in a conflict or refuse to pay sufficient respect to the national symbols. For Fromm, this represents a deplorable collapse into a 'herd conformity' and irrationality, a major obstacle preventing the building of a world based on 'human solidarity and justice' (Fromm 1990: 60). In another attack he points out the 'group narcissism' displayed in nationalism but warns that it is less easy to recognise than individual narcissism. An individual who extolled the superiority of himself and his family and the inferiority of everyone else would be considered crude and unbalanced, if not insane, but when a politician does something similar, substituting the nation for family, he is likely to be praised and admired for showing his love of country (Fromm 1964: 79).

A similar anti-nationalist line is taken by Michael Billig in *Banal Nationalism*, in which he argues that the uncritical adulation of the nation is brought to people on a daily basis through a process of 'flagging', in which politicians and the media bombard their audience with linguistic iterations of 'we', 'our' and 'here', routinely playing the patriotic card with such frequency and insistence that it becomes difficult to stand outside the discourse and open it up to criticism (Billig 1995: 93–127). In times of war the nationalist discourse is even more difficult to gainsay, with talk of 'our boys' making the 'ultimate sacrifice' for 'our freedom' contributing to an atmosphere in which it is difficult to develop a rational discussion of whether or not the state should be involved in the conflict. This nationalist mindset is frequently racialised and directed against refugees, immigrants and ethnic minorities.

Ghassan Hage has argued that the weakening of the welfare state and the creation of the new poor has produced a decline of hope in society at large and a proliferation of 'paranoid nationalism' directed against those who do not conform to the majority stereotype of a 'true' national (Hage 2003: 20, 47).

Can strong cosmopolitanism allow for the emergence of a less malign form of national identity? Fromm concedes that there can be a legitimate 'loving interest in one's own nation, which is the concern with the nation's spiritual as much as with its material welfare – never with its power over other nations' (Fromm 1990: 58). This an important qualification, for it recognises that developing an appreciation of the culture and traditions of one's own community can promote an active interest in other cultures and therefore build towards a wider, human solidarity. Indeed it could be argued that respect for place, community and the particularities of culture is a necessary part of a global ethic. This viewpoint was articulated by a number of writers in a major debate in the United States in the mid-1990s, prompted by an appeal to cosmopolitanism by Martha Nussbaum that first appeared in the *Boston Review*. In it she expresses her concern that patriotic appeals to the 'us' of the nation is likely to sustain parochialism and discourage people from developing an awareness of the needs of others in the world, as well as our collective responsibility for human wellbeing. Instead she proposes a cosmopolitan education to encourage people to aspire to becoming citizens of the world (Nussbaum 1996: 3–17).

Most of the respondents to Nussbaum's article clearly considered that she had gone too far in rejecting not only nationalism but patriotism as well. Charles Taylor emphatically asserted that 'we cannot do without patriotism in the modern world' (Taylor 1996: 119), while Benjamin Barber argued that 'pathological patriotism can be cured only by healthy patriotism' (Barber 1996: 36). Kwame Anthony Appiah insisted that we can be both cosmopolitans and patriots and that caring for others in a nation or a state can prepare us for a meaningful global citizenship (Appiah 1996: 26–7). Yet however much the defenders of 'benign' patriotism sincerely think it can be combined with cosmopolitanism, patriotism has an underlying emotional power that obstructs attempts to develop the cosmopolitan consciousness required by global solidarity. As Appiah observes, the prevailing emotion of patriotism is pride, but what he does not say is that more often than not this is an instance in which the individual takes credit for something others have achieved, or, conversely, feels shame for something that is not her or his responsibility. I would suggest that this form of false pride and feigned shame is a form of irrationalism that becomes part of a cycle of manipulation of the sort described by Billig as banal nationalism.

There is, however, a danger of exaggerating the extent to which appeals to the nation or patriotism necessarily pander to reactionary instincts. In the case of Billig, although he identifies a phenomenon that often reproduces puerile displays of national supremacism, it is too easy to see each and every mention of the nation as nothing more than banal bombast and trite flattery. Billig cites Nelson Mandela's speech on the night of his election victory in South Africa's first democratic election in 1994 as an example of banal nationalism. Mandela addressed his audience as 'my fellow South Africans' and exhorted them to build a new South Africa of 'one people with a common destiny in our rich variety of culture, race and tradition' (Billig 1995: 97). However, in those extraordinary circumstances this speech was anything but banal, for it was both an affirmation that the once excluded were now fully included in the body politic, and also an appeal to the minority who had lost their privileged position to embrace the new democracy. It was an effective rhetoric of reconciliation following a protracted and often bloody struggle. The following year, Mandela's open support for the predominantly white Afrikaner-based South African rugby team, which had long seemed to emblematise white supremacy, proved to be a master-stroke of reconciliation. Many had predicted that a peaceful solution could never be achieved in South Africa, and these gestures, although using the emotional pull of the nation, could be regarded as solidarity-building.

This brings us to the second part of the section, in which we consider the difficulties involved in trying to overcome the dangers of nationalism and patriotism. Renan's approach to the question of nationality constitutes a landmark in our understanding, for in stressing the continual social and political construction of the idea of the nation he departs from attempts to provide an objective definition that attempts to locate the nation as some sort of natural entity integrated through ethnicity, language, religion or territorial contiguity (Özkirimli 2000: 35–6). It is now generally accepted that any such attempts do not work, and that to a great extent the nation is an actors' concept that draws on the elements listed above in disparate fashion. 'Modernist' theories of nationalism stress the relatively recent construction of national consciousness, usually dating back to the late eighteenth century, and at times they provide some persuasive evidence, as when Eric Hobsbawm points to the fact that at the time of the great French Revolution half the people in France did not speak French, and at the time of Italian unification in 1860 less than 3 per cent of the people spoke Italian for everyday purposes (Hobsbawm 1990: 60–1). Other theorists adopt an ethno-symbolist approach which stresses the importance of long-established ethnic associations as an underpinning for modern nationalism (Leoussi and Grosby 2007). Obviously the modernist interpretations are more open to the idea that national identity should weaken as the conditions for its sustenance change in the age of globalization, but however cheering this is for cosmopolitans, it is beyond dispute that today nationalism remains a powerful and emotional form of identity that threatens any appeal to global solidarity.

National identity can be linked with social solidarity in three concrete ways. In the first place, the growth of nation states coincided with the emergence of movements for democracy. While it is true that many nation states endured long periods of dictatorship, it is possible to interpret the development of legal, political and social rights as a sequence of social struggles, as T. H. Marshall did in his discussion of citizenship (Marshall 1973: 65–122). A similar trajectory of the onward march of

Global Solidarity

liberal democracy is contained in Francis Fukuyama's post-Cold War tract, *The End of History and the Last Man* (1992). It may be disputed that it is a kind of reification to attribute the achievement of political democracy to the nation state, rather than understanding it as the outcome of generations of often violent social struggles. Nevertheless, as political and social inclusion spreads within the polities that comprise the nation states, it is inevitable that attachment or identity also develops. Even in instances where this consciousness falls well short of uncritical acceptance of institutions and traditions, the attachment is strongly implicit, well captured by Pierre Bourdieu's notion of *doxa*, a disposition assumed without conscious choice which nevertheless exerts a powerful social control (Bourdieu and Eagleton 1994).

A second way in which the idea of nation can exert a solidaristic force is in trumping other identities that impair social cohesion, such as religion, ethnicity or language. For example, religious friction in Scotland has been symbolised by the often vicious rivalry between two Glasgow football clubs, Celtic and Rangers, but this is overcome when the fans come together to support the national team. Another football example of the nation being reclaimed, this time from racist prejudice, is France's victory in the 1998 World Cup. The French team had been criticised by National Front leader Jean-Marie Le Pen for having too many black players, and their victory was popularly acclaimed as an achievement of the multicultural nation. In the United States, the assimilation of a range of ethnic and religious immigrants into the body politic has arguably been an important factor in the strong emotional attachment to the idea of 'patriotism'. However, it must be doubted that such examples do little more than mask the divisions that remain untouched. Le Pen may have been rebuffed in 1998, but in 2012 his daughter Marine won 18 per cent of the vote in the first round of elections for the French presidency on an openly racist platform. In the United States there is a very high level of inequality, and, as we saw in Chapter 2, a hugely disproportionate number of black men serving jail sentences.

Finally, and more convincingly, national identity is likely to be particularly strong in those nation states that have had to fight for independence. The imposition of rule from an external power has invariably been experienced as intolerable, and the memories of the struggles for independence are kept alive in new national histories and commemorations of key dates in the achievement of political autonomy. The involvement of activists in the liberation struggles is passed through generations of families. Appiah, in the essay responding to Nussbaum mentioned above, openly states that his attachment to patriotism stems from the Ghanaian patriotism embraced by his father in the course of that country's struggle for independence from Britain. People who have experienced imperialist domination will be in no doubt about the legitimacy of national liberation, although the experience of national oppression should militate against the development of an aggressive form of nationalism.

In the face of the persistence of nationalism and patriotism, how can cosmopolitanism hope to grow? A wider discussion of this can be found in Chapter 7, but at this juncture we can propose five principles on which progress can be made. First, there can be no concession on the argument of the equal moral worth of all individuals, and therefore the liberal nationalist claims that nationalism offers a 'set of moral values worthy of respect' (Tamir 1993: 95) have to be rejected. Although moral obligations are involved in all forms of association, they are no more than local applications of universal principles. Second, banal nationalism needs to be exposed and scrutinised for the xenophobia or supremacism that often lurks beneath its rhetoric. This is no easy task, as people can become aggressive if their national emblems are called into question, even though they may be implicitly presenting a 'my country right or wrong' sense of allegiance. Third, images of the nation that present it as essentially belonging to a dominant group should be confronted for their partial and racist implications. Fourth, appreciations of aspects of a nation's culture and history should be promoted as positive when those aspects can be seen as a contribution towards the building of global solidarity. Fifth, the development of a deep appreciation of the cultures of other nations should be encouraged in order to break the monocultural laziness that feeds reactionary thought. This can be done through travel, the learning of other languages, or the development of a deep interest in the music, art or literature of other nations.

It may well be that globalization is already promoting a greater cosmopolitan consciousness through global geographical mobility, the development of cultural hybridity and the gradual emergence of a global public sphere around issues such as economic governance, global warming and world poverty. It is interesting that Fromm begins his condemnation of nationalism in *The Sane Society* by accepting that most people obtain their sense of identity from belonging to a nation rather than belonging to the global species (Fromm 1990: 58), for this already appears outdated. In the World Values Survey (WVS) conducted in the late 1990s, only 38 per cent of people considered national identity to be their principal identity, compared with 47 per cent for local identity and 15 per cent for supranational identity (cited in Archibugi 2008: 78). A subsequent survey in 2005 did not ask the same either–or question, but simply asked respondents whether or not they saw themselves as world citizens, members of a local community or nationals, without these categories being mutually exclusive. In this round of the WVS, involving surveys in fifty-seven countries, 77 per cent agreed or strongly agreed that they saw themselves as a world citizen. Although this figure is lower than the percentages that identified with local community (91 per cent) and with the national community (96 per cent), it is still remarkable evidence of a growing cosmopolitan consciousness (World Values Survey 2005).

Race

There is a clear link between nationalism and racism, the latter being perhaps the most virulent form of supremacist nationalism. Etienne Balibar argues that racism presents itself as a supernationalism that has meaning and a chance of success only 'if it is based on the integrity of the nation, integrity both towards the outside and on the inside' (Balibar and Wallerstein 1991: 59). Racism is a great simplifier, offering easily identifiable scapegoats for all social problems and readily available 'solutions'. The extent and intensity of racism cannot be over-stated, for the evidence of it spreads much further than the daily occurrence of racist physical assaults. It can be heard in every utterance about 'them' and 'that lot', in the standard political rhetoric that accepts the immediate need to restrict immigration and refugees, and in the hugely disproportionate criminalisation of ethnic minorities.

In trying to understand racism it is necessary to grasp where the idea came from and why it became ingrained in popular prejudice. In order to obtain a deeper understanding of the experience of racial hatred we can still benefit from the writing of Frantz Fanon (1925–61), for although he died more than half a century ago, his contribution still raises key questions about the pain of racism and the solidaristic response to that pain. Finally, we must attempt to discern some tendencies that might indicate that from this sorrowful history some hope might yet emerge.

Racism, as contempt for others solely because they belong to another ethnic group, raises issues similar to those faced in defining nationalism and nation. Although ethnic identities are created and recreated as part of a cultural process (Rattansi 2007: 88–90), clearly there are visible biological differences between groups that make it easier for racists to identify their enemy. An important issue here is the significance attached to those biological differences. Ivan Hannaford, in his history of the idea of race, has argued that no such significance attached to the biological differences between groups of human beings in the ancient world (Hannaford 1996: 17–60). Rather he sees the earliest ideas about 'types' of people emerging in the religious texts of the Hermeticists and Cabalists in the late Middle Ages, before the word 'race' enters the Western languages in the sixteenth century (Hannaford 1996: 147–8). Ali Rattansi argues that although the expulsion of the Moors and Jews from Spain at the end of the fifteenth century was driven by religious, political and economic motivations, an element of 'blood purity' was introduced that developed in later centuries (Rattansi 2007: 16–17).

One of the consequences of the European conquest of the Americas was the open discussion as to whether groups of human beings could be considered to be not fully human. In a theological court in Spain in 1550 Ginés de Sepúlveda argued that the American Indians were closer to apes and could therefore be enslaved, but he was opposed by Bartolomé de las Casas, who proclaimed them fully human and 'convertible' to Christianity. The las Casas view was taken up as the official position, but it has been pointed out that it was not until much later that he thought there might be a problem with the enslavement and trafficking of Africans (Rattansi 2007: 22). Indeed before his change of heart las Casas actively encouraged the importation of African slaves; as Hugh Thomas observes, 'like all enlightened men of his time, he believed that an African enslaved by a Christian was more fortunate than an African in domestic circumstances' (Thomas 1997: 98).

The slave trade lasted for more than 300 years and involved the imprisonment and transportation of eleven million Africans to the Americas (Thomas 1997: 804–5). The inhumanity of this practice prompted the first intellectual justifications of the natural or developmental superiority of Europeans. Some of the leading philosophers of the seventeenth and eighteenth centuries, such as Thomas Hobbes, John Locke (1632–1704) and Montesquieu (1689–1755), categorised black people as 'inferior' and 'primitive', providing the building blocks of the racist mindset (Hannaford 1996: 191–213; Lentin 2008: 23–31). Despite the arbitrariness and inconsistencies of such classifications, and the blatantly ideological nature of their attributions, the pervasiveness of this thinking shaped the dominant racism of educated white Europeans and North Americans. It is a way of thinking that has left its mark, for the term 'Caucasian', first used by Johann-Friedrich Blumenbach in 1781 to describe white people as 'the most beautiful and pre-eminent' of the races, is still in official use today, despite lacking any scientific foundations (Hannaford 1996: 207–8).

The 'science' of race took on a more menacing form with the development of theories of racial determination in the mid-nineteenth century. A British scientist, Robert Knox (1791–1862), published *The Races of Men* in 1850, arguing a strict hierarchy of distinctive and impermeable races with the white Europeans at the top and the negroes at the bottom in terms of achievement and potential. In 1854 Arthur de Gobineau's (1816–82) *Essay on the Inequality of the Human Races* argued that the European civilisation was degenerating because of mixing with inferior races. These ideas were the foundations on which modern racism developed (MacMaster 2001: 13–30; Lentin 2008: 9–12). The overall thrust of the new science of race was to justify the economic and political power of the core states and to fix the peoples of other countries as naturally and irrevocably inferior. Although its scientific claims were groundless, it received a boost from the genuine scientific breakthrough made by Charles Darwin (1809–82) in *On the Origin of Species* (1859) and *The Descent of Man* (1871). Although his theory of evolution by process of natural selection affirmed the essential unity of the human species, the emphasis on the driving power of heredity was applied to the social world in a deterministic and prejudiced way by Social Darwinists such as Karl Pearson, Benjamin Kidd and Herbert Spencer (Hannaford 1996: 272–6; Lentin 2008: 13–15). It also prompted the enthusiastic promotion of eugenics, a term coined by Francis Galton (1822–1911) in 1883 to refer to selective breeding, either to reproduce what were considered to be the superior beings, or to eliminate the weakest (Rattansi 2007, 54–5). Eugenics was manifested in the policies of sterilisation and euthanasia applied in Nazi Germany (Hannaford 1996: 366–8; Kershaw 2000: 252–61), and contributed to the development of an 'eliminationist' mindset towards the Jews (Goldhagen 1997: 80–163).

A specific product of the pseudo-science of racism was anti-Semitism, a term coined by Wilhelm Marr (1819–1904) in a pamphlet published in Germany in 1879 entitled 'The Way to Victory of Germanicism over Judaism'. Although hatred of Jews by Christians is a recurring feature of European history, this was the first time that it had been justified in biological terms through the use of the pseudo-science of race (Rattansi 2007: 5; Lentin 2008: 58). The trend quickly spread to France, where Edouard Drumont's (1844–1917) diatribe *Jewish France* (1886) extolled the virtues of the mythical Aryan race and its historic struggle against the corrosive force of the Semites. He embellished his account with accusations that Jews smelled and spread disease (Hannaford 1996: 319–20). At the time there were only about 80,000 Jews in the whole of France, but anti-Semitism quickly established itself as a unifying prejudice of right-wing nationalism. Drumont's book went through 200 reprints in fifteen years and anti-Semitism became a key idea for the development of extremist groups such as *Action Française* and *La Croix* (Magraw 1986: 263–7). In Germany, in the late nineteenth century, no fewer than nineteen publications called for the physical extermination of the Jews (Goldhagen 1997: 71). Thus a 'race war', fomented by disaffected nationalists and fuelled by false science, opened the way for the extermination programme of the Nazis that claimed the lives of six million Jews and 220,000 gypsies during the Second World War (Gilbert 1993: 245, 141).

The enormity of the Holocaust might be taken as evidence that humanity can never achieve the tolerance and cooperativeness required for the advance of the normative goal of global solidarity. Not only were whole human groups marked for extermination, but the scale of the destruction was such that it was processed with meticulous planning and the use of modern technology in the gas chambers. This gave the appearance not of a frenzied loss of human self-control but rather a cool and calculated fulfilment of a judgement that went unquestioned. This was exemplified in the demeanour of 'dutiful' bureaucratic detachment assumed by one of the leading functionaries of the Holocaust, Adolf Eichmann, at his trial in Jerusalem in 1961, prompting Hannah Arendt to coin the term 'the banality of evil' (Arendt 1984: 252). Arendt notes that Eichmann was 'normal' in the sense of being unexceptional within the Nazi regime, commenting that in that regime only 'exceptions' could be expected to react normally (Arendt 1984: 26–7).

Although some historians have ascribed the complicity of soldiers and civilians in these crimes to a process of 'desensitisation' developed through a mixture of terror and propaganda, others have stressed the active and often enthusiastic support for the slaughter. This is the thrust of Daniel Goldhagen's *Hitler's Willing Executioners*, in which he amasses evidence of horrific cruelty, concluding that the executioners individually made choices 'as contented members of an assenting genocidal community, in which the killing of Jews was normative and celebrated' (Goldhagen 1997: 406). In the light of such detailed accounts of inhumanity it may be difficult to cling to the humanist conviction that humanity can learn from its past and preserve an ethical code that renders such obscenities impossible. We recognise the human capability for evil, but under what circumstances is this triggered, and how can we avoid a repeat? Ivan Hannaford's major argument in his book on the history of the idea of race is that the emergence of racism involves the destruction of politics, where 'politics' refers to the original Athenian ideas of public processes, the accommodation of difference by compromise and the emphasis on public discussion (Hannaford 1996: 11–12). In a similar vein, Arendt argued for the vital importance of a permanent public realm (Arendt 1969: 50–8) and warned of the danger that the isolation of human beings invites totalitarian terror (Arendt 1986: 474–9). The collapse of political association entails the disabling of the established moral framework, and racism accomplishes its crimes in ways that indicate this breakdown. The science of race is used either to deny the 'true' humanity of the victims, or to portray them as a mortal threat to the 'pure' race. Then the exterminators act with extreme brutality, feeling compelled to prove the inferiority of the victims by humiliating them and showing their abjectness (Goldhagen 1997: 376–89).

Nevertheless, it is vital to recognise that this collapse of moral integrity was never total, and that thousands of people showed extraordinary courage to rescue Jews during the Holocaust (Block and Drucker 1992). The question is, as Norman Geras has posed it, to what extent does the example of their moral courage raise the possibility of an alternative 'ethical landscape' (Geras 1999: 56)? Geras's own answer is to appeal to a 'positive universal right to aid and the universal obligation to bring it' and he emphasises the need to make this demand explicit in our social practice (Geras 1999: 48–77). On the other hand, his depiction of an alleged 'contract of mutual indifference' to describe the prevailing tendency in human relations as a 'model of our world' reflects a more pessimistic frame of mind (Geras 1999: 28–9). Zygmunt Bauman laments that in the Holocaust, people elected for self-preservation rather than moral duty, and comments that 'in a system where rationality and ethics point in opposite directions, humanity is the main loser' (Bauman 2000: 206–7). However, he adds an important caveat, that it does not matter how many people chose moral duty over self-preservation; what matters is that some did. This affirms that 'evil is not all powerful' and that 'it can be resisted' (Bauman 2000: 206–7). Bauman, like Primo Levi and many others, points to the imperative of remembering these horrors, so that humanity may be preserved (Bauman 2000: 248–50; Levi 2000: 231–4).

In 1951 the recently established United Nations Educational, Scientific and Cultural Organisation (UNESCO) issued a Statement on Race attacking the scientific credibility of attempts to ascribe superiority or inferiority to particular groups of people. Attempts to create lists of races based on genetic or phenotypical variations simply do not work, and, as Ali Rattansi has concluded, 'the concept of race is now regarded by the majority of biologists as having no credible scientific foundation' (Rattansi 2007: 75). Studies arguing for hereditary explanations of superior and inferior IQ performance among different groups consistently fail to take into account more plausible physical and social explanations (Rattansi 2007: 78–85). The debunking of attempts to provide scientific justification for racism is a welcome development, since we have noted the significant role it played in preparing the way for eliminationist policies, as in Nazi Germany, or segregation, as in the southern United States before the civil rights movement of the 1960s, or in South Africa under apartheid. However, the theoretical defeat of racist science does not dispel the persistence of the phenomenon. Immanuel Wallerstein sees the replication of racism as springing directly from the process of capitalism itself, whereby visibly different groups compete in a world economy that allocates distinctive economic roles to groups identified as 'races' (Balibar and Wallerstein 1991: 34). In this perspective, racism helps the functioning of the system for capitalists on a divide-and-rule basis, in which competition among workers is racialised, a phenomenon noted by Marx himself (Fraser and Wilde 2011: 175–6) and examined in detail in the American case by Theodore Allen in *The Invention of the White Race* (1994–7). However, explanations of the causes and function of racism tell us little about how it is experienced and how it can be confronted and resisted in the capitalist society that still has some life left in it. This is where the work of Frantz Fanon comes into its own.

Born into a black, middle-class family in the French colony of Martinique, Fanon moved to France towards the end of the Second World War and served in the Resistance and then the Free French Army. He studied medicine and psychiatry in Lyons before working in hospitals in France and then Algeria. There he became deeply involved in the Algerian struggle for independence from France, publishing his most famous work, *The Wretched of the Earth*, a damning attack on colonialism, in 1961 (Fanon 1985). In the same year he died of leukaemia. It is obvious from his first book, *Black Skins, White Masks*, published in 1952, that he was appalled by the racism he encountered in France, but what gives his account a special power is the way he links his personal struggle against alienation to the wider political struggle against every kind of racism and colonialism. The chapter entitled 'The Fact of Blackness', which Alana Lentin points out should be translated as 'The Lived Experience of the Black Man' (Lentin 2008: 33), opens with the descriptions that he is forced to hear, of 'dirty nigger' or simply 'look, a negro!', and his despair at being 'sealed into that crushing objecthood' (Fanon 2008: 82). His education had taught him all about European culture, and his learning was orientated to that culture, but he had no knowledge of any authentic culture of his own. No matter how he excelled as a soldier, student or doctor, the white world would never accept him. He recounts one incident as a student comparing black and European poetry, and a white acquaintance had praised him: 'At bottom you are a white man' (Fanon 2008: 25). He declares that when people like him it is in spite of his colour, and when they don't like him they insist that it is not because of his colour. He realises that he is 'hated, despised, detested ... by an entire race' and he adds in anger, 'For a man whose only weapon is reason there is nothing more neurotic than contact with unreason' (Fanon 2008: 88–9). In answer to this Fanon wants to assert himself as a black man (Fanon 2008: 87), and he comes to see that this struggle for recognition needs to be a *fight* for recognition, a concrete struggle through which the black person forges authenticity. Interestingly, Fanon rejects Hegel's dialectic of recognition as portrayed in the master–slave relationship in *The Phenomenology of Mind*, where the labour of the slave compels recognition from the master. In the existing situation of the black person, no such peaceful mediation is possible. Recognition will be achieved 'only through conflict and through the risk that conflict implies' (Fanon 2008: 168–70; cf. Hegel 1971: 229–40).

Fanon was in no doubt that racism came in many forms, and he talks about 'the racial distribution of guilt', pointing out that he had found to his astonishment that some north Africans despised black people, but that when in Algeria he had also found that some French soldiers considered a Martiniquan to be distinctly superior (Fanon 2008: 61–81). Fanon identifies with all who are oppressed by racism, with Jews attacked by anti-Semites to those in apartheid South Africa, 'a boiler into which thirteen million blacks are clubbed and penned in by two-and-a-half million whites' (Fanon 2008: 64–6). Ultimately, he feels that racism will be defeated only through conflict, and he points approvingly to the struggles only then being initiated to win the battle for civil rights in the United States. He says 'yes' to life, love and generosity, and a resounding 'no' to scorn, degradation, exploitation and 'butchery of what is most human to man: freedom'. The aim is to be 'actional', but with the important qualification that what is preserved in all relations are 'the basic values that constitute a human world' (Fanon 2008: 173). The specific inhuman expression of racism is his target, but in the context of a wider commitment to universal human freedom:

> If the question of a practical solidarity with a given past ever arose for me, it did so only to the extent to which I was committed to myself and to my neighbour to fight for all my life and with all my strength so that never again would a people on the earth be subjugated. It was not the black world that laid down my course of conduct. My black skin is not the wrapping of specific values. (Fanon 2008: 177)

Fanon indeed went on to fight for freedom with all his strength, identifying the collective struggle as necessary for overcoming the depersonalisation that colonialism had inflicted, not only on the individual but in the 'collective sphere' (Fanon 1985: 237). The outcome of the battles against colonialism will preserve some of the 'prodigious theses' put forward by Europe, but it will also remember Europe's crimes, 'of which the most horrible was committed in the heart of man, and consisted of the pathological tearing apart of his functions and the crumbling away of his unity' (Fanon 1985: 254).

Some of Fanon's concerns seem dated to the modern reader, particularly his emphasis on the need for colonised people to reject the shame felt by many for being black. At that time, the colonised were taught the grandeur of European history and the inferiority of their own race. Thanks to the success of independence movements and struggles for civil rights, this aspect of colonial psychological domination depicted in *Black Skins, White Masks* is not now so directly relevant. When that book was written, the indigenous populations of the colonies were not only denied political rights but were treated with varying degrees of brutality by the imperial powers. Independence from colonialism removed a cursed oppression, but it was not always followed by government 'by the people, and for the people, for the outcasts and outsiders', as advocated by Fanon (Fanon 1985: 165). Nevertheless, the election of Nelson Mandela as President of South Africa following the first free elections there in 1994 symbolised the defeat of state racism, achieved primarily through the struggles of black South Africans but also through a worldwide anti-apartheid movement. In the United States, segregation was widely practised in the south, forcing black people to attend separate schools, drink from different water fountains and ride in the back seats of buses. Not only did the civil rights struggle break down these and other discriminations, but it inspired anti-discrimination legislation in many other countries. It is a measure of the advancement of the recognition of black people in the United States that Martin Luther King Junior Day was adopted as a national holiday by all fifty states in 2000, including those states where there had been bitter resistance to the civil rights struggle that he led. Above all, the symbolic power of a 'new age of freedom' was invoked by Barack Obama when he was inaugurated as the first black President in January 2009.

Progress in combating officially sanctioned racism may also call into question Fanon's recognition of the necessity of violence in achieving racial justice. In fact Fanon's endorsement of the liberation struggles was always quite specific to the task in hand, and always regarded as a necessary measure of self-assertion against the violence of the colonisers. His humanistic aims were frequently iterated, and he proclaimed the need to build democracies that would 'give back their dignity to all citizens, fill their minds and feast their eyes with human things' (Fanon 1985: 165).

Racism continues to be the most vicious expression of what Raimond Gaita has condemned as the 'denial of a common humanity' (Gaita 2002: 57–72). Racist political parties of the extreme right have had some alarming successes in Europe since the 1970s and have participated in coalition governments in Italy, Austria, Poland, Slovakia and Switzerland (Bale 2008: 317). In France in 2002 the leader of the National Front, Jean-Marie Le Pen, with six convictions for racism or incitement to racism behind him, won a place in the run-off elections for the French

Presidency. Even though he was soundly defeated, receiving only 20 per cent of the vote, it was a frightening indication of the continuing appeal of racism as the great simplifying explanation and answer to all social ills. It is this that has been combated by civil society groups like *SOS Racisme* in France and Hope Not Hate in Britain and by teachers and other citizens everywhere.

There is no single anti-racist approach to solidarity. Paul Gilroy argues that, as the development of genetic science has wiped away all claims for biologically discrete races or nations, we should reject race as a category and work towards 'a radically nonracial humanism' with a stress on human dignity (Gilroy 2004: 15–17). Juliet Hooker, on the other hand, argues that such a renunciation of race would leave unchallenged those apparently 'neutral' practices of the liberal state that reproduce racial injustice (Hooker 2009: 113–14). She favours a more active identification and rejection of the often hidden practices of racism. For her, the development of 'genuine solidarity' cannot be achieved by 'suturing the wounds created by past racial injustice and continuing racial inequality', but rather by recognising that the polity comprises radically different cultures, some of them suffering deep injustice (Hooker 2009: 172–5). Although the argument of this book clearly chimes with Gilroy's vision of 'planetary humanism' (Gilroy 2004: 356), it can only be realised through an ever-vigilant opposition to racism in all its forms.

Religion

Religion continues to be one of the most important modes of identity in the world, despite rationalist predictions that it would lose its significance with the development of modernity (Norris and Inglehart 2011: 9–13). In reality, although religion in general plays a less significant role in most of the world's affluent societies, findings from the WVS indicate that 'the world as a whole has more people with traditional religious views than ever before – and they constitute a growing proportion of the world's population'

(Norris and Inglehart 2011: 240). It follows that religion must be taken into account in any exploration of the possibility of global solidarity. Richard Falk, in his work on humane global governance, suggests that religion has a double-coded message. On the positive side, its ethical dimension transcends the obsession with economic growth, but, on the negative side, it can produce political extremism associated with the imposition of fundamentalist beliefs that deny the human rights associated with the advance of secularism (Falk 2001: 25–6). We will return to this possible positive 'opening' at the end of the section, but first we need to look seriously at the argument that religion has been and will continue to be a source of social division. This will be done primarily by looking at the arguments put forward recently by a number of writers who have launched strong attacks on religion from a rationalist, atheist perspective, a position I have labelled 'aggressive atheism' (Wilde 2010). It is important to consider their aims, their rhetoric and their assertion of the dichotomy between faith and reason. I will then advocate constructive dialogues of various kinds that can help to soften differences and make a positive contribution to human solidarity.

The recent spate of books attacking religious faith reflects the alarm felt by rationalists at the threat posed to secularism by the resurgence of religion as a social power. Not content to criticise the excesses of religious fundamentalism, the writers view all expressions of belief in God as an affront to rationality and an invitation to prejudice and judgementalism (Dawkins 2006; Dennett 2006; Harris 2006; Grayling 2007; Hitchens 2007; Onfray 2007; Stenger 2007). For the most part this aggressive atheism is intent on attacking religious thought and its influence on society, setting to one side the question of what a radical secular alternative might look like. The scientist Richard Dawkins has been the most outspoken, making a two-part television programme, *The Root of All Evil?*, for Channel 4 in the UK in 2006, and later that year publishing *The God Delusion*, which went on to sell over two million copies. In 2009, in conjunction with the British Humanist Association, he set up the Atheist Bus Campaign, taking the antireligious message across the country, and he has also conducted speaking tours in Britain and the USA to break down what he considers to be the protected respect that privileges religious positions. In the course of his attacks on religion he raises many serious examples of intolerance and abuse, and quite reasonably questions religious control of education in secular societies. However, the aggressive nature of his attack on religion is clearly not conducive to promoting a human solidarity that embraces people of all faiths as well as non-believers.

Polemics, of course, revel in their controversial nature and are designed to raise hackles in order to bring out controversial arguments into the public sphere. However, in this case, when attacking the self-righteous certitude and vehemence expressed by religious zealots, it is surely self-defeating for Dawkins to adopt a rhetorical strategy that mirrors that of the position he abhors. He protests at the 'moral outrage' and 'frenzied malevolence' displayed by the fundamentalists (Dawkins 2006: 211, 214), but he attacks religion with the same temper. Dawkins claims that the device of 'ridicule' is the only weapon against 'unintelligible' propositions (Dawkins 2006: 34). He then proceeds to savage not only religious fundamentalists but those who adopt the stance of pantheism or deism. According to Dawkins, pantheists like Einstein, who identify God with nature itself, run the risk of associating their position with the 'miracle-wreaking, thought-reading, sin-punishing, prayer-answering God', and, as such, are guilty of 'intellectual high treason' (Dawkins 2006: 19). Similarly the many scientists who declare themselves to be deists, on the grounds that the immense complexity of the world suggests a creator, are derided as partaking in a 'dreadful exhibition of self-indulgent, thought-denying skyhookery' (Dawkins 2006: 155). These scientists, it should be remembered, are not supporting the idea of a God that intervenes in the social world, nor are they seeking to convert others to their belief, but are merely expressing a strong intuition that the immense interactive complexity of the world suggests some sort of unifying principle. The sense of wonderment which sparks this intuition is a spiritual feeling, a source of ethical commitment of respect for life and nature, but Dawkins's intemperate denunciation closes off this area of spiritual needs to intellectual inquiry.

The issue of faith is bound up with Dawkins's refusal to accept the conventional boundaries between the concerns of religion on the one hand and science and philosophy on the other. He rails against the distinction made by Stephen Jay Gould (1941–2002), an atheist and scientist, in his formula of 'non-overlapping magisteria' whereby science covers the empirical realm and religion covers the realm of ultimate meaning and moral value (Dawkins 2006: 54–61). Gould is in a long line of scientists who have acknowledged the limitations of science in this way. Einstein, for example, argued that science 'can only ascertain what *is*, but not what *should be*, and outside of its domain value judgements of all kinds remain necessary'. Religion concerns itself not with facts and relations between facts but only of 'evaluations of human thought and action' (Einstein 1984: 22, original emphasis). Of course it might be argued that issues of value judgement should be the province of philosophy rather than religion, but that would be to overlook the historical role played by religion in inscribing fundamental ends and values into the emotional lives of individuals and societies. According to Einstein, the authority of these ends and values is derived only in the 'powerful traditions which act upon the conduct and aspirations and judgements of the individuals' (Einstein 1984: 19). This approach will not do for Dawkins, who insists that there is nothing beyond the range of science. One is tempted to say that this is a misplaced 'faith' in science, but for Dawkins science deals only in evidence, and faith is an 'evil' because 'it requires no justification and brooks no argument' (Dawkins 2006: 308). There is a problem here, for this rigid separation of faith and reason elides important questions about how we give meaning to our lives, the 'big' questions concerning human commitment and the purpose of social life.

Einstein argues that science is concerned only with the 'is' and religion with the 'should be', but he suggests that there are strong reciprocal relationships and dependencies between the two spheres. He argues that the urge for truth and understanding springs from the sphere of religion, and that faith in the possibility that the regulations valid for the world of existence are comprehensible to reason is a 'profound faith' shared by all genuine scientists (Einstein 1984: 22). This view is also endorsed by Erich Fromm, who uses the example of science in his discussion of faith in *Man for Himself*. The scientist, he argues, does not proceed by making experiment after experiment and gathering fact after fact without some sort of vision of what he or she expects to find. This 'rational vision' is a necessary part of all creative thinking, and although it is based on observation and study rather than sheer fantasy, it is nevertheless a manifestation of rational faith. Fromm argues that at every step in the scientific process, '*faith* is necessary'; it is expressed in terms of the vision as a rationally valid aim to pursue, in the conviction that the hypothesis is a plausible proposition, and in faith in the final theory, at least until a general consensus about its validity has been reached (Fromm 2003: 154, original emphasis). Einstein describes the 'religious feeling' of the scientist in 'rapturous amazement at the harmony of natural law', a feeling which is 'the guiding principle of his life and work' (Einstein 1982: 40). The general point here is that pre-evidential intuitions play an important role in the scientific process, and Charles Taylor makes a telling comment against Dawkins's position when he points out that 'to hold that there are *no* assumptions in a scientist's work that are not already based on evidence is surely a reflection of *blind* faith' (Taylor 2007: 835 n. 27, original emphasis).

Dawkins does not consider the possibility of a rational faith, insisting as he does on defining faith by its opposition to reason. His conception of faith is more accurately rendered as 'irrational faith' (Fromm 2003: 152). Justifying an assertion or practice by stating that it says so in a sacred text is a clear example of blind faith and also an affront to reason, but that is an extreme form of faith, and it is possible to identify forms of faith that are not only *not* an affront to reason but are part of the reasoning process itself. Fromm argues that we should think of faith as an inner attitude rather than something primarily directed at something, and the original Old Testament use of 'faith' (*emunah*) means firmness, a character trait, rather than the content of a belief in something (Fromm 2003: 149). More recently, Alain Badiou has asserted the centrality of this sort of faith, which he terms *pistis* (conviction), to our current philosophical tasks (Badiou 2003: 15). Dawkins displays that sort of faith in his allegiance to science, and in particular to Darwinian evolutionary theory, but he rejects the accusation that he is a fundamentalist because his belief is based on studying the evidence rather than on obedience to a holy book. He claims his belief in evolution through natural selection is not faith because he knows what it would take to change his mind, and, furthermore, he would 'gladly do so if the evidence were forthcoming' (Dawkins 2006: 282–3). However, there is a problem with this assertion. Since scientific discovery involves surpassing previous knowledge, it is not always obvious within a scientific community what counts as valid evidence. This is well illustrated by the account of the great physicist Werner Heisenberg (1901–76) of the immense difficulties he shared with Niels Bohr (1885–1962) in accepting the truth of quantum theory, a difficulty which even Einstein could not overcome. Heisenberg was forced to ask himself, 'Can nature possibly be as absurd as it seemed to us in these atomic experiments?' (Heisenberg 2000: 12–13; Kumar 2008: 225–50).

Although Dawkins trumpets reason over faith, rationality involves the formulation of goals, and when it comes to deciding to what ends we employ our reason we enter the sphere of morality. This is the 'substantive rationality' discussed as one of the key human potentials in the previous chapter, adopted by Max Weber to refer to the choices made in accordance with their efficiency in achieving 'ultimate ends' and which inevitably involve some sort of ethical commitment (Weber 1978: 85–6). Substantive rationality involves a commitment to a goal that is not susceptible to empirical verification. There is, therefore, a tension between the radical doubt at the heart of science and the firm conviction that necessarily accompanies scientific progress.

On the issue of evaluating the social impact of religion, where aggressive atheism sees only a vengeful God demanding sacrifice, radical humanists such as Ernst Bloch (1885–1977) and Erich Fromm have detected a message of human liberation in the biblical depiction of the unfolding relationship between God and humanity. Bloch calls this the 'underground Bible', in which the 'Cannibal' version of God is periodically confronted and eventually gives way to the idea of the 'Son of Man', symbolising humanity's 'emancipation' from God (Bloch 1972: 86, 176, 148). Whereas Dawkins sees only the vindictiveness of God in sending the Great Flood, Fromm focuses on the covenant which follows, revealing a startling retreat by God, who repents his action and promises it will never happen again. Fromm interprets this not simply as a decisive step in the religious development of Judaism, but 'a step which prepares the way to the concept of the complete freedom of men, even freedom from God' (Fromm 1991: 24–5). The wholly negative reading of religious stories has been described by Charles Taylor as 'subtractionist', in which human progress involves the gradual elimination of degrees of superstitious attachments until we arrive only at the human good, which, in Dawkins's account, is the realm of science. However, as Taylor argues, being left only with human concerns does not in any way tell us what our fundamental goals are, individually or socially, and modern humanism displays a striving for justice which can not be explained simply in terms of the jettisoning of religious belief (Taylor 2007: 572). This commitment to a framework of values is common to radical humanism and religion, and it invokes a realm of ideas and emotions which are commonly termed 'spiritual'. When Marx described religion as 'the sigh of the oppressed creature, the heart of a heartless world and the soul of soulless conditions' (Marx 1975: 244), he was not calling for the spiritual categories of heart and soul to be discarded but rather for them to be *realised* in the social relations of the future. It is precisely on this ethical plane, in striving for social justice, that the concerns of radical humanism and religion meet. Aggressive atheism precludes such a meeting and closes off the possibility of conciliatory dialogue.

To achieve meaningful dialogues there need to be processes that foster greater understanding of difference and promote mutual recognition and respect. Who talks to whom, what forms do dialogues take, in what social context, and what outcomes are achieved? In general three kinds of dialogues on religion have been developed, between theists and atheists, between representatives of different faiths, and between different denominations within faiths. For dialogue to be meaningful there needs to be some shared ground, and this is particularly true when the issues are likely to evince emotive responses. So, while a comparison of religious precepts might form the basis of inter-faith dialogue in formal or academic contexts, for dialogue to produce reflexivity among those who live by these precepts, the interlocutors would almost certainly need to share the same faith. On the other hand, reports of discussions between 'experts' at a formal level may trigger responses at informal levels, encouraging greater tolerance. In terms of the contexts in which these dialogues take place it is important to avoid restricting the idea of dialogue to formal meetings or exchanges between renowned representatives. The cultural level of dialogue involves the opening up of discussion of religiously grounded cultural practices through novels, films, drama, music and also comedy. At the level of everyday life, dialogues are conducted in workplaces and social situations through processes of familiarisation that encourage curiosity where suspicion may once have prevailed. Often it is children who lead the way here, learning at school about the variety of religious beliefs and practices and conveying this positive interest in different creeds to their elders. Finally, in terms of outcomes, they range from the minimal goal of avoiding conflict to the maximal goal of a global ethic of peace and harmony. Realistically, what is to be gained is some form of multiculturalism that is actively building greater understanding rather than a minimalist 'toleration of the co-presence of mutually indifferent communities' (Modood 2007: 65).

A few examples may help to show the potential of these reconciliatory dialogues. In terms of dialogues between atheistic and theistic positions, from the perspective of social theory the contribution of Jürgen Habermas offers an excellent example. His commitment to communicative rationality and discourse ethics elicited a response from theologians, and he has responded in a constructive way which not only clarifies essential points of difference but also shows some common ground. For example, Habermas engages with the theologian Jens Glebe-Möller on the issue of reconciling secular and religious 'language games', finding agreement in the idea of cross-generational solidarity, expressed in materialist terms yet carrying strong spiritual overtones (Habermas 2002: 77–8, cf. Glebe-Möller 1987: 112). Habermas has also engaged in constructive dialogue with theologians Michael Theunissen on 'negative theology' and Johannes Baptist Metz on multiculturalism (Habermas 2002: 110–38). Such exchanges do not dissolve differences, but rather point to hitherto unsuspected commonalities. The meeting that produced much greater publicity was Habermas's debate with Cardinal Joseph Ratzinger (now Pope Benedict XVI) in Bavaria in 2004, and their willingness to seek some common ground was symbolically important. Cardinal Ratzinger, not noted for his openness on matters of doctrine, nevertheless expressed agreement with Habermas's remarks 'about a postsecular society, about the willingness to learn from each other, and about self-limitation on both sides' (Habermas and Ratzinger 2006: 77).

There remains, of course, a dividing line between theistic and atheistic perspectives that will not go away. Believers may well feel that atheistic interest in religion is condescending, but in the past such dialogues have revealed strong affinities in different approaches to concepts such as reconciliation, transcendence and justice. Today the challenges for dialogue between atheism and theism cover a number of areas, as Richard Falk argues, including an ecological concern for 'wholeness', a concern for human and animal suffering, a trust in the cooperative potential of human beings, and a commitment to 'a pervasive pedagogy of tolerance as the foundation of citizenship, nationally and globally' (Falk 2001: 96).

In the sphere of inter-faith dialogue, the religious idea that seems most closely connected to the normative goal of multicultural harmony is that of the 'universal ecumene', which acknowledges that there is a truth in all religions. From this perspective, a sense of universal religiosity can inspire initiatives on peace, the eradication of poverty and the protection of the environment. As Susanne Rudolph argues, the deep commitment to the idea that there is truth in all religions is incompatible with actively seeking converts, and this is one of a number of obstacles, but it is an idea that has already developed a major following (Rudolph 2005: 189–99). In terms of global institutional developments, an initiative launched through the UN Conference for Interfaith Cooperation and Peace in New York in 2005 has led to the emergence of the Tripartite Forum for Interfaith Cooperation for Peace. Other bodies that contribute to the process of seeking common religious ground and defusing differences include the United Religions Initiative, which has special consultative status with the UN, and the World Congress of Faith.

One of the most influential of these inter-faith initiatives has been the Parliament of the World's Religions. The parliament met in Chicago in 1993 as part of a centennial celebration of the first parliament, also in Chicago, and the major discussions focused on a document, 'Towards a Global Ethic', drafted mainly by the Catholic theologian Hans Küng. He later developed the ideas into a text, *A Global Ethic for Global Politics and Economics*, which has become an important point of reference for discussions of global justice. Here he invokes the many expressions of the Golden Rule to affirm the commonality and longevity of this moral principle, the oldest form coming from Confucius in the sixth century BC – 'What you yourself do not want, do not want to do to another person' (Küng 1997: 97–9). The parliament now meets regularly, focused on specific issues of global justice, although certain important religious groupings are absent from the process, such as evangelical Protestants, orthodox Jews and fundamentalist Muslims. Besides these international initiatives there are many thousands of groups at work in communities all over the world, assisting social harmony and working actively for social justice (Smock 2002). Work by the sociologist Paul Lichterman in the United States has shown via a detailed ethnographic study just how significant religions are when acting as civic groups dedicated to healing social divisions (Lichterman 2005).

Finally, in situations in which religion is associated with aggression, an intra-faith dialogue becomes virtually the only communicative means through which violent fundamentalism may be restrained. It is perhaps the most difficult of dialogues to develop, since fanatical sects are aware of the need to dissociate themselves from their most closely related denominations. Nevertheless, it is only through this discourse that the selectivity of the fanatical use of sacred texts can be held open to scrutiny. Examples can be found within all religions, but here I will mention only a few examples, from Christianity and Islam. Within Christianity, Randall Balmer's *Thy Kingdom Come* provides an evangelical Christian's critique of the dramatic move to the Right taken by the evangelical movement in the United States. Balmer questions the 'selective literalism' which places overwhelming emphasis on attacking abortion and homosexuality while ignoring other messages from the Bible such as 'care for the poor and opposition to war' (Balmer 2006: 33–4). In the conclusion to his book he contrasts his own reading of the principal Bible messages, emphasising social justice and equality, to the militaristic aggression of the 'religious Right', which continues to ignore issues such as torture and poverty (Balmer 2006: 167–91). Evangelical Christians will never listen to Dawkins, but they may listen to Balmer, a former editor of the leading US evangelical journal *Christianity Today*.

Within Islam, attempts have been made by Islamic scholars to question interpretations of the religion which support violence and intolerance (Modood 2007: 139–45). For example, Bassam Tibi argues at length that the history of Islam reveals a great deal more flexibility of interpretation than modern jihadists are prepared to accept. In particular he argues that *sharia* or sacred law is a post-Koranic construction which should not be rigidified and proposed as a complete replacement for state law (Tibi 2005: 153–66). He also expresses concern that the current politicisation of Islam will produce 'gated' communities within non-Muslim societies, leading to the alienation of Islam from the rest of humanity (Tibi 2005: 269–72). Seyyed Hossein Nasr argues against the modern emphasis on jihad as 'holy war', for its literal meaning of 'exerting effort' in the name of God has always lent itself to a call for spiritual and social renewal without necessarily any implication of violence. Nasr points out that even where 'jihad' has obviously referred to holy war, as in the defence against the Crusades, strict rules of conduct deplore injustice, including attacking the innocent (Nasr 2002: 256–72). Nasr also argues for an Islamic defence of human rights and responsibilities capable of contributing to the creation of harmony between religions and peoples throughout the world (Nasr 2002: 275–306). It should be noted here that although dialogue within fundamentalisms may be effective only within a faith or sect, the content of that dialogue need not be contained to 'internal' religious affairs, and Abdullahi An-Na'im makes the point that it is vital for such dialogues to discuss the implications for Islamic identity in modern societies, including the right to dissent, and that it be supplemented by cross-cultural dialogues (An-Na'im 1999: 110–11).

Constructive dialogues of the types described above are discouraged by aggressive atheism's wholly negative view of the social impact of religion. A standard rhetorical ploy is to highlight the worst excesses of fundamentalist religions and warn that any accommodation of religious identity in the public sphere will involve a 'return to the Dark Ages' (Grayling 2007: 47). Another is to suggest that multiculturalism involves a dangerous relativism by declaring that any set of views is as worthy of respect as any other. Michel Onfray, for example, is particularly scathing in his attack on what he terms 'today's dominant branch of secularism', alleging that in decreeing the equality of all religions and of those who reject them it is accepting the 'equality of magical thinking and rational thought' (Onfray 2007: 216). Daniel Dennett alleges that 'some multiculturalists' claim that people from the affluent world can never understand the subjectivity of Third World people (Dennett 2006: 260). The commitment to reach understanding between different viewpoints does not open the floodgates to fundamentalisms of various kinds, but rather serves to draw fundamentalisms into a terrain in which they will not flourish.

The equation of multiculturalism with an 'anything goes' relativism is a gross caricature. Supporters of multicultural societies are committed to the core values of inclusive democratic states, and claims for the accommodation of religious views and practices will be weighed against those values. The outcomes will vary according to the prevailing conditions and circumstances, but the commitment to the process of accommodation through negotiation is a *sine qua non* for the emergence of societies capable of becoming comfortable with their differences. What is important is the encouragement of a disposition which intuitively seeks to reach a better understanding of positions that may seem arcane or even offensive. The intention is not to tolerate the intolerable or condone practices that breach human rights, but rather to create a fair society which is sensitive to the variety of deeply held values in its midst, and is eager to explore the possibilities for their accommodation.

The desirability of a more conciliatory relationship between secularism and religion can be justified in pragmatic and normative terms. Pragmatically, Bhikhu Parekh urges the inclusion of religious identities into the political process because it provides a better chance of accommodating difference:

> Nothing in human life is an unmixed good and we should not take an unduly rosy or irredeemably bleak view of religion. Rather than keep it out of political life and allow it to sulk and scowl menacingly from outside it, we should find ways of both benefiting from its contribution and minimizing its dangers. (Parekh 2000: 330)

This defence of accommodation will have a widespread appeal to those who intuitively recognise the benefits of living together in an atmosphere of tolerance and understanding. From the perspective of promoting global solidarity, we may take the argument further and suggest that for social movements to push for social justice, an active ethics of human solidarity is required, and this is inconceivable without the contribution of the faith groups.

Gender

Given the centrality of the drive to ever-greater social inclusion in the definition of solidarity, the fact that women were excluded from positions of power in social life for the vast majority of recorded history raises important questions about the role of gender in the struggle for human solidarity. It was not until the twentieth century that women achieved the vote in liberal constitutional states, as late as 1945 in France and 1971 in Switzerland. And in parts of the world today there are serious problems not simply of exclusion from the political process but of extreme physical aggression against women. In a survey conducted by the Thomson Reuters Foundation in 2011 a range of offences such as rape, female infanticide, sex trafficking, forced marriages and genital mutilation made certain parts of the world very dangerous places for women, with Afghanistan, the Democratic Republic of Congo, Pakistan, India and Somalia being the most dangerous (Bowcott 2011). This section will explore the development and justification of patriarchy and outline the struggles that women have conducted in order to combat it. It will also discuss the emergence of women's transnational solidarity activism and assess the impact of feminism on the goal of global solidarity.

Patriarchy refers to 'the manifestation and institutionalization of male dominance over women and children in the family and the extension of male dominance over women in society in general' (Lerner 1986: 239). Through the establishment of descent through the male line and the exclusion of women from the public sphere, men not only asserted their superiority, but, over thousands of years, took it for granted as the natural order of things. This view

Social Division and Reconciliation

was explicitly challenged by two 'waves' of feminism, the first referring to demands for political rights in the late nineteenth and early twentieth century, and the second developing out of the 1960s to strike down both legal discriminations against women and also the social discriminations which had become embedded in an area of life that had historically been regarded as 'personal'. In second-wave feminism, the personal became political.

In fact, women's objections to being treated as inferior beings had been articulated long before the first wave. Marie le Jars de Gournay (1565–1645) wrote *The Equality of Men and Women* in French in 1622, defending the honour of women 'oppressed by the tyranny of men' (Lerner 1994: 197). The Enlightenment commitment to reason also opened up the issue of the status of women for public debate, well illustrated by the response of Mary Wollstonecraft (1759–97) to the sexism displayed by Jean-Jacques Rousseau (1712–78) in *Emile*, published in 1762. Rousseau sets out an enlightened educational programme for the development of Emile as an autonomous, rational man, and denies the same opportunity to Sophie, and by extension to all girls, on the basis of the 'natural' dependence of women on men. Rousseau writes that whereas the man should be 'strong and active' the woman should be 'weak and passive', and whereas the man must have 'both the power and the will' the woman 'should offer little resistance' (Rousseau 1993: 322). He asserts that 'it is impossible to controvert' that when 'woman tries to usurp our rights, she is our inferior' (Rousseau 1993: 327). In arguing that a man can do without a woman 'better than she can do without him', he concludes that nature has decreed that woman 'should be at the mercy of man's judgement' (Rousseau 1993: 328). Wollstonecraft, in *A Vindication of the Rights of Woman* (1792), rejected the idea that woman was formed only to please and be subject to man, although she was aware that this was the version propounded in the Bible. Above all, she denounces the 'pernicious tendency' of those books that 'degrade' the sex of women while glorifying their personal charms (Wollstonecraft 1992: 157–73).

A number of generalisations can be taken from this particular exchange about the devices used to justify patriarchal domination. In the introduction to her pathbreaking text of 1949, *The Second Sex*, Simone de Beauvoir observes that men effectively denied that women were autonomous beings by defining them only as adjuncts to themselves (Beauvoir 1993: xxxix). She points out that antifeminists have 'proved' women's inferiority by drawing on religion, philosophy and theology, as well as science in the form of biology and psychology. At most they have been willing to grant 'equality of difference', justifying extreme discrimination by declaring it to be appropriate to their natural needs (Beauvoir 1993: xlvii–xlviii), which is precisely the strategy deployed by Rousseau that most angered Wollstonecraft. Another point is the way in which the subordination of women is assumed to be natural. Gerda Lerner, in her history of the creation and development of patriarchy, points out that, despite evidence that some ancient societies used maternal lineage, by the time the historical record begins, the sexual division of labour had somehow developed into one based on the hierarchy and power of 'some men over other men and all women' (Lerner 1986: 53). This order of things is sustained ideologically in monotheistic societies by two myths, that life itself is created by a male God, and that only men are capable of actually speaking directly to God (Lerner 1986: 180–98).

An important step in challenging the assumption of male superiority was the opening of the history of gender relations to intellectual inquiry in the late nineteenth century. In *Mother Right* (1861), the Swiss jurist and anthropologist Johann Jakob Bachofen (1815–87), on the basis of work on the myths, drama and archaeology of the ancient Mediterranean world, concluded that there were clues to the existence of societies in which women played a significant leading role. He argued that descent through the female line indicated a 'cultural period preceding that of the patriarchal system' in which women exerted far greater power (Bachofen 1992: 70–1). Although Bachofen, a conservative, considered the emergence of patriarchy to be a progressive development and did not favour the emancipation of women, he wrote in a very romantic way about the prevailing qualities of love, union and peace in the matriarchal societies of the pre-Hellenic period. He acknowledged that the progress of patriarchy had destroyed the hegemony of woman and reduced her from a 'lofty position' to a condition of 'bejewelled servitude'. This deep historicisation of gender relations had potentially radical implications (Bachofen 1992: 171). Although modern anthropological evidence has falsified the idea of women's hegemony in matriarchal societies, it has confirmed the existence of relatively egalitarian societies and 'complex and varied solutions' to the problem of the division of labour (Lerner 1986: 29–31).

It is hardly surprising that the first considerations of the history of gender relations should be by men, given their domination of the public sphere. As Simone de Beauvoir observes, 'the whole feminine history has been man-made' (Beauvoir 1993: 135). Nevertheless, the opening up of the historical record of gender roles encouraged a vigorous challenge to the exclusion of women from public life, and first-wave feminism campaigned for decades for the right to vote until full citizenship was won in the early twentieth century (Hannam 2012: 29–46). One of those campaigners, Charlotte Perkins Gilman (1860–1935), produced a radical critique of patriarchy and a staunch defence of women's autonomy in the form of a utopian novel, *Herland*, originally published in 1915 in her own small circulation magazine, *The Forerunner*. The novel only became widely known when it was published in book form in 1979, when the great skill and humour she uses to expose the irrationality and hypocrisy of patriarchal thinking and practice became a notable contribution to second-wave feminism. The book is also impressive because it imagines an applied ethics of care of the sort discussed in Chapter 4, decades before this approach was developed theoretically, and because the women's society described demonstrates the highest possible level of solidarity.

Set in the remote highlands of South America, the story of this society of three million women and girls is related to the reader through the account of one of three stereotypical male explorers.

Global Solidarity

The Herlanders lived without men for 2,000 years, following a natural calamity that claimed the lives of all the men at a time of war (Gilman 1999: 56). They live a communistic existence marked by cooperation, sustainability, intelligence and innovation. The problem of reproduction has been resolved by the miracle of parthenogenesis; originally a woman conceived without male assistance and gave birth to a daughter, followed by other daughters. It was from this mother than the entire society developed, and she became venerated as a form of divinity (Gilman 1999: 57–9). At first each woman produced five daughters, but when this eventually caused a problem of over-population the women learned how to control their fertility and produce only one daughter each, once they had reached the responsible age of twenty-five. Nurturing and education are collective responsibilities, and the most able carers take the leading role (Gilman 1999: 104, 84). A collective reverence for motherhood, viewed as the 'sacrament of a lifetime', is the most valued ethic, and is the foundation for an incredibly strong sense of solidarity (Gilman 1999: 89, also 70, 102, 138). This strong sense of solidarity among the women is not intended to be exclusivist, for the Herlanders look forward to reinstating a two-sex society, and celebrate the marriage of one of the women with one of the explorers as the harbinger of a new global solidarity (Gilman 1999: 119).

Although Gilman's novel is an important text in the emergence of 'maternalist' or 'difference' feminism, many second-wave feminists had strong reservations about a version of feminism that extolled the virtues of motherhood, for this appeared to conform to the stereotypical view of women's nature that had been used to subjugate women throughout the history of patriarchal society. In the light of this long history of ascribing a biologically determined inferiority to women, it is not surprising that most second-wave feminists were anxious to demand equality with men without recourse to arguments about biological difference. As well as that, there are aspects of social life depicted in *Herland* that are deeply problematic and may illustrate the danger of relying solely on an ethics of care. The Herlanders punish women who display possessiveness towards their children or who exhibit vestigial sexual feelings, for they are seen to be acting in ways that would corrode collective stability (Gilman 1999: 83, 93). This has prompted Joan Tronto to argue that the novel demonstrates the inevitability of suppressing individuation if private caring values are made the sole ethical principle in public life. As mentioned in Chapter 4, Tronto concludes that care is not a 'sufficiently broad moral idea to solve the problems of distance, inequality and privilege' and needs to be supplemented by other forms of deliberative justice (Tronto 1994: 158–60). Be that as it may, the elevation of care and compassion to a much more significant place in ethical thinking is a very positive response to the reconsideration of the relations between men and women that flourished in twentieth-century feminism.

The achievements of second-wave feminism, beginning in the late 1960s, have been immense (Hannam 2012: 75–92). Legal discriminations against women were challenged, with legislation requiring equal pay for the same work, an end to sexual discrimination in employment and other spheres of society, the availability of abortion and, for the first time in Catholic countries, the right to divorce. These developments, mainly in the 1970s and 1980s, coincided with that phase of feminism when large national associations and mass movements campaigned for specific and enforceable demands. There was also a sustained attack on what might be called institutionalised sexism, whereby the oppression of women was sustained through the operation of male-dominated social structures and state agencies. The family structure itself and the traditional household were challenged because they reproduced injustices for women, giving rise to the slogan 'the personal is political' (N. Fraser 2009: 103). The 'neutrality' of 'universal' social benefits was also challenged, as in the case of male-dominated health services that routinely opted for unnecessary invasive operations on women, and police services that ignored domestic violence and were frequently insensitive to the victims of rape. Feminist networks set up women's health groups and rape support centres. Combating sexual harassment in the workplace became and remains a major issue. Related to these projects was a sustained cultural assault on the depiction and social judgement of women, rejecting the extreme roles of objects of male desire or dutiful wives and mothers tied to the home. Women demanded the same freedoms as men, to assert themselves and to aspire to all positions of power. The women's movement was massively effective, but the diffuse nature of the concerns of women from various groups in different cultures militated against the development of homogeneous, hierarchical organisations that would have followed the institutional format of patriarchal society.

From the late 1980s on, numerous disagreements arose within feminism about how women should prioritise issues raised by differences of race, religion, class and sexual orientation, and how women should respond to various aspects of consumerism. Large-scale national groups gave way to local networks organised around specific concerns, yet still able to respond to attacks on newly won rights, such as abortion and child care. Although this might appear to constitute a weakening of feminist solidarity, it coincided with the widening of feminist concerns to the global level. The first United Nations conference on women took place in Mexico in 1975, attended by 5,000 delegates. It inaugurated the UN Decade for Women and drew the attention of national governments to the specific problems faced by women, while the UN conference on women in Beijing in 1995 was attended by 25,000 delegates. The UN now disaggregates its data on quality-of-life indicators, enabling the targeting of improvements in those areas most significant to women in the Millennium Development Goals. Despite different theoretical differences about how women can benefit most from development strategies (Haynes 2008: 171–9), international solidarity work is one of the most significant aspects of modern feminism.

Two examples of women's transnational solidarity highlight both the potential and the problems involved in developing global solidarity. The first is the Latin American Network of Women Transforming the Economy, created in 1997 by a diverse group of women from ten Latin American states, and seeking to promote ideas and initiatives around women's relationship to the economy. Against a background of developing free trade and IMF-imposed structural adjustment programmes, these women began to show how policy shifts impacted on the lives of women generally, and brought women to the forefront of campaigns against neoliberal policies such as the privatisation of water and energy services (Diaz Alba 2010: 199–200). They have also worked within existing organisations such as the World Social Forum and the Campaign against the Free Trade Agreement of the Americas, bringing home to those organisations the particular impact on women's lives that might have otherwise been overlooked by adopting a 'gender blind' perspective. In this way, an international feminist movement works with broader groups as part of a broader humanist struggle (Diaz Alba 2010: 205–22).

The second example is the Women in Black movement, which campaigns for peace and reconciliation by campaigning and demonstrating in conflict zones. It began when Israeli Jewish women demonstrated in sympathy for the Palestinians during the first *intifada* in 1987. New groups developed in Italy, Yugoslavia during its wars of disintegration, India and the United States. It was estimated that by 2006 there were 360 groups around the world, although there is no constitution, no headquarters and no official membership (Cockburn 2009: 156–62). This form of loose networking in which the organisation is a flexible forum has the advantages of spontaneity and the simplicity generated by empathy with women suffering the consequences of conflict, but Cynthia Cockburn asks an important question – is it an instance of global solidarity? (Cockburn 2009: 162–3). Her answer is cautious, for she argues that global solidarity, like global sisterhood, is an optimistic notion that overlooks differences in the positions of individuals and groups within the movement. Solidarity, she argues, can only be secured by respectful listening to differences through democratic processes that are not in place in that particular movement. Nevertheless, she concludes that Women in Black 'does embody an aspiration to global solidarity', even though such a grand aspiration 'may prove forever out of reach'. The caution expressed here is wise, but what is amazing about this example and many similar instances of transnational solidarity is precisely the strength of that aspiration, the determination to realise global justice.

Despite the achievements of feminism, particularly in the more affluent parts of the world, women continue to bear the brunt of global poverty, environmental degradation and violence. As Nancy Fraser has commented, it can be argued that 'the movement's relative success in transforming culture stands in sharp contrast to its relative failure to transform institutions' (N. Fraser 2009: 98). The advance of feminism coincided with the crisis of international capitalism that gave rise to neoliberalism. As feminism stressed the need for recognition rather more than redistribution, its central concern was not with macro-economic policy. Furthermore, the attack on the patriarchal state also lent itself to a general opposition to state intervention as such, making it harder to defend the role of the public sector against market incursions. Feminist demands for greater freedom have been met, to some extent at least, with greater inclusion in the workforce and increased professional opportunities, but the free-market solutions that have accompanied these developments have also weakened the bargaining power of labour in general and created more poverty, especially for women (N. Fraser 2009: 108–13). Fraser states her 'what is to be done?' conclusion in very general terms, but it chimes with the theme of this book:

> Having watched the neoliberal onslaught instrumentalize our best ideas, we have an opening now in which to reclaim them. In seizing this moment, we might just bend the arc of this impending transformation in the direction of justice – and not only with respect to gender. (N. Fraser 2009: 117)

Writing at the onset of the financial crisis, Fraser assesses it as an opportunity for feminism to recover its social emancipatory instincts after the failure of neoliberalism. The latter, however, has proved to be a frighteningly resilient opponent of human solidarity.

For Simone de Beauvoir, the subordination of women turned on the denial of women's autonomy. Towards the end of *The Second Sex*, in the chapter titled 'Toward Liberation', she writes of the need for women to throw off their vassal status:

> When she is productive, active, she regains her transcendence; in her projects she concretely affirms her status as subject; in connections with the aim she pursues, with the money and rights she takes possession of, she makes trial of and senses her responsibility. (Beauvoir 1993: 713)

She is at pains to point out that this is not only within reach of those with access to education and prosperity, but can be and is experienced by all women. Perhaps we can go further, and say that this emphasis on productiveness calls for commitment to the development of a key potential for all human beings, and this can be realised only when the other potentials of compassion, substantive rationality and cooperation are combined in human solidarity.

Conclusion

The broad areas discussed above do not, of course, exhaust the list of divisive issues that have generated antagonisms. Yet it is not difficult to see that progress has been made, for example, in the way that Western societies have moved, in the past half century, from punishing homosexuality as a crime to accepting same-sex marriage, and, despite the persistence of homophobia in some quarters, to general social acceptance of difference in sexual orientation. There has also been great progress made in understanding and addressing the issues arising from physical and mental disability. The rise of the green movement has challenged the conquistador mentality that prevailed in attitudes towards nature, and questions the 'growth at any cost' idea of progress that has been driving economic globalization so far. There is so much to build on, and yet the first point of division, social class, embedded in the social relations of capitalist production, continues to reproduce levels of inequality wholly incompatible with progress towards solidarity. A cultural shift is needed to challenge the power structures that dominate world society, and it is to this issue of the culture of solidarity that we now turn.

6 Culture

The radical humanist approach outlined in Chapter 4 requires a movement away from a narrowly conceived pursuit of self-interest through instrumental rationality to a broadly conceived pursuit of the interests of the social self through substantive rationality. Insistence on conceiving the self as always a social self overcomes the implication of 'loss' associated with the notion of self-sacrifice, which is sometimes seen as a necessary element of solidarity (Baurmann 1999: 248). In acting solidaristically, we experience the effulgence of expressing the realisation of our finest potentials, of doing the right thing for our 'common humanity' (Monroe 1996: 197–216; Gaita 2002: 276–85). It must be conceded that the structures of a competitive world economy do not encourage the development of this social self, and yet, despite the exigencies of everyday life, the hope for a kinder and fairer world has not been extinguished.

This chapter explores the possibility of developing a culture of solidarity in which there is a growing consciousness of our inter-dependence and a growing commitment to a more just and sustainable world. A solidaristic consciousness can emerge, based on the development of the potentials identified in Chapter 4. This requires a process of contestation taking place at two levels. The first is the level of everyday life, through inter-personal relations in communities and workplaces and through attitudes affirmed or demonised by the media and through education. The second is through art in its most general sense, including literature, music and visual arts that prompt powerful emotional reactions that may generate an intuitive appreciation of the need for human solidarity. Such cultural products are able to illuminate the subjective experience of the struggle for solidarity in dramatic detail, often in extreme and inauspicious circumstances. Two examples will be discussed here, Barbara Kingsolver's novel *The Poisonwood Bible* and Walter Salles's film *The Motorcycle Diaries*.

Everyday life

One of the principal features of globalization is the migration of people, bringing with it tangible changes in the lived experience of everyday life. It has been estimated that in almost all western European countries 'the population of immigrants and their children approaches or surpasses ten per cent' (Caldwell 2010: 8). This cultural mélange can be viewed either as enriching or as a serious threat. For Ulrich Beck, the breaking down of national borders and differences opens up the possibility of 'cosmopolitan empathy', in which differences can be recognised and the perspectives of others more readily understood (Beck 2006: 6–8). For Christopher Caldwell, immigration in general, and Muslim immigration in particular, is something to be greatly feared, a mortal threat to some imagined culturally homogeneous European civilisation (Caldwell 2010; Lentin and Titley 2011: 51–62). This is a crude European variation on the global theme developed by Samuel Huntington in *The Clash of Civilizations*, in which he argues that globalizing forces of integration have provoked counter-forces of 'cultural assertion' that threaten the dominance of Western civilisation, and, therefore, civilisation in general (Huntington 1997: 36, 320–1). A litany of global ailments can then be ascribed to the toxic mix thrown up by globalization, without much or any attempt to understand the multiple ways in which people are managing cultural diversity and transcending insularity. Rabble-rousing politicians and newspapers have often resorted to predicting that indigenous populations will be 'swamped' by immigrants, with the implication that society as a whole will be dragged down into the mire. Caldwell, reflecting on the infamous 1968 'rivers of blood' speech by the Conservative minister Enoch Powell, asks why, given that the level of immigration has been as Powell predicted, the violence he foresaw did not materialise (Caldwell 2009: 6). He struggles to find an answer, because it is simply too damaging to his alarmist thesis to admit that peaceful multiculturalism is developing because the majority of people are learning to live together.

What does such a learning process consist of? The disruption to traditional modes of living caused by economic globalization has been immense, and the experience of loss and insecurity sometimes leads to rising support for parties and movements of the extreme Right (Bale 2008: 316–19). Geographical mobility is often accompanied by the emergence of 'gated' communities in which old ways are preserved and group resentment festers. This contributes to the flashpoints that make the headlines and feed the alarmists, leading to attacks on multiculturalism when the problem is rather one of 'culturalism', the failure to reach out to other cultures. Despite this the cosmopolitanisation of cities develops apace, and through interaction in workplaces, leisure activities and other social places, people from different cultures learn their differences and learn to live with them (Hopper 2007: 159). Merely tolerating difference does not in itself actively generate solidarity, but the meeting and mixing of cultures in a process of 'hybridisation' opens the possibility of developing solidaristic relations. Cultures have never been 'pure' and unchanging, but long-standing norms and customs now change rapidly, in a self-conscious and often liberating way (Tomlinson 1999: 141–9). One notable example of this is the development of world music in recent years, in which musicians from all over the world have fused their styles with music from different cultures to produce distinctively new sounds. As Simon Featherstone has noted, this 'hopelessly hybrid' phenomenon both affirms 'a distant localness' and renders that localness 'universally comprehensible and adaptable' (Featherstone 2005: 40). This, I would argue, contributes to a culture of human solidarity.

The experience of cosmopolitanism is not limited to affluent elites who travel the world, but rather, to use Beck's phrase, it has 'taken up residence in reality' (Beck 2006: 2). Indeed it is an experience that is more familiar to people in less developed countries as a result of colonialism and economic domination exerted by Western-based transnational corporations (Beck 2006: 69–70). Increased global inter-dependence opens up solidaristic possibilities, but the particular form that economic globalization has taken in the past three decades has had divisive consequences. The neoliberal emphasis on the ability of unregulated markets to deliver prosperity has widened inequality both internationally and within states, creating simultaneously an illusion of freedom and a reality of greater dependency. The advertisements celebrate speed, change and choice, but the consumption of the products encourages obsessions with assorted trivia and fashions. Neoliberalism's ideological elevation of freedom and competition is confirmed in the 'rolling back' of the state. In Britain, for example, one of the richest countries in the world, instead of society ensuring that there are no children in need, there is an annual charity television event of that name that has been in existence since 1980. Despite the enormous sums raised, Britain has four million children – one third of the total – living in poverty, one of the highest rates in the industrialised world (Child Poverty 2012). It must be emphasised that this is not to impugn the generous motives of donors and fundraisers, but to suggest that perhaps the event might also become a forum for discussing what could be achieved through increasing progressive taxation. Charity should develop into solidarity. How can solidaristic principles of social inclusion and respect for the environment permeate our individualist culture? Can the social self prevail? Two sites of contestation that need to be considered are the media and education.

Many theorists sympathetic to the goal of human solidarity have lamented the corrosive effects of popular culture, damned by Theodor Adorno and Max Horkheimer as 'mass deception' (Adorno and Horkheimer 1986: 120–67; Adorno 1992; Marcuse 2002). The 'culture industry', to use Adorno's term, presents major problems from a solidaristic perspective, since it is a direct beneficiary of the low tax, anti-regulation model that has led to widening inequality and social exclusion. Nor do we need to look far for the products of popular culture that are destructive of the very idea of solidarity. For example, popular 'reality' television shows in which participants are manipulated into displaying selfish and aggressive behaviour encourage a bleak view of human nature. Much television and film entertainment offers an invitation to peek and sneer, to laugh at others' humiliation, or to delight in the latest transgression of moral norms. However, it may be doubted that cheap shock has an enduring impact, and it is vitally important to see the positive potential there is in popular entertainment for developing a solidaristic consciousness.

There are countless examples of films and television programmes that have succeeded in drawing attention to social injustices and can be seen as important contributions to healing the social divisions discussed in Chapter 5. Looking back fifty years, it is possible to see the positive social impact of these dramas. Harper Lee's 1960 novel, *To Kill a Mockingbird*, exposed the deep racism of the American South, and when it was made into an outstanding feature film by Robert Mulligan in 1962 it was seen by millions around the world. It provided an awakening moment for race relations in the United States and was an important contribution to the struggle for civil rights in that decade. Its enduring relevance was affirmed when Gary Ross 'quoted' a famous courtroom scene from *Mockingbird* in his own solidaristic masterpiece *Pleasantville* in 1998. In Britain, Brendan Behan's brilliant play about capital punishment, *The Quare Fellow*, was made into a feature film by Arthur Dreifuss in 1962, and the harrowing nature of the execution scene led to increased pressure to abolish the death sentence. The last judicial hanging took place in 1964 and the sentence for murder was formally abolished in 1969.

Many television dramas have succeeded in putting social justice on the political agenda, and a famous example in Britain was Jeremy Sandford's *Cathy Come Home* (1966), directed by Ken Loach, which shocked the nation by showing that even in a period of full employment and prosperity, people could become destitute through no fault of their own. It led to support for the newly opened charity Shelter and triggered the formation of another one, Crisis, as well as developing approval of the redistributive policies of the Labour government of the day. The popular media have also played a significant role in gaining public acceptance of gay and lesbian sexual orientations. Basil Dearden's 1961 film *Victim*, starring Dirk Bogarde, was effectively a plea for the decriminalisation of homosexuality, and although it was banned in the United States, in Britain it contributed to a significant shift of public opinion that cleared the way for legalisation in 1967. At the same time that these dramatic interventions were having such an impact, Bob Dylan was railing against social injustice as popular music took a decidedly radical turn (Wilde 2009). The end of the decade saw the release of the quintessential solidarity song, John Lennon's 'Imagine', with its hope that 'the world will live as one'.

So, despite the acuity of so much of their cultural analysis, Adorno and Horkheimer were quite wrong to state that 'all mass culture is identical' (Adorno and Horkheimer 1986: 121). On the contrary it is an important site of contestation, and one in which developments in communications technology have, to some extent at least, wrested power away from the monopolies and towards independent producers. The internet and new forms of social media have helped to circulate critical viewpoints, and, crucially, to expose the ideological nature of the old media. They have enabled the networking and mobilisation of protest movements, from revolutionary situations in the 'Arab Spring' to the Occupy movements that spread across the world in 2011. Digital networked communications have the potential to be an important vehicle for solidaristic political action. There is a danger, of course, that new technology becomes fetishised, with the circulation of information encouraging passivity rather than mobilisation. However, even while heeding these warning, Joss Hands is justified in concluding that 'global webs of mutual support and solidarity contribute greatly to the global justice movement' (Hands 2011: 190).

Turning now to education, can it help to promote a solidaristic consciousness? The realm of education has not been immune to the pressures of the market, reflected in the incessant testing of discrete 'bits' of knowledge with a view to making students better fitted for a more flexible workforce. It has also seen the rise of business studies and enterprise initiatives, although as Hans Schattle points out, there has also been a positive response to the idea of global citizenship (Schattle 2008: 93–116). On the darker side, corporate sponsorship can lead to unhealthy consumer exploitation, as illustrated by Leslie Sklair, who cites a letter from Coca-Cola to a school principal in Colorado Springs in the USA in which the school is given the imperative of selling seventy cases of products during the first three years of the contract (Sklair 2003: 169–70). More generally, Martha Nussbaum has complained of a growing neglect of the study of the humanities at all levels, arguing that the profit motive has caused systems of education to 'heedlessly' discard the skills 'needed to keep our democracies alive' (Nussbaum 2010: 2). Following the example set by John Dewey, whose *Democracy and Education*, first published in 1916, used to be a standard text in teacher-training colleges, Nussbaum opposes passivity in education and calls for the development of Socratic methods of dialogical investigation, in order that society can produce active and informed citizens (Dewey 2007: 212–22; Nussbaum 2010: 25–6). She is particularly critical of the prevailing 'teaching to the test' style of rote learning prevailing in schools (Nussbaum 2010: 134), instead recommending an education to inspire citizens of the world, with a focus on world history and economic understanding (Nussbaum 2010: 79–94; cf. Fromm 1964: 92n). Nussbaum's reminder of the significance of historical knowledge brings to mind the sage warning issued by Herbert Marcuse (1898–1980) that the triumph of functional discourse involves the 'suppression of history', not simply as an academic problem but as a political problem, because it closes off the imagination of historical possibilities (Marcuse 2002: 100–1).

Alain Touraine and Roberto Unger have also emphasised the importance of reforming the content and pedagogy of education. In both cases they are concerned to create learning environments in which students are encouraged to develop their powers of substantive rationality. They want to see a fundamental change of direction whereby societies openly prioritise human welfare above the narrow growth needs of market-driven economies. Touraine emphasises the importance of a radical reform of education in his chapter 'A School for the Subject' in *Can We Live Together?*, calling for the adoption of three principles, through which the freedom of all individuals is recognised and encouraged, diversity is acknowledged and celebrated, and equality of opportunity becomes a reality (Touraine 2000: 269–71). Touraine insists on the need for secularism in the provision of education, which need not jeopardise multiculturalism. He also wants schools to be centres of communication rather than authoritarianism, and wants them to encourage a critical consciousness that will promote a democratic awareness (Touraine 2000: 271–87). There is a similar thrust to Unger's comments on education in *Democracy Realized*, for he also argues for a departure from the rote-learning, authoritarian and nationalistic aspects of traditional education. He envisions a school that encourages the independence of children so that they can look critically at society and develop critical and innovative powers, 'enabling them to become little prophets', an experience which requires 'a large measure of detachment from the dominant culture' (Unger 1998: 231). At the post-school level, he suggests a scheme of social inheritance, partly financed by heavy taxes on personal inheritance, whereby a social endowment account would enable adults to engage in further and higher education, as well as retraining programmes (Unger 1998: 205). In a later work, *The Self-Awakened*, he places great emphasis on avoiding 'entrenched inequalities' of opportunity, respect and recognition, avoiding at all costs the 'hereditary transmission of economic and educational advantage'. He also calls for an increased awareness of people's need to care for others, the 'principle of solidarity' (Unger 2007: 175–6).

Ironically, many of the qualities demanded by these solidaristic thinkers are actually evident in much of the educational entertainment directed at young children. Modern capitalist societies seem happy to encourage the very young to be caring, cooperative and appreciative of the supreme value of friendship, only to abandon them to the imperative of competitive success once the harsh reality of adolescence arrives. Nevertheless, the continued spread of basic, further and higher education carries with it the potential for expanding knowledge of human inter-dependence and challenging fatalism. The second of the UN's Millennium Development Goals commits the global community to ensure that by 2015, 'children everywhere, boys and girls alike, will be able to complete a full course of primary schooling' (Black 2008: 93). Unfortunately it is doubtful that this goal will be achieved, with lack of schooling in sub-Saharan Africa and southern Asia proving hard to overcome. There is also a marked gender imbalance, as shown in the case of India, where the male literacy rate is 65 per cent but the female rate is only 50 per cent (Nussbaum 2010: 11). The progress that has been made, however, indicates that more ambitious targets for basic education and literacy can be set, while it has been estimated that the expansion of higher education across the globe should produce two billion graduates by 2015 (Hopper 2007: 165). Paul Hopper is surely right to conclude that the expansion of education has the potential 'to engender more critical, liberal and enlightened attitudes', which he regards as a prerequisite of a cosmopolitan disposition. He is also right to argue that more educated citizens are 'more likely to question the claims of nationalists and national leaders, to challenge racial and cultural stereotypes, and to resist the essentialising of other peoples' (Hopper 2007: 165). However, to nurture global solidarity there needs to be explicit attention to issues of global justice and global history from an early age, in an atmosphere in which rote learning and constant testing give way to discursive and reflective education, as in the literal sense of *educare*, 'to lead out'.

The aesthetic dimension

The title for this section is borrowed from Herbert Marcuse's final book, and the approach adopted here owes much to his insight that art achieves a degree of autonomy from existing social relations, enabling it to protest and transcend those relations, thereby subverting the 'dominant consciousness' (Marcuse 1998: ix). A prerequisite for a major shift of consciousness in favour of the normative goal of human solidarity would require the emergence of a critical and popular art, depicting people striving to overcome social division and insisting on the recovery of humanity. This is why Marcuse sees the aesthetic dimension as a necessary element in the struggle for solidarity:

> The emergence of human beings as 'species beings' – men and women capable of living in that community of freedom which is the potential of the species – this is the subjective basis of a classless society. Its realization presupposes a radical transformation of the drives and need of the individuals: an organic development within the socio-historical. Solidarity would be on weak grounds were it not rooted in the instinctual structure of individuals. (Marcuse 1998: 16–17)

The two case studies considered here show how art, conceived in its broadest sense, can contribute to a re-evaluation of values and promote an affective shift in confronting injustices and striving for solidarity.

Kingsolver: The Poisonwood Bible

Since its publication in 1998 Barbara Kingsolver's *The Poisonwood Bible* has sold over four million copies and helped to bring attention to the complicity of Western political and economic power in the ruination of the Congo. In addition to exposing different forms of oppression, the novel presents moments of solidarity in which the affirmation of shared human needs and aspirations overcomes prejudice and destructive anger. Specifically I focus on two forms of human solidarity in the novel, cross-cultural solidarity and what I term dependency solidarity, which in this case involves disability. However, before looking at how Kingsolver brings these ideas out in her narrative, it will be helpful to recount the major forms of oppression revealed in the novel, the parallel imperiums of Western colonialism inflicted on a whole people and the patriarchal tyranny inflicted by Nathan Price on his wife Orleanna and their four daughters.

The novel is organised in seven parts or 'books', named after books of the Bible or other biblical references, for this is the story of a missionary family. They are brought to Kilanga, a remote village in the Belgian Congo, by Nathan Price, a Baptist preacher from Georgia who is driven to bring the truth of the Bible to the natives of the Congo. It is 1959, just prior to independence. The story is told in multiple narratives by Orleanna and the daughters: Rachel, seventeen at the start of the mission; twins Leah and Adah, two years younger; and Ruth May, aged seven. Nathan is a tyrant who beats his wife and children and routinely punishes the children by getting them to write out verses from the Bible. The daughters are destined to be denied higher education because the Reverend Price deems it unnecessary for women, just as the Belgians had deemed it unnecessary for the Congolese. He considers that he has nothing to learn from the villagers, whom he considers to be ignorant heathens who need to be civilised. His failure even to attempt to understand their values and concerns leads to the collapse of his mission and the break-up of his family. The subjugation of the females parallels the colonial subjugation of Africa, and Orleanna makes this link explicit by describing her position in the marriage as being 'lodged in the heart of darkness', referring to Joseph Conrad's Congolese novel.

The failure of Nathan Price to communicate with his potential flock, and the broader glaring cultural chasm between the West and the Congo, is encapsulated in the title of the book. The poisonwood tree gives off a nasty burn to all who break its bark, symbolising the Congo's resistance to a foreign hand. Nathan ignores warnings from their cook, a villager, not to touch it when clearing land for planting, and consequently he develops a severe rash (Kingsolver 1998: 46). The Kikongo word for the tree, *bängala*, means both 'most precious' and 'most insufferable', depending on how it is pronounced. The Reverend ends every sermon with 'Tata Jesus is *bängala*', but although he thinks he is saying 'Father Jesus is most precious', he is understood by the locals to be saying either that Jesus is insufferable or that Jesus is a poisonwood tree, much to their bemusement (Kingsolver 1998: 312). Because he speaks neither French nor Kikongo he relies on Anatole, the young village teacher, to translate for him. Anatole is an honest mediator, but when he conveys the message from the local chief and his spiritual advisor that the Christian Church should be respectful of the local traditions, Nathan is outraged by their effrontery and turns angrily on the messenger (Kingsolver 1998: 145–53). For Nathan, there can be no respect for local traditions; they have to be renounced and replaced by the truth as revealed in the Bible. Anatole is initially the only character aware of the impending withdrawal of the Belgian colonial power, and he has to prepare the people for independence by showing them how to vote. As one would expect, Nathan is contemptuous of the idea that the people could hold elections and form a nation, declaring that 'you might as well put a fence round sheep, wolves and chickens, and tell them to behave like brethren' (Kingsolver 1998: 192).

One example of how this contempt for local knowledge brings the family down is Nathan's attempt to apply Western horticultural methods to the jungle. He plants his seeds in a level garden, and his cook, Mama Tataba, warns him that they will not grow unless they are placed in small hillocks. She even does it for him, but this act of kindness enrages him, and he restores his level garden, only for all the plants to be washed away in the first deluge (Kingsolver 1998: 47–8, 73). Mama Tataba eventually gives up her duties, and without knowledge of the local food or hygiene, Orleanna struggles to feed the family. Towards the end of their seventeen-month stay they survive only through the assistance of their neighbours (Kingsolver 1998: 234–5). On another occasion Nathan wants to impress the locals by giving them fish, but, when he dynamites the river to catch some, he kills so many that they are left to rot on the banks, a waste that is deeply offensive to the villagers. He also wants to baptise the village children in the wide river nearby, but it takes him six months to learn that a child had been killed by a crocodile the previous year and the children are expressly forbidden from going in the water (Kingsolver 1998: 93).

The decisive year in the disintegration of the country and the family is 1960. The Congo's independence from Belgium in the summer is quickly followed by the assassination of the first democratically elected leader, Patrice Lumumba, in a CIA plot, and his replacement by the corrupt and brutal dictator Joseph Mobutu, who guarantees that Western interests will prevail in the country. For the family, their situation deteriorates rapidly when they lose their small income as their church pulls out of missionary activity following independence. Nathan refuses to heed the warnings to leave, and Orleanna and the children turn against him completely. His obduracy has already created bad relations with the local chief, and the tensions become unmanageable when Kilanga is ravaged by disease and crop destruction from ants. The chief eventually demands an election in the church to decide whether Jesus Christ should have the office of village god, and Jesus loses by fifty-six votes to eleven. Following the death of the youngest daughter, Ruth May, from a snake bite, Orleanna takes the other girls and walks away from the village, surviving immense hardships only through the help of the Congolese, often at great risk to themselves. Orleanna returns the USA with Adah, while Leah, too ill to travel, stays in the Congo with Anatole, marrying him and supporting him in his political opposition to the Mobutu regime. Rachel offers herself to the sleazy smuggler who had brought them to Kilanga by plane in return for escape to Johannesburg. She stays in Africa and has various relationships with wealthy white men, eventually becoming a hotel proprietor in the former French Congo. Nathan, according to a story told many years later to Leah, moved to another village and repeated his mistake of threatening to baptise the children in the river. The enraged villagers chased him to a *tour de maître* – the towers used by the Belgian foremen to pick out the lazy coffee pickers for whipping – and burned it down.

The final quarter of the book shows the development of the

surviving members of the family over the next thirty years, and their attempts to achieve an understanding of the events they lived through and their relationships with one another. Despite the harrowing nature of the events, Kingsolver constructs images of solidarity that offer hope that, despite all the odds, we may learn to remedy such injustices. In 1985 the surviving sisters hold a reunion. Leah is waiting for the release of Anatole following his latest imprisonment for opposing the Mobutu regime. Rachel, a racist, considers him a criminal, and she is not prepared to permit Leah and Anatole to share a room in her 'whites only' hotel.

Leah begins to tell her sisters that she heard that their father had been killed. She mentions that she still has a lot of contact with Kilanga, and that 'some of the people we knew are still there' (Kingsolver 1998: 547). Rachel simply does not understand. The pilot had taken her out of the Congo and there were no other white people there, so how can people 'we knew' still be there? Unthinkingly, she denies recognition as 'people' to the black Congolese villagers. It is a small but telling example of the blindness of the coloniser to the humanity of the colonised. Five years into her life in the Congo, Leah Price learns that the black people she lives among simply know that they count for nothing in the eyes of most white people: 'It's dawning on me that I live among men and women who've simply understood their whole existence is worth less than a banana to most white people. I see it in their eyes when they glance up at me' (Kingsolver 1998: 494).

However, in the relationship between Leah and Anatole, Kingsolver creates a symbol of cross-cultural solidarity. Their relationship develops after the fashion of a utopian novel in which people from different worlds inform each other of the realities of their life, seeking to overcome their bewilderment at the alien practices they learn about. The bond between them is strengthened in a functional way, with Leah taking on the teaching of numbers at Anatole's school and Anatole teaching her how to hunt, which she does far better than him. However, her prowess at hunting provokes a cultural clash that marks the end of the Price family's stay in Kilanga. Above all their love is portrayed as a 'reaching out', with both wanting to gain knowledge of the worlds beyond the boundaries of their upbringing. When Leah asks Anatole what object he would like more than anything he replies that he wants a picture of the world, that is, a map or globe of the planet (Kingsolver 1998: 323), something that every Western child would take for granted. In 1968 the couple move back to the USA to study at university, and Anatole thinks of the library as 'heaven', but what impresses Leah is the racist ignorance directed at Anatole and their children (Kingsolver 1998: 531). They finally return to the Congo, by then renamed Zaire, in 1981, only for Anatole to be immediately arrested and imprisoned. Leah has to raise three children among the Congolese while being largely shunned by them; as she puts it, 'they know just one thing about foreigners, and that is everything we've ever done to them' (Kingsolver 1998: 535). Despite the hardships, she is totally committed to her husband and children and their unceasing struggle against injustice:

> I crave to stop bearing all the wounds of this place on my narrow body. But I also want to be a person who stays, who goes on feeling anguish where anguish is due. I want to belong somewhere, damn it. To scrub the hundred years' war off this white skin till there's nothing left and I can walk out among my neighbours wearing raw sinew and bone, like they do. (Kingsolver 1998: 537–8)

When Anatole is finally released the family move to a cooperative in the southern part of the country, near Angola, and then to Angola itself, where the government is more welcoming.

Leah's emotional reaction to the oppressions she has witnessed is contradictory. When awaiting Anatole's first release from prison she angrily tells a nun that if God is intervening he is 'bitterly mocking the hope of brotherly love' (Kingsolver 1998: 477). Yet she knows that they would never have survived their ordeal without the decisive help of the villagers of Kilanga, and she knows that her sister Ruth May is still mourned there. More than twenty years later Leah maintains that she still has the conviction that life will be fair, that goodness will be rewarded and evil punished, despite the years in which she has seen 'rewarded evils and murdered goodnesses' (Kingsolver 1998: 571). She still lives in hope because 'the Americans are losing in Angola' (Kingsolver 1998: 573). After another ten years we see her in despair, cursing the absence of justice, bemoaning that 'this world has brought one vile abomination after another down on the heads of the gentle, and I'll not live to see the meek inherit anything'. However, she still does not discount the possibility that this might happen one day, speaking wistfully about the 'unbearable burdens that the world somehow does bear with a certain grace' (Kingsolver 1998: 590-1).

Although cross-cultural solidarity is affirmed strongly in the relationship between Leah and Anatole, there is no underestimation of the difficulties involved in living this enlightened principle. *The Poisonwood Bible* points to real cultural differences that will remain extremely difficult to mediate. At one stage Leah tries to defend African complicity in the early slave trade with the Portuguese by a completely unconvincing moral relativism, simply because she cannot bear the idea that the Africans would be blamed for their own enslavement. Other contentious issues raised are the Congolese hostility to twins and the subordinate position of women in the village societies. The point is not that cultural difference is illusory or superficial, but that different cultures can at least reach the point where they can identify what their differences are about, thus creating space for dialogues about particular practices. Kingsolver illustrates this by describing Anatole's relief to have left their cement house in Kinshasa because it had an indoor toilet and he could never accept the propriety of defecating in the middle of his home (Kingsolver 1998: 567). This attitude would no doubt puzzle a modern Western reader, but the same objection was made not so long ago by people in Western cities resisting plans to modernise their houses by replacing the outdoor toilet with an indoor one.

'Dependency solidarity' is concerned with our appreciation that all human beings, at different times of their lives, are heavily dependent on others. Dependency can produce a life-affirming response, but is all too often dealt with in insensitive and demoralising ways. 'The arrogance of the able-bodied is staggering', concludes Adah Price when she has fully overcome her disability, many years after her Congolese experience (Kingsolver 1998: 559). She is born a hemiplegic, paralysed down one side, and is therefore bent and with a pronounced limp. The damage to her brain delayed the development of speech and caused her to see words differently, reading them backwards as easily as forwards. She also has an uncanny ability at mathematics (Kingsolver 1998: 39–40, 64–7). She does not talk and remains silent by choice, and from an early age she recognises the common human failing that responds to the dumb as if they are also deaf and feeble minded (Kingsolver 1998: 40). Her teacher recognises that Adah is as intellectually gifted as Leah, but this does not impress Nathan, who is adamant that it is wasteful for girls to go to college. Her fascination with words is an important part of the book, for she is the one who hears the different meanings of the same Kikongo words through pronunciation, and she is able to understand how the language reflects a different outlook on nature and life.

In Western eyes, Adah is marked out not only as different but as inferior. The Congolese recognise her difference and name her *bënduka*, meaning either 'the crooked walker' or a sleek bird that dips on the river banks. There is no stigma attached to disability because disability is so common among the Congolese. Their next-door neighbour, whose support is essential to their survival, has lost both legs in an accident, and many other villagers are missing limbs. Adah's complaint about the arrogance of the able bodied is that they judge the disabled in terms of their inability to perform the tasks dictated by the able bodied in the manner prescribed by them. She counters that 'we would rather be just like *us*, and have that be all right' (Kingsolver 1998: 559, original emphasis), and it is the experience of it being all right in the Congo that has a profound effect on her. Nevertheless, when she goes to medical school in Atlanta she is advised that by now her brain should have compensated fully for the damage that occurred at birth, and that she should be able to train herself to walk straight. She accepts the challenge, but then feels uneasy at leaving behind an identity which she had grown comfortable with. 'Will I lose myself entirely if I lose my limp?' she asks (Kingsolver 1998: 499), and it is not just the limp she loses but also her strange way of seeing words. Because she used to think in palindromes she had thought of herself as Ada, without the 'h', but when she becomes able bodied she loses that identity. She becomes a famous medical researcher specialising in viruses, locked into her work but retaining that feeling of exclusion. Her complaint about the arrogance of the able bodied is a plea for a wider form of inclusion, a solidarity that recognises that we are all dependent, for long periods in our lives and in a variety of ways (cf. MacIntyre 1999).

Kingsolver is one of the most overtly politically committed novelists of our day, and her support for solidarity is evident not just in her novels but in her non-fictional account of the strike of women copper miners in Arizona in the 1980s. As she says in the introduction to that book, she grew up in a part of rural Kentucky 'that teaches nothing if not the lessons of class struggle and the survival value of collective action' (Kingsolver 1996: xix). At the age of seven she was taken to the Congo by her parents, public health workers trying to combat smallpox and malaria, and this was her initiation into cultural diversity. The outrage she felt when eventually discovering the complicity of the US administration in the installation of the Mobutu regime is expressed in the novel. Sometimes the politics in *The Poisonwood Bible* is posted in didactic or contrived ways, but there is more to this than simply preaching to the converted, for the vast majority of readers of the novel will have had little or no knowledge of Western complicity in African despotism, and many may share the view that Africa's misfortunes are the sole responsibility of Africans. Kingsolver seeks to jolt readers into questioning the economic and political structures that reproduce the gross inequalities in the world. *The Poisonwood Bible* serves as an act of disclosure and an appeal for solidarity, a fine example of how the radical artist can contribute to the development of a new cosmopolitan consciousness.

Salles: The Motorcycle Diaries
Radical art in its widest sense has a significant role in stimulating a solidaristic consciousness, and, occasionally, feature films can prompt a humanistic engagement with a mass audience. Walter Salles's *The Motorcycle Diaries* (2004), based on the young Ernesto Guevara's account of a journey through South America with his friend Alberto Granado, is an outstanding example of this political-cultural engagement. A useful way of understanding its power to provoke a solidaristic reaction is to draw on the theoretical insights of Giorgio Agamben. He sees that cinema can move us away from 'image', conceived as static and uncritical, towards 'gesture', a dynamic display of mediation which 'opens up the ethical dimension for human beings' (Agamben 2007: 155). In Agamben's terms, Salles succeeds in transforming image into gesture, in the process of showing Guevara's transformation from observer to actor, from Ernesto to Che. After sketching the main themes of the film I will summarise Agamben's insights into the possibility of film as a medium for moving us from a world of static images to that of the critical 'gesture'. I will then examine three examples to show how the film uses gesture to convey a 'reaching out' to others in a radical humanistic way.

The film takes its title from Guevara's account of his journey through Latin America with fellow Argentinian Granado in 1952, when Guevara was a 23-year-old medical student taking a break prior to completing his studies in Buenos Aires. Granado was six years older, a biochemist specialising in treating leprosy, embarking on a last adventure before settling down to full-time work. Granado's own account of the journey, *Con el Che por Sudamerica*, appeared in 1978, and Granado acted as chief advisor to Salles about the experience and the impact it had on both men. The title is somewhat misleading, for the motorcycle concerned, a 1938 Norton named *La Poderosa* (The Mighty One), gets them no further than Santiago in Chile. As Granado confirms, abandoning the motorcycle made the trip a much more valuable and rewarding experience, for they had to secure a number of short-term jobs – drivers, seamen, porters, dishwashers and at one stage even copper mine guards – to finance their journey, thereby establishing much closer relationships with the people of the continent (Sinclair 2006: 6).

The film follows the actual path of their journey, down to the cone of South America, up through Chile to Peru, and on to Colombia and Venezuela. Shortly after starting out they stay for a few days in Miramar, south of Buenos Aires, at the home of Ernesto's girlfriend. The family is extremely wealthy and clearly disapproving of the relationship, while Chichina, the young woman, does not want him to make the journey, but, rather, would have him settle down, complete his studies and live a conventional bourgeois life. She asks him what he wants, but he clearly is not certain. On the journey they witness exploitation and brutality, extreme poverty and the racial oppression of the indigenous people, treated as inferior beings in the land that was once the empire of the Incas. Ernesto feels a bond with peoples who were defeated by the Spanish invaders, and asks himself in puzzlement, 'How is it possible to feel nostalgia for a world I did not see?' Towards the end of the journey they work as volunteers for three weeks in the leper colony of San Pablo in Peru, and this is seen as key to Ernesto's transformation, as I shall discuss in the final section.

The transformation of Ernesto is shown inter-subjectively, in terms of his friendship with Alberto, and introspectively, in his developing awareness of the intolerable nature of the life of the dispossessed. Alberto, as the older and more streetwise character, sets out as the leader, but he knows by the end of their travels that it is his friend who is now prepared for leadership. This is conveyed in a scene at Ernesto's twenty-fourth birthday party, in which Alberto sees his friend make the sort of speech he would never attempt, an impassioned speech for solidarity and Latin American unity. Above all, however, the film shows the transformation within Guevara from a restless middle-class student into a person ready to commit everything to fight the injustices he saw on the journey. In dramatising this, the film leads us to an affective understanding of revolutionary subjectivity as compassionate commitment. As Salles himself argues, the trip does not present Guevara's conversion to a revolutionary consciousness as a single point of rupture, but rather a layered disengagement with the world his parents would have chosen for him and a growing conviction that only revolution could overcome the desperate social injustices that he witnessed (Salles 2004).

Although the film focuses on the young Ernesto, most viewers will know that this is a formative experience for the man known to the world as Che Guevara, the great revolutionary leader. The film, therefore, also has a retrospective power, symbolised at the end by the substitution of the actor by the real Granado, aged eighty-two, gazing at the plane that took Guevara back to Argentina. The friends part in Venezuela, where Alberto has accepted a position to work in a clinic specialising in developing treatments for leprosy. In their parting conversation, Ernesto confesses that something has happened to him that he will have to think about for a long time. He registers the extent of the injustice they have witnessed and the fact that he has been radically changed by the experience: 'I am not me any more; at least not the same me as I was.' The postscript to the film announces that the friends were not to meet up for another eight years. By then, Guevara was one of the leaders of the Cuban revolutionary government and he invited Granada to set up a clinic in Cuba, which he did. Guevara, after serving in government, went on to fight in the Congo and in Bolivia, where he was killed by government forces in October 1967.

The power of the film is helped by outstanding performances from Gael García Bernal as Guevara and Rodrigo de la Senna as Granado, a powerful, unsentimental script by José Rivera, and a wonderful, under-stated musical score by Gustavo Santaolalla. In returning to the key original locations, Salles sought to be faithful to the spiritual truth of the experience. When Granado revisited the San Pablo leprosarium with the film crew, he met and was remembered by some of the people he had treated half a century earlier. To compete with commercial cinema in terms of production values requires massive funding, and this was provided by producer Robert Redford. His Sundance organisation supports independent film makers, and Salles had been the recipient of funding for his breakthrough film, *Central Station*, which appeared in his native Brazil in 1998. Redford, convinced of Salles's directorial skills and artistic integrity, committed to the Guevara project, and was able to facilitate what he describes as a humanistic film full of heart, spirit and transformation (Redford 2007).

One way of appreciating the emancipatory power of the film is by using Giorgio Agamben's idea of the movement from image to gesture. In his 'Notes on Gesture', appended to his 1978 book *Infancy and History*, Agamben argues that 'gesture rather than image is the cinematic element' (Agamben 2007: 153). He argues that towards the end of the nineteenth century the close analysis of human movement, conducted by the French pre-Freudian psychologists Georges Gilles de la Tourette and Jean-Martin Charcot, and also through the multi-camera work of Eadweard Muybridge, began a period of introspection through which bourgeois society lost its ability to communicate through spontaneous and subtle gestures. Agamben cites cultural attempts to protest the reduction of gesture to a collection of static images, such as the philosophy of Friedrich Nietzsche, the dancing of Isadora Duncan and the fiction of Marcel Proust, but clearly he feels that, as part of a process of modern alienation, bourgeois society as a whole lost the ease of its gestures (Agamben 2007: 149–52).

Earlier in the book he mourns the 'destruction of experience' that accompanies modern life, whereby even when everyday life includes disruptions of various kinds they will not become experience, since there is nothing for us to learn and no prospect of us being able to change that world. Even when we witness wonders of the world, such as the Alhambra, we leave the experience of it to the camera (Agamben 2007: 16–17). Cinema, however, possesses the potential to 'lead images back into the realm of gesture' (Agamben 2007: 153). Images have a paralysing power, but gesture can break the mythical fixity of image. Gesture is understood as 'a display of mediation, the making visible of a means as such', and this, for Agamben, 'opens up the ethical dimension for human beings' (Agamben 2007: 155). In its ability to deliver these inspiring gestures, cinema thus ranks with ethics and politics, and not merely with aesthetics (Agamben 2007: 154).

In the notes, Agamben's sole reference to filmic work is Samuel Beckett's *Nacht und Träume* (mistitled *Traum und Nacht* by Agamben), which focuses on the dream of a gesture with hands, inspired by the close-up drawing of hands in prayer by Albrecht Dürer that Beckett had grown up with in his home in Dublin. The film maker's task, according to Agamben, is to bring 'the element of awakening' into this dream. While this is, indeed, a brilliant example of the direct relationship between gesture and human solidarity, it is also a self-consciously 'serious' work of art not intended for popular appeal. Agamben's appreciations of film, such as Guy Debord's short films and the unfinished *Don Quixote* by Orson Welles (Noys 2004; McCrea 2009), again discuss works either not intended for mass audiences or posing insuperable problems for the director. However, I would argue that *The Motorcycle Diaries* moves beyond the iconic image of Guevara to a humanistic understanding of his commitment conveyed by gestures at key moments in the film. Salles moves us from image to gesture by taking us back to Ernesto as he began to develop into Che, by revealing the friends as 'true humanists' who were plagued by doubts rather then driven by certitudes (Salles 2007).

The first example of gesture comes when the two friends have been walking across the Atacama desert in order to get to a mine further north on their journey. They meet a destitute couple and engage in conversation with them over a campfire on a freezing night. The husband reveals that they have been forced off their subsistence farm by land speculators and threatened with imprisonment by the police. When Alberto asks why, the friends are visibly shocked when the wife replies that it is because they are communists. The couple are travelling towards the Anaconda Mining Company in the Chilean Andes, because the work is so dangerous that the company is not interested in the political affiliation of the workers. The woman asks the friends if they too are

Global Solidarity

travelling to find work, and when the friends say no, she inquires why they are travelling. The two friends look at each other, embarrassed by the contrast of their chosen adventure with the plight of these desperate people. 'We travel just to travel,' Ernesto responds, tentatively, and the couple exchange uncomprehending looks. The woman then replies, 'Then bless you,' and, after a pause, 'Blessed be your travels.' Ernesto hands over his blanket to keep the thinly clothed woman warm, and Alberto shares his food with them. Those in real need cannot grasp the motivations of those who suffer hardship for adventure, but the response of the couple is to respect and bless their endeavour. It is a reaching out that is reciprocated.

There is also another aspect to this meeting of two worlds. The scene has just been preceded by Ernesto receiving a letter from his middle-class girlfriend, ending their relationship. She had earlier given him some money to buy a bathing costume from Los Angeles, their original destination. Later in the film, when Alberto wants the money, Ernesto reveals that he gave it to the couple at the mine. Just as that experience moved them from middle-class comfort to empathy with the downtrodden, so a small redistribution of wealth symbolises the future action that must remedy these wrongs.

Another example of solidaristic gesture occurs during their three-week stay at the San Pablo leprosy colony in Peru, where 600 patients on the south side of the river are treated by doctors and nursing nuns who are housed in the hospital and other buildings on the north side of the river. On their first visit to the lepers they are advised by the doctor to put on rubber gloves, even though the patients are not contagious when under treatment. Ernesto argues that the gloves are purely symbolic and that they will refuse to wear them. When they are greeted by Papa Carlito, the head of the community, Ernesto thrusts out his hand to exchange a handshake, but the close-up shot of the unshaken hand changes to register the shock of Carlito, who asks the doctor if he has not explained the rules. The doctor merely nods and gives a sideways glance at Ernesto as if to say 'He knows and it doesn't matter to him'. There is then a close-up shot of the handshake, followed by similar exchanges all round, with Carlito concluding that 'those guys are real gents'. The friends are then reprimanded by the head nun who insists that they have no right to flout the rules. The handshakes affirm solidarity, whereas the wearing of gloves doubly affirms the 'untouchable' nature of the patients and the righteous magnanimity of their carers. It is a fine illustration of the distinction between solidarity and charity as expressed by the first theorist of solidarity, Pierre Leroux, back in 1840. Later on the nuns refuse to feed Ernesto and Alberto because they have not attended mass on Sunday – 'You can't feed the body if you haven't fed the soul,' says the nun – but the lepers give them food.

The third example of solidaristic gesture comes on the night before the friends' departure from San Pablo, after a party among the staff to celebrate Ernesto's twenty-fourth birthday. It's very much an expression of solidarity, with the carers giving the friends a present of a raft to take them on the next stage of their journey, and Ernesto makes a speech calling for the end to illusory nationalism and the creation of a united Latin America. But the patients are, of course, absent, and Ernesto resolves to swim across the river to celebrate his birthday with them. Despite Alberto's entreaties he sets out, and between each stroke we hear the desperate inhalation of his asthmatic breath. Alberto discovers that nobody had been known to swim across to the other side. The shouts from the southern side for him to return recede while the shouts from the northern side to keep going get louder. He arrives exhausted, to be carried to safety by the lepers. This gesture displays extraordinary determination to overcome the barriers that keep us apart, and also to overcome the physical disabilities that, in so many modern societies, exclude the 'imperfect'. Earlier, Ernesto persuaded one of the women with leprosy to have an operation that could save the use of her arm, striking a rapport with her precisely because she could hear him wheezing and drew strength from his determination to overcome his physical disability. The use of the river by Salles reflects his view that in the course of their journey the two characters change dramatically, and 'in layers' rebaptise themselves (Salles 2007). Their farewell to the lepers is portrayed in a soft-focus sequence of waving and clapping hands as the raft drifts into the mist and rain, inspired by Alberto's own description: 'It seemed dreamlike: everything was embellished by the affection and sense of brotherhood that we all felt in that moment' (in Sinclair 2006: 8).

Returning now to Agamben's conception of the potential of film to move us from static image to gesture of true human experience, it seems to me that *The Motorcycle Diaries* succeeds in at least two ways. The first is the rather literal one of reclaiming Che the human being from the ubiquitous image which at times has become no more than a fashion item. The most famous picture of Guevara was taken by Alberto Korda and brought to the world via the cover of *Time* magazine. In 1968 it was turned into a pop-art poster by Irish artist Jim Fitzpatrick, who deliberately forswore copyright so that radical movements could have free use of it. Now disgusted by the commercialisation of the image, in 2011 Fitzpatrick began legal action to establish copyright with the intention of handing it over to the Guevara family in Cuba. The film helps to restore the humanity of Guevara in a more subtle and effective way than Steven Soderbergh's two-part *Che* of 2008, whatever the merits of that film. More specifically, in the focus on human gestures such as the eye-to-eye look, the handshake, and that rhythmic, wheezing front crawl across the river, Salles evokes a deep humanity reaching out for reciprocation, determined to overcome all barriers.

In revealing Guevara's formative experiences, the film will certainly enlighten viewers as to why he chose the revolutionary path in the Latin America of the 1950s. It also, I would argue, conveys well Che's frequently expressed view that exploitation and oppression involve a tragic waste of human potential. In a speech to young Cuban communists in 1962 he exhorted them to be 'essentially human', responding to the best in human beings and bringing out the best they can offer 'by means of work, study, and the exercise of continued solidarity with your people and with all the peoples of the world'. He went on to call for them to develop their sensibilities to the maximum so that they would feel anguish at the loss of life anywhere in the world, and joy at every progress towards liberty (Guevara 1972: 311). The humanistic thrust of the film is emphasised by both Salles and Redford, but they are careful to avoid discussion of its wider political implications. Nevertheless, the dramatisation of the call to resist the injustices in South America sixty years ago may well prompt a questioning of today's global injustices, and some sort of commitment to challenging them.

Films such as *The Motorcycle Diaries* offer a radical alternative to the uncritical, formulaic, image-pounding product of mainstream cinema. They challenge the prevailing disposition in which established structures and processes are regarded as unchallengeable and radical alternatives are unimaginable. This film makes a notable contribution to the recovery and redevelopment of the gestures of solidarity.

Conclusion

It may well be objected that, in general, Marx was right when he remarked in *The Communist Manifesto* that 'the ruling ideas of each age have ever been the ideas of its ruling class'. There can be little doubt that, as Martha Nussbaum has argued, educational systems are modified to prepare flexible and technically able people best equipped to contribute to national success in a highly competitive world economy rather than to train young people to become good citizens of the world. Nor can there be any doubt that in the daily diet of television and popular feature films a range of destructive and selfish attitudes are paraded before us as being a normal and acceptable way of responding to the reality of that competitive world. This chapter has argued that that is not the whole picture, and that the contestation of the assumption that 'there is no alternative' is alive and well, creating a culture of solidarity that insists that another world is possible.

7 The Politics of Global Solidarity

What are the preconditions for moving the global community towards solidarity? There have been many proposals for global policy changes and institutional innovations that would make global governance more accountable and responsive to the social needs of the world's population (e.g. Falk 1995; Held 1995; Unger 1998; George 2004; Gould 2004; Held 2004; Patomäki and Teivanen 2004; Unger 2005; Archibugi 2008; Tännsjö 2008). Invariably, these ideas are abstracted from the unpromising reality of international and national politics and say little about the political processes that might trigger such restructuring. Other theorists have considered how social forces might develop to propel the world along a more solidaristic path, conceptualising the work of global activists in terms of an emerging global citizenship that challenges global decision-making on issues such as development, the environment, war and peace and human rights, in an emerging global civil society (Dower and Williams 2002; Heater 2002; Dower 2003; Kaldor 2003; Keane 2003; Carter 2006; Schattle 2008). These contributions tend to abstract the 'global' from the lived experience of citizens struggling to make improvements to their social lives within nation states. This chapter assesses the politics of global solidarity in a way which links potential policy innovation with institutional reform, and global political activity with the struggle for solidarity at regional, national and local levels.

It is important to understand the politics of global solidarity as a historical development, fashioned by the past experiences of solidarity movements and confronted, as in the past, by powerful defenders of the status quo. Accordingly, the first section looks at how the gains of the welfare state era have been eroded and how inequality and poverty have grown as a consequence of three decades of neoliberal policies. It will also introduce the growing resistance to this anti-solidaristic process. The second section will consider redistribution and regulation policies that would effectively sound the death knell of global neoliberalism. Particular attention will be paid to global taxation and tax justice. It will also look at the institutional changes that would be needed to operate these policies. The third section looks at the social forces that are mobilising in support of global solidarity, at a number of levels, including actors directly confronting justice issues at the global level, those engaged in politics at regional and national levels, and also solidaristic actions at the level of everyday life. The final section will discuss the prospects for a change of direction in global governance that would open the way towards global solidarity. Inevitability, major factors such as the future policy orientation of the United States and the political direction of China are in the realm of speculation, but it is useful to note the sort of possibilities that could provide an enormous fillip to solidaristic hopes.

Social solidarity under attack: inequality, poverty and resistance

As we saw in Chapter 2, Peter Baldwin argues that the limited measures of social solidarity attained by the welfare state can be explained as 'the outcome of a generalised and reciprocal self-interest' rather than as the result of some sort of moral consensus (Baldwin 1999: 299). In pointing to the decisiveness of the political balance of class forces, he underlines the fragility of the welfare state settlement. T. H. Marshall's 1949 depiction of three stages of citizenship suggests that social rights are the culmination of a long historical process, a teleology unlikely to be reversed

(Marshall 1973: 65–122). However, Baldwin's emphasis on the balance of class forces is potentially lethal to solidaristic hopes if that balance turns decisively against the working class. As noted in Chapter 2, the welfare state settlements were secured between the political representatives of capital and of labour, with the state operating as guiding mediator, in an arrangement later known as 'tripartism'. The dominant interests, however, were challenged from within, by the emergence of a variety of other interests, and without, by the transformation of primarily nation-based capital into a more powerful and mobile international capital. In more favourable economic circumstances, the internal challenge might have been met by more diverse, sensitive and participatory forms of social provision, but the economic crisis of the late 1970s presaged a very different sort of response. This has produced perhaps the most formidable obstacle to the achievement of global solidarity, the persistence of extreme inequality in the world as a whole and the intensification of inequality within affluent nation states.

In terms of global inequality, in 2005 the richest 5 per cent of the world's population owned 33 per cent of global income while the poorest 5 per cent owned 0.2 per cent, a ratio of 165:1. If the bands are widened, the disparity is slightly reduced but still enormous, with the richest 10 per cent owning 50 per cent of global income while the poorest 10 per cent own just 0.7 per cent, a ratio of 71:1 (Milanovic 2007: 40). In terms of trends, the situation is mixed. The most widely accepted measurement of inequality is the Gini coefficient, whereby 0 indicates perfect equality and 100 perfect inequality. So, a country with a strong egalitarian tradition, Sweden, scores 25, whereas Britain scores 36 and the United States scores 41. Latin American countries tend to be even more unequal, with Mexico at 52, and South Africa is one of the most unequal large states, with a Gini score of 67 (Gini Index 2011). If we look at the Gini for all world citizens, it has fluctuated around the mid-60s since 1980 (Dollar 2007: 84–5; Milanovic 2007: 39), a shockingly high figure.

Looking at trends in global poverty, there was a reduction in the numbers suffering extreme poverty, that is to say with an income below $1.25 a day (adjusted according to purchasing power parity), from 1.82 billion to 1.37 billion between 1990 and 2005, with a provisional figure of 1.2 billion for 2008 (Oneworld 2012). Given the large rise in the world's population, the decrease in the numbers of those in extreme poverty looks greater in percentage terms, and this has enabled neoliberals to claim that their policies are bringing massive numbers out of poverty. This argument loses force when it is noted that there has been a similar *increase* in the numbers living beneath the threshold of $2 a day in the same period, leaving about half the world's population in this category (Dollar 2007: 83). Despite large reductions of the numbers in poverty in China, the situation has worsened in other parts of the less developed world. The reality of life for the world's poor can be gauged from some of the statistics. The United Nations Food and Agriculture Organization estimates that there were 925 million under-nourished people in 2010, one in seven of the world's population, an increase on the figure of 780 million in 1995–7 (World Hunger Education Service 2012). Approximately eighteen million people die of poverty-related causes each year, about one third of all human deaths (Pogge 2008: 2).

Turning to inequality and poverty within affluent states, perhaps the first thing to observe is how little has been made of this as a political issue, so strong has been the neoliberal consensus among policy makers. According to figures from the Organisation for Economic and Co-operative Development, the gap between rich and poor in those countries widened from 5:1 in the 1980s to 6:1 in 2011 (OECD 2011). In the USA, the top 1 per cent of earners increased their share of national income by 275 per cent between 1979 and 2007, whereas the lowest 80 per cent saw their share decrease by 49 per cent over the same period (Congressional Budget Office 2011). The top 20 per cent of US citizens own 85 per cent of all their country's wealth, with the top 1 per cent enjoying a 34.6 per cent share (Mutnick 2011). Figures like these, showing the enormous gains made by the very richest people, prompted the slogan 'we are the 99 per cent', displayed by Occupy protesters in cities across the world during 2011.

In the case of Britain, inequality fell greatly from 1918, when the share of national income of the richest 1 per cent was 17 per cent after tax, to 1979, by which time it had dropped to 4 per cent. The Conservative period in power then brought a remarkable increase to 10 per cent by 1997, when Labour won the general election, and there was a further increase to 13 per cent by 2005 (Dorling 2010: 176, 191). It is also clear that, while a massive increase in poverty took place during the 1980s and early 1990s, the Labour government did no more than stabilise the numbers living in poverty, at about 23 per cent of the population (Horton and Gregory 2009: 5). From being one of the most equal countries in the developed world in 1979, Britain has become one of the most unequal (Lansley 2012: 13). By 2008/9 there were over thirteen million people living in households below the official poverty line, or 22 per cent of the total population (Poverty 2012). These inequalities have grown ever wider since the financial crisis, with cuts in public expenditure driving unemployment towards the three million mark. This 'austerity' does not apply to the rich, however, and the number of millionaires in the UK rose by 17 per cent from 2008 to the end of 2010, to a total of 619,000 (*Daily Mail*, 21 March 2011).

What this means globally is that billions of people lack the material resources to develop the potentials required for a fulfilled life. Our definition of solidarity specifies 'ever-widening social inclusion', and it is all too clear that this is not possible in a world that perpetuates massive social deprivation. As for the human potentials of rationality, compassion, productiveness and cooperation, all of these are stunted or perverted. There is evidently no substantive rationality in the neoliberal model of globalization. It has delivered the most skewed income distribution since the 1920s, pushing the swollen ranks of the super-rich to engage in disastrous high-risk speculation, and encouraging aspirants to go into unprecedented levels of private debt (Lansley 2012). The destructive logic of neoliberalism annuls all alternatives. The imminent collapse of huge banks is avoided by state rescues, but dependence on the financial sector in Britain and the United States means that governments are reluctant to curb bankers' soaring remunerations on the grounds that they will take their skills elsewhere if they are forced to forgo their 'entitlements'. Enormous national debts run up as a result of the bank bail-outs have led to cuts in public services that hit the poorest, the only people who did not benefit in some way from the boom. The severity of the cuts is justified by warnings that the credit ratings agencies – Moody's, Standard and Poor's and Fitch – may downgrade the sovereign debt status and make it more difficult and expensive to borrow, leading to a repeat of the low growth and mass unemployment recipe of the 1930s (Kingsley 2012). Ironically, these were the same agencies that gave the banks the all-clear before the crash of 2008 (George 2010: 52–5). It is deemed heretical to attack the deficit by raising taxes, as this might hinder investment. Finally, the neoliberal argument runs, state spending has been so swollen in the past that it must be cut back drastically, so that good pensions for public-sector workers are no longer affordable, and they must work more years for lower pensions. All of these seemingly unavoidable measures are largely accepted by a compliant media, and their inevitability goes largely unquestioned.

On the face of it, then, to return to Peter Baldwin's functional explanation of the conditions for solidarity, the massive shift towards the interests of global industrial and financial power appears to have undermined hopes of building solidarity at national, regional or global level. Another way of seeing this is through the lens of class struggle, as David Harvey has done:

> The first lesson we must learn, therefore, is that if it looks like class struggle and acts like class war then we have to name it unashamedly for what it is. The mass of the population has either to resign itself to the historical and geographical trajectory defined by overwhelming and ever-increasing upper-class power, or respond to it in class terms. (Harvey 2009: 202)

This formulation returns us to an old tension in Marx's original model of working-class solidarity between the structural and subjective aspects of class struggle. At the structural level, Harvey is undoubtedly correct to see neoliberalism as a strategy for advancing the interests of an increasingly globalized economic elite, but when he observes that this has been 'effectively disguised' (Harvey 2009: 201) he is already pointing out the difficulties of generating an alternative in class-conscious terms. Class consciousness, historically associated with industrial struggles at the point of production and national political strategies based on state ownership and planning, has evanesced. Certainly it will manifest itself in newly industrialised areas of the world economy, but not as a unifying guide to effective political alternatives at the global level. However, it is important to recall that the commitment to human freedom was immanent and frequently explicit in Marx's class struggle model, as was his adherence to internationalism, and it is surely these universal elements that are uppermost in the consciousness of 21st-century activists campaigning for 'another world'.

Today's struggles are increasingly grasped as struggles for global justice. This moral motivation is particularly clear in environmentalism, where the struggle for sustainability is an appeal for generational solidarity, a demand for a new substantive rationality based on the conviction that the future of life on earth is in danger. The difficulty faced in finding a binding global agreement on cuts in greenhouse emissions offers a clear example. The United Nations summit on climate change in Copenhagen in December 2009 resulted in no agreement on specific targets because the states responsible for most emissions calculated that such targets would be too costly for them in a competitive world market (Heywood 2011: 403). The response from global activists provides a clear picture of their motives and values. The Alternative Declaration from the Forum of International Non-Governmental Organizations at the Copenhagen summit emphasised principles of community participation, empowerment, equity, self-reliance and sustainability, while highlighting the role of women and the young (Thomas and Evans 2011: 468). Its rejection of neoliberalism and its demands for democratic control over the global economy could be construed as elements of class struggle, but they are conceived from a consciousness of the pressing need for humane governance and the subordination of economics to the needs of people.

In the struggle to extend democratic accountability to the processes of global governance, and in the concrete struggles around the environment, poverty, women's rights, anti-racism and human rights, the ethical claim for social justice becomes a practical force. In exposing injustice it creates the space in which social forces can be mobilised to create a more humane system of global governance, and to further the cause of solidarity on a national and global level. In this process, ethics helps to create and nourish an anti-systemic politics that can contest the neoliberal status quo. As Manfred Steger has argued, justice globalism has begun to fight back against market globalism in the form of 'a comprehensive ideology offering an alternative translation of the rising global imaginary' (Steger 2008: 211). With this in mind we shall next turn to two concrete areas that have been the subject of high-level debate since the financial crash of 2008, namely taxation and reform of the institutions of global economic governance, and also consider the implications of some radical reform suggestions for the democratisation of global politics.

Reclaiming solidarity: policies and institutions

When the US investment bank Lehman Brothers went out of business in September 2008 it triggered a collapse of share prices worldwide and a run on banks that threatened to destroy the economies of the richest countries in the world. Almost instantly, the myopic instrumental rationality of deregulated financial markets was recognised for the madness that it was (Peck 2010: 8–9). It was generally acknowledged that much tighter regulation needed to be put in place, and that in the short term governments would be obliged to rescue banks from failure and guarantee the safety of deposits. It was decided, through international cooperation at the G20 meeting in London in April 2009, to ensure that there was sufficient financial stimulus put into the world economy to prevent a repeat of the great depression that followed the financial crash of 1929. There was also an expressed determination not to revert to national policies of protection which had proved so disastrous for the world economy in the 1930s. The exposure of the destructive logic of neoliberalism persuaded many that this ideology had been dealt a death blow, as is clear in the subtitle of Paul Mason's book on the crash, *Meltdown: The End of the Age of Greed* (2009). Walden Bello, announcing that 'neoliberal approaches are thoroughly discredited', advised radicals to prepare for the next big struggle against the weak reformism of 'global social democracy' and to push for a more comprehensive rejection of market economics (Bello 2009: 57–64). These hasty dismissals of neoliberalism failed to recognise how neoliberal principles have thoroughly embedded themselves, through economists and advisors, in governments, inter-governmental bodies, think-tanks and corporations around the world (Peck 2010: 28–31). As Jamie Peck has commented, 'neoliberalism's demonstrated capacity to rise phoenix-like even from crises of its own making suggests that it has acquired a kind of flexibility in practice that it may some time ago have lost in theory' (Peck 2010: 275). Neoliberals have exploited the huge indebtedness forced on states by the bank bail-outs to urge savage cuts on a public sector that is declared to be 'unaffordable', without even discussing raising revenue by progressive taxation. Mass unemployment becomes 'a price worth paying' to finish the job of rolling back the state first announced in the 1980s. In these circumstances solidarists must support proposed reforms that negate the logic of neoliberalism and have already been aired among key decision makers in global politics.

Two radical proposals on taxation were widely discussed in the immediate aftermath of the financial crisis, which, if implemented, would have far-reaching consequences. The first of these is the idea of a global Tobin tax, or financial transactions tax (FTT), suggested at various times by the then British Prime Minister,

Gordon Brown, and supported by the then French President, Nicolas Sarkozy (Peck 2010: 253). The idea is named after the economist James Tobin, who suggested it in 1972 as a tax on currency transactions designed to discourage financial speculators. At the time he envisaged a tax of about 0.5 per cent, but this was before the explosion in financial transactions that has taken place over the past thirty years. In the early 1980s foreign exchange dealing amounted to $70 billion a day, a figure which rose to $3.2 trillion a day just before the financial crisis (Mason 2009: 65). Astonishingly, despite the crisis, this figure rose to a new high of $4 trillion a day by 2010, according to the Bank of International Settlements (King and Rime 2010). To put this figure in some sort of perspective, it represents more than 98 per cent of all financial transactions, with the remainder, less than 2 per cent, representing all transactions in the real economy (George 2010: 246). The annual figure that would be available for an FTT is a staggering $960 trillion, which means that a tax of only 0.05 per cent would yield $480 billion, more than enough to meet the United Nations' Millennium Development Goals, and, furthermore, to meet more ambitious ones for the 2015–30 period. Susan George comments that an FTT would 'amass enough to eliminate virtually every problem the world has ever known – hunger, environmental destruction, climate change, blatant inequalities' (George 2010: 246). In fact the tax yield would be lower than my estimate if the FTT had the desired effect of curbing speculation, but the sums involved would still be enormous. Addressing the injustice of world poverty is by far the strongest candidate for the disbursement of such funds, but it should be noted that at least part of the revenue could be used as an insurance fund against future crashes, until governments finally separate the retail and investment arms of the major banks.

There are no insuperable practical impediments to the implementation of a global FTT, and there have already been taxes in Sweden and Britain based on the same principle. In January 2012 Sarkozy announced that France would introduce an FTT of 0.1 per cent in August of that year (Hickley 2012). As the vast majority of Europe's financial trading takes place outside France, in Frankfurt and London, the impact will be limited, but even so it was claimed that the new tax will raise $1.3 billion. The principal argument against imposing an FTT on a national or regional basis is that states like Britain and the United States run the risk of losing their enormous financial services sector if the banks could move to states where there was no FTT. For this reason British Prime Minister David Cameron rejected the idea of an FTT applied only to the European Union, on the grounds that such a tax would be feasible only on a global basis (Parker and Masters 2011). However, in reality neoliberals would never support such a global tax. They would argue that it would hinder investment flows to the real economy, but this can hardly be taken seriously. Rather, their real fear would be the precedent set for global redistribution, which would be seen as a limitation on the freedom of the market. For them, an FTT would mark a major surrender in the battle over the regulation of the world. On that point, solidarists would agree.

Neoliberal opposition to redistributive taxation is the equivalent of the resistance of property owners to the introduction of income tax in the nineteenth century. The commitment to a progressive income tax, through which more would be paid by those who could afford it, was shared by communists and social liberals alike. Marx and Engels's *Communist Manifesto* of 1848 outlined practical measures to be undertaken by a workers' party upon achieving power, the second of which was 'a heavy progressive or graduated income tax', and they made a similar demand in the revolutionary struggles in Germany later that year (Marx 2010a: 86, 110). In 1896, the leader of the French solidarist movement, Léon Bourgeois, emphasised the significance of introducing a progressive income tax in his programmatic text, *Solidarity* (Bourgeois 2009: 141–56). His brief tenure as Prime Minister came to an end that year when the Senate threw out his attempt to introduce the tax, and the resistance of French property owners was so strong that it was not introduced until 1917, after three years of war (Cobban 1974: 67). The motivations of Bourgeois and Marx were quite different, of course, with the former intent on ameliorating poverty in order to achieve solidarity between classes, and the latter intent on creating a classless society. Marx was convinced that reforms such as progressive taxation would develop a momentum that would 'necessitate further inroads upon the old social order' and were 'unavoidable as a means of revolutionizing the mode of production' (Marx 2010a: 86). It was a sound argument then, and now it could equally apply to the idea of a global FTT.

Global taxation would require a tax-raising body, and might well trigger the adoption of the suggestion made by the 1995 Commission for Global Governance for an Economic Security Council of the United Nations (Commission on Global Governance 1995: 153–62). The political implications of making the United Nations a tax-raising body are immense. At the moment the UN is reliant on the subscriptions of member nations calculated according to their economic capacity, as well as voluntary contributions to various funds (Hanhimäki 2008: 45–8). The budget for 2012 was just under $5.2 billion, with an extra $7 billion agreed separately for peacekeeping missions (UN News Centre 2011). This is a fraction of the sum that could be raised through very low rates of global taxation. It is inconceivable that such an expansion of the power of the United Nations could take place without reforms to make the institution more accountable, both to governments and citizens. Many schemes for this have been touted in recent years, but only a massive functional shift in the power of the UN would enable an equivalent political shift. If the precedent was set by the introduction of a global FTT, the way would be cleared for other taxes to be levied, and such is the inequality of global resources that very low rates of taxation would make an enormous difference to ameliorating the most pressing problems, and in doing so provide an opening to develop global solidarity.

One candidate for such a tax could be Thomas Pogge's proposal for a global resource dividend (Pogge 2008: 202–21). This would allow for a small tax on any resources employed by a particular state, on the grounds that 'the global poor own an inalienable stake in all limited natural resources'. Proceeds could go to fulfilling the basic needs of the poor and to supplying the means for them to free themselves from poverty. Pogge has calculated that a tax of 0.67 per cent of the 2005 global product would have yielded $300 billion, roughly the amount that it would take to lift 2.5 billion people out of poverty. The idea could also be targeted on certain resources deemed to be environmentally problematic, such as oil. Even if oil producers passed on the tax to consumers, that would deter over-consumption of an environmentally dangerous product.

Another idea for a global tax, proposed by environmental activists, is the greenhouse gas tax, a carbon tax on coal, oil and gas, which would almost certainly prove more effective than the limited cuts in emissions agreed at Kyoto in 1997 (Patomäki and Teivanen 2004: 178–81). It would also provide a source of funding for the Green Climate Fund, agreed at the Cancun climate summit in 2010, which targeted $100 billion by 2020 for the development of cleaner energy supplies without identifying where the money would come from. Novel ways of redistribution might also be considered, as for example, the idea of a global pension, proposed in 2007 by Robin Blackburn. A pension of $360 a year, paid to those over sixty-five in prosperous societies and over sixty in less developed countries, would cost $205 billion (Blackburn 2007). A pension of half that sum would still make an enormous amount of difference to the poorest in the world, while those who chose to redonate would feel a connection with the less well off. In terms of forging global solidarity, the symbolic value would be enormous.

Another area of reform that has been widely discussed since the financial crash has been tax evasion and avoidance, and in particular tax havens. In the summer of 2009 US President Barack Obama set down a comprehensive plan to combat tax avoidance, including the use of tax havens. This included eliminating the loopholes whereby corporations avoid tax by shifting income from one foreign subsidiary to another, and also cracking down on tax avoidance by individuals hiding their money in offshore accounts (*Huffington Post*, 4 June 2009). Before taking office, Obama had co-sponsored the Stop Tax Haven Abuse Act of 2008 (Tax Justice Network 2008), but its effectiveness was blunted by powerful lobbying. However, even stricter national regulation does not get to the heart of the problem of so-called 'offshore' havens, where corporations and individuals can move their money to minimise their tax bills, an attraction so powerful that more than half of world trade passes through tax havens (Shaxson 2011: 8). In *Treasure Islands*, Nicholas Shaxson argues that the havens offer secrecy above all, which benefits not only rich individuals and corporations but also international criminal gangs and terrorists. The havens are not illicit, but rather established at the heart of the global financial system, operating mainly in Europe, from the City of London – using dependencies such as Jersey and the Cayman Islands – and the United States, including states like Florida and dependencies such as the Virgin Islands and the Marshall Islands (Shaxson 2011: 14–21). While it is impossible to quantify accurately how much potential revenue is lost because of tax havens, the reality is that the richest corporations and individuals are paying a tiny percentage of their incomes in tax compared with ordinary working people (Christensen 2009: 115–25). In Britain, for example, in 2009, when the rate of corporation tax was 28 per cent, Barclays Bank paid £113 million out of a profit of £11.6 billion, about 1 per cent, amounting to a shortfall of over £3 billion (Lansley 2012: 245).

The effrontery of tax avoidance has even produced arguments for lower rates of taxation on the basis that higher rates will not bring in the income. In other words, corporations and rich individuals are effectively letting governments know just how little they are prepared to pay. In a world-system of competitive states this is allowed to happen because the mobility of capital allows it to play off state against state, all of which are desperate to attract inward investment and hold on to their business. The substantively rational course of action would be to make the whole system transparent and subject to global regulation. Since 2008, there has been a shift in public opinion against tax avoidance in

Europe and the United States, where it was reflected in Barack Obama's budget announcement early in 2012. He proposed to abolish a range of tax breaks and apply the so-called Buffett rule, whereby all households earning more than $1 million a year must pay at least 30 per cent tax (*The Guardian*, 14 February 2012).

The second part of this section looks at ideas for new global institutions which date back to the 1990s. The 1995 publication of *Our Global Neighbourhood*, the report of the Commission on Global Governance, brought these issues to a worldwide readership. The commission was created in 1992, at the end of the Cold War, and comprised twenty-eight leading politicians and administrators with wide knowledge of international politics. It was endorsed by the UN Secretary General and partly funded by UN bodies. A number of the suggested reforms have since become commonplace on the reform agenda, but only the call for a Criminal Court of Justice has actually been heeded. Nevertheless, the report provided a direction to an alternative, more solidaristic future that has helped shape many subsequent ideas for reform. Significantly, it recognised the need to develop a 'global civic ethic' in order to 'help humanize the impersonal working of bureaucracies and markets and constrain the competitive and self-serving instincts of individuals and groups' (Commission on Global Governance 1995: 55). As mentioned above, the commission urged the creation of a UN Economic Security Council (ESC) equal in status to the existing Security Council, to deliberate on the overall coordination of global policy, including development and environmental issues, thereby adding a strong social dimension to policy (Commission on Global Governance 1995: 153–62). Although it fell short of proposing that the ESC should have executive power over bodies such as the World Trade Organization, the International Monetary Fund and the World Bank, if it were to administer the global taxes outlined above it would need to have such power. At present there are no social duties in the rules adopted by the WTO, and all too often the policies of the institutions of global economic governance frustrate attempts to make progress on the UN's Millennium Development Goals. The commission also proposed the creation of a Forum of Civil Society, comprising representatives of the international non-governmental organisations (Commission on Global Governance 1995: 345). In general, however, despite suggesting a phase-out of the veto in the Security Council (Commission on Global Governance 1995: 241), the commission's report was cautious, designed as it was to attract a consensus around the need for reform to come sooner rather than later.

Also published in 1995, David Held's *Democracy and the Global Order* points to the urgent need for political democracy to catch up with the dispersal of power that flowed from globalization, a relatively new concept at that time. Held eschews any idea that world government would provide a feasible or desirable way forward to democratise the new global order (Held 1995: 228–31). Instead he envisages a democratic network of all groups and associations that have the capacity for self-determination, provided that they agree to guarantee human rights and require certain obligations. These rights and obligations must cut across each network of power, so that democracy can operate in specific spheres of social life, such as formal politics, economic life, the environment, health, welfare or culture, and at different levels, from the local and national all the way to the global. Held anticipates the emergence of multiple citizenships, with people being empowered in decision-making in various spheres and at different levels. In his view, this cosmopolitan model of democracy creates the possibility of 'an expanding institutional framework for the democratic regulation of states and societies' (Held 1995: 232). The cosmopolitan democracy project aims at democratising all aspects of social life, including decision-making at the global level.

Held originally set down the institutional requirements of the project as short-term and long-term goals, and even the short-term goals were more radical than the proposals of the Commission on Global Governance. These included the creation of a second chamber of the United Nations, reform of the Security Council, compulsory jurisdiction before international courts and an international military force. The specifically economic goals included limitations on markets and private ownership in key public spheres, and also the adoption of a guaranteed basic income for all adults (Held 1995: 279–80). Latterly, Held has advocated global social democracy, emphasising the 'taming of global markets', the formation of a global anti-trust authority, and a tighter regulatory framework for the global economy (Held 2004: 164–5). In a more recent contribution to the cosmopolitan democracy project, Daniele Archibugi, in *The Global Commonwealth of Citizens* (2008), has put forward similar political proposals, emphasising the central importance of a reformed UN and recommending a World Parliamentary Assembly that could protect human rights, audit internal democratic processes and promote democracy at the global level (Archibugi 2008: 282–3; cf. Falk and Strauss 2001; Patomäki and Teivanen 2004: 139–46).

In the crucial area of global economic governance, the existing institutions – the WTO, the IMF and the World Bank – reflect, in their structures and policies, the economic interests of the most powerful states and transnational corporations (Patomäki and Teivanen 2004: 41–93). The WTO has overseen a massive reduction in world tariffs, while doing nothing to prevent the USA and Europe from providing massive subsidies to selected economic beneficiaries, making it impossible for the less developed states to compete. The conditionality imposed by the IMF has transferred public services to the private sector and deprived millions of free health care and affordable water and energy supplies (Palast 2002: 44–75; George 2010: 153–7). The fixation on growth as the single indicator of economic health has prised open the poorer countries to transnational corporate investment, at the expense of subsidised public services and vital subsistence production (Peet 2009). In the process, the strictures of the IMF have displaced democratic control of economic policy in a new form of economic imperialism. It is therefore imperative either to radically reform the existing institutions or, preferably, to create new institutions compelled by statute to place the needs of people above the needs of capital.

New institutions would need to administer the redistributive measures outlined above, as well as ensuring the effective regulation of the activities of transnational corporations. This would include ensuring minimum levels of taxation for corporations to mitigate the 'race to the bottom' outcome whereby states desperate for inward investment offer tax holidays that capture the investment but produce little or no social benefits. It would also include the strict monitoring of laws and codes of practice to ensure the payment of a minimum wage rate and the elimination of child labour, excessive shift working and lax safety standards. The institutions would also have to guarantee states the right to preserve the public control of services vital to the wellbeing of their people, such as health, education, water and energy supplies. Even the Director General of the WTO, Pascal Lamy, appears to be sympathetic to the creation of just this sort of democratic legitimacy in global economic governance (Lamy 2005), so what is it that prevents this solidaristic progress?

There are three major obstacles to the radical reforms outlined above. The first is the perceived self-interest of powerful states in a competitive world-system, which seems to confirm the continued relevance of the 'realist' approach to international relations theory as the best way of understanding how international politics really works (Dunne and Schmidt 2011). Certainly it is the most powerful states that have maintained a controlling hand in the IMF and the World Bank through the weighting of voting rights and control over appointments. The foreign policy of US President George W. Bush (in office 2001–9) was aggressive towards and at times openly contemptuous of the United Nations. The failure to agree strict limitations on greenhouse gas emissions at recent summits also testifies to the difficulties in overcoming narrowly conceived national self-interest. Nevertheless, with the business of corporations no longer confined to individual states or regions, there is a general determination to avoid a return to the protectionism of the 1930s. There is also a widespread recognition that more multilateral cooperation is needed to secure economic stability, an agenda that is likely to be pushed at G20 meetings by the representatives of the BRICS nations – Brazil, Russia, India, China and South Africa.

The second obstacle is the power possessed by neoliberal ideologists who are embedded in leading policy-making and advisory roles at international and national levels and whose worldview is shared by many media organisations. Unlike some of the famous 'isms' of the past, neoliberalism is an ideology that makes no claim to be an ideology, and although the dogma is easy to spot for those with a basic knowledge of political economy, it is rarely identified as such in media exchanges. As Manfred Steger has argued,

> the presentation of globalization as some sort of natural force, like an earthquake or gravity, makes it easier for globalists to convince people that they must adapt to the 'discipline of the market' if they are to survive and prosper. (Steger 2008: 187)

Blind faith in the curative powers of the free market has survived the bank failures of 2008, and neoliberal politicians continue to locate the underlying problems not in casino capitalism but in a 'swollen' public sector where spending has 'spiralled out of control'. As for unemployment, increasingly it is presented as the fault of individuals who lack the necessary skills or attitude to work, even though there are no jobs for them to find. A significant part of the mass media supports this worldview by the iteration of the message that the public sector is parasitic, and by regularly accepting the ideological opinions of neoliberal economists and politicians as incontrovertible. Cowed by the power of the media, social democratic politicians have often been deterred from mentioning even the possibility of increasing progressive personal taxation or nationalising private monopolies. Suggestions for legislation to ensure plurality in media ownership and regulation of media practices are welcome, but in the meantime, from a solidaristic point of view, it is essential that parties proclaiming to pursue social justice, as well as journalists, stop giving neoliberal rhetoric a free run and expose it for the divisive ideology it is.

The third obstacle is the relative weakness of the social and political forces needed to secure the change of direction discussed above at the global level, in a context in which political activity is still largely state bound. It is one thing to identify global issues and criticise the flawed processes through which the international community struggles to deal with them, but quite another to develop social and political movements capable of creating that elusive 'better world'. Craig Calhoun quite reasonably observes that 'cosmopolitanism needs an account of how social solidarity and public discourse might develop enough in these wider networks to become the basis for active citizenship' (Calhoun 2003: 96). This vital issue will be addressed in the next section, as well as the tasks facing social democracy at regional and national levels.

Forging solidarity: the social forces

The 'Battle of Seattle' in December 1999 has been described as the 'coming-out party' of a movement that represented an alternative to the neoliberal vision of globalization that had prevailed in the 1990s, and as the moment when 'the world woke up' (Klein 2002: 3–6; Kingsnorth 2003: 61–2). Something like 60,000 protesters arrived at a meeting of the WTO to protest about the social consequences of accelerated free trade. They came from a variety of backgrounds, including American labour unions, environmental protection groups and delegations from the less developed world. They were met with a strong police over-reaction that helped bond the various groups and add to the symbolic significance of the confrontation (Tormey 2004: 38–40). The WTO meeting, determined to push through even more liberal terms of world trade, broke up in disarray without agreement. Something of a myth has been created around Seattle, for it is more likely that the meeting broke up because of internal divisions within the WTO rather than as a result of the protest. There were already many organisations of global activists at work throughout the 1990s, such as Global Trade Watch and ATTAC (Association for the Taxation of Financial Transactions for the Aid of Citizens), and subsequent

Global Solidarity

protests, such as those at the meeting of the G8 at Genoa in 2001, drew much larger numbers (Pleyers 2010: 18–21). Nevertheless, the events at Seattle announced to the world that global governance was up for contestation, and they triggered the emergence of what became known as the 'anti-capitalist movement'.

The first World Social Forum (WSF) met in Porto Alegre in Brazil in January 2001, at the same time as the thirty-first meeting of the World Economic Forum (WEF) at Davos in Switzerland (Pleyers 2010: 5). Whereas the WEF can be seen as a think-tank for neoliberal globalization, the WSF, with its slogan 'Another world is possible', symbolises global resistance to the social consequences of that version of globalization. It has since burgeoned into a worldwide network of groups embracing activists in a range of areas from environmentalism and feminism to economic reform, with massive turnouts at annual global meetings as well as those at a more accessibly continental level. The 2005 meeting in Porto Alegre drew a record attendance of 170,000, with fewer 'set piece' addresses and more open and decentralised meetings (Pleyers 2010: 194–8). In 2001 the WSF adopted as its first principle that it would be an open meeting place for debate by groups and movements of civil society 'opposed to neoliberalism and to domination of the world by capital and any form of imperialism, and committed to building a planetary society directed towards fruitful relationships among humankind and between it and the earth' (World Social Forum 2012). Its determination to remain as an open network, avoiding specific policy commitments and eschewing centralised membership or leadership, is widely regarded as its strength. Inevitably, some will see this as a weakness, given the daunting nature of the mission of what Naomi Klein calls the 'movement of many movements' (Klein 2004: 220), but in recent years it has become more closely allied to progressive political developments, such as the egalitarian programmes brought in by the leftist regimes elected in Brazil, Venezuela, Bolivia, Ecuador and Paraguay, whose presidents all attended the WSF meeting in Belém, Brazil, in 2009. The WSF was also highly involved in the campaigns to secure a just international agreement on greenhouse gas emissions at Copenhagen in 2010 (Pleyers 2010: 246–57). As Geoffrey Pleyers has commented, there is now a widespread feeling within the alter-globalization movement that 'the time has come to focus on concrete alternative outcomes' (Pleyers 2010: 239).

The activists involved in WSF networks belong to a wide range of civil society groupings, many of whose members would be reluctant to become involved with direct action of the sort that was witnessed at Seattle and Genoa (Della Porta and Tarrow 2004). Work within INGOs is frequently done on a local or national basis, often with considerable success. Perhaps the best example was the pressure exerted to secure international agreement on debt cancellation and increased aid for the world's poorest countries. Jubilee 2000 was set up in Britain in the early 1990s and then developed into a number of international Jubilee campaigns early in the present century. In 2005 it operated as the ONE Campaign in the USA and as Make Poverty History in Britain, mobilising brilliantly to exert maximum pressure on world governments at that year's meeting of the G8 in Scotland. Greeted by a demonstration of 150,000 activists, against a background of solidarity concerts by leading stars of popular music, the Gleneagles summit delivered some significant outcomes on debt cancellation for the poorest countries and commitments to higher levels of aid (Willetts 2011a: 157). Even though these measures have been criticised by activists as insufficient, the official acknowledgment that global poverty was a global social responsibility signalled a progressive shift and gave encouragement to civil society movements to press for more significant structural change. The issue of global poverty is now addressed by myriad civil society movements, often combining forces in large coalitions such as the Trade Justice Movement.

Relatively new forms of social organisation harness expert help, particularly in the areas of development, international political economy, and the science of climate change and alternative energy sources. A good example is ATTAC, mentioned above, which started in France in 1998 and now has affiliates in Europe, Africa and Latin America. Its initial impact came from its coordination of expert knowledge and its educational activities, but since 2006 it has reached out successfully to a wider group of activists (Pleyers 2010: 115, 146–9). In Italy, the Social Centre movement, active since the 1970s, has provided a community basis for involvement in global justice issues. Other global activists operate within the thousands of established INGOs that have flourished since the 1970s. They exert pressure for change through their practical activities and the publicity they generate, and can also influence global policy-making through the Economic and Social Council of the United Nations (Willetts 2011a: 32–63).

At this point in the discussion it is important to note that although we are dealing with something relatively new in global politics, it is not only new social movements that are involved in this great contestation. For example, the struggles of organised labour, central to the achievement of social rights within the old industrialised states, are replicated, albeit in new forms, across the world. Internationally, the organised labour movement was split along Cold War lines between communist and non-communist federations until the 1990s, but eventually, in 2006, a new International Trades Union Confederation was founded in Vienna, and by 2010 it represented 175 million workers in 151 countries (ITUC 2012). Although we may think of this activity as an extension of an 'old' form of social struggle, as Ronaldo Munck has argued it is very much 'new' as a transnational social actor, learning the networking techniques of the new social movements while displaying more internal democracy than many of the newer INGOs (Munck 2002: 193–4). In the present struggles, in which union recognition brings vital material benefits to the poorest workers, the emphasis is increasingly on solidarity, not simply within the union and within the working class, but with all those on the receiving end of punitive processes in an unjust world economic system (Bieler *et al.* 2008; Waterman 2008). So far, there has been only limited collaboration between the WSF and the ICTU, but it is not only at that global level that this meeting of the old and the new occurs. At local and national levels coalitions of non-governmental organisations will often include trade union affiliates, while global causes are introduced into trade union meetings and trade unionists become involved both as global activists and as local unionists.

It should be clear that oppositional movements responding to the policies enacted by unelected global bodies are acting as concerned citizens of the world, in an arena that is the global equivalent to the civil society that developed in the nation state. However, the objection has been raised that 'citizenship' and 'civil society' are indissolubly linked to the processes of state-building and are therefore inappropriate for understanding the political process at the global level. David Chandler expresses deep scepticism about the notion of the global citizen, arguing that 'blurring the distinction between the citizen, with rights of formal democratic accountability, and the merely moral claims of the non-citizen, cannot further democracy under any normative framework' (Chandler 2005: 194). This is an overly formalistic and ahistoric view of political action still at an incipient stage. In the era when democratic rights were being demanded, the activists mobilised in ways which we associate with modern citizenship. Unable to vote for social inclusion, they wrote letters and pamphlets, signed petitions, held mass meetings and organised huge demonstrations. At the time this was regarded by the authorities as a threat to social order and drew a coercive response, but what was being fought for was social inclusion, and those in struggle were acting as good citizens for the society that was to come. There is no question that decisions that have an architectonic significance on the lives of billions of people are taken at global or inter-governmental level with hardly any accountability to the people affected by them, and that the demand for that accountability should be seen as a continuation of a long historical struggle for social inclusion. As for global civil society, it is important to recognise that it is currently dominated by 'the allies of transnational business who promote a market framework at global level' (Kaldor 2003: 107). Alter-globalization activists are radically contesting a sphere that is dominated by those actors who use their vast resources to protect their own interests. Pleyers rightly comments that although global democratic institutions remain to be invented, the movements of global activists represent 'a valuable contribution to fostering global democracy and citizenship' (Pleyers 2010: 259–60).

There are enormous differences in the motivations of those engaged in the range of radical action protesting the social consequences of the form of globalization driven by neoliberalism. Does this produce a debilitating fragmentation, or rather a complex articulation of the strands of resistance, combining into a movement reaching out for 'global solidarity' (Waterman 2001: 230–45)? When the first demonstrations against the global economic institutions began to attract media attention, it was common to hear the protesters labelled as the 'anti-globalization' movement. This immediately opened them up to the accusation that they wanted to reverse an unstoppable historical phenomenon, a new version of the Luddite movement that destroyed machinery at the beginning of the nineteenth century. The label 'anti-capitalist movement' then became more common, and had the merit of identifying the systemic causes of global injustice. Again, the stress on what they oppose begs the question of what they stand *for*. The term 'alter-globalization' is now gaining wider circulation, making clear that what is at stake is a new form of global society, rather than an attempt to turn back the clock to some unattainable communitarian social settlement within existing nation states. Whatever the label, the multiple movements pushing to make poverty history, to secure environmental justice or to guarantee human rights for all can be seen as a global movement, as broadly conceived in the first principle of the WSF mentioned above, dedicated to building a 'planetary society' of fruitful relationships among humankind and between it and the earth. Only a general appeal to global solidarity can encompass the breadth of concerns. More formal methods of representation and decision-making would be counter-productive, although a worldwide membership scheme would have a powerful symbolic effect.

Pleyers makes a distinction between two general dispositions in the alter-globalization movement, the 'way of subjectivity' and the 'way of reason' (Pleyers 2010: 22–3, 210–13). The 'way of subjectivity' tends to be suspicious of ideology as such, and tends to emphasise the autonomy of individuals and groups. This could apply to anarchists or single-issue activists in the affluent societies, but also to land resistance movements such as the Zapatistas in Mexico or the Landless Workers Movement (MST) in Brazil. The Zapatistas, who have been an inspiration to global activists throughout the world, started their ongoing campaign for the protection of their livelihoods in the Chiapas region on the day that the North American Free Trade Agreement came into effect, 1 January 1994 (Olessen 2005). The MST has put pressure for land reform on successive Brazilian governments and has seen 800,000 families settled on reclaimed land. These movements of resistance do not set out to transform global structures, but their influence, first through spontaneous networking and later through the WSF, has contributed to a developing solidarity between groups and causes that in the past would never have made the connections. Zapatista arguments have been couched in openly ethical terms, around issues such as democracy, autonomy, racism and gender, emphasising the concepts of human dignity, mutual aid and social justice, and this has appealed to a solidarity that goes well beyond the particular context of their own struggle (Holloway 1998: 159–90; Olessen 2005: 116–21). The second disposition, the 'way of reason', refers to the involvement of experts of every description that have given their knowledge to the alter-globalization cause without necessarily being concerned about democratic accountability. This contribution has been particularly vital in all areas of environmental and developmental politics, but also in the development of alternative economics and international law. These approaches might lead to different attitudes towards compromise with those in a position to influence global decision-making, but the global justice movement should be able to accommodate a plurality of identities, special interests and methods.

We now turn to the development of a politics of solidarity within regions and states. This is essential because a radical change of direction could only be initiated through decisions made at inter-governmental bodies such as the G20 or a new version of the Bretton Woods agreement that set the framework for the world economy back in 1944. A significant number of the G20 governments must therefore respond to the need for policy coordination and institutional reform. They are unlikely to do this unless they are committed to building social cohesion in their own states. As Joseph Schwartz argues, 'the road to greater international solidarity cannot transcend the politics of the state, but, rather, must run through it' (Schwartz 2007: 131–2). More specifically, it is the affluent states that need to renew their commitment to solidarity in their own communities, as they are in pole position to propose new global institutions that can remedy global injustices. However, inspired by the leadership of Ronald Reagan in the United States and Margaret Thatcher in Britain in the 1980s, political parties of the Right and Centre enthusiastically promoted economic neoliberalism (Lansley 2012: 34–5), while social democratic parties buckled under the pressure of the 'no alternative' momentum of deregulation and marketisation. The failure of earlier attempts at establishing distinctive social democratic paths to recovery paved the way for the abandonment of defining commitments to full employment and strongly progressive taxation.

Many European social democrats concluded that in an increasingly inter-dependent world economy it would be difficult to defend strong welfare systems at national level, but it might be possible to do so at the level of the European Union. The leading advocate of 'Social Europe' was Jacques Delors, President of the European Commission between 1985 and 1994. He presided over the creation of a single market in the EU, which was of obvious benefit to European business, but he ensured that the Maastricht Treaty of 1991 contained a commitment to high levels of employment and social protection, with its Social Chapter guaranteeing maximum working hours and robust health and safety regulation (Wilde 1994a: 179–80). Delors boldly declared that the EU could be 'the theatre in which social democracy accomplishes its mission' (Delors 1989: 32). In order to achieve this in the medium term he wanted to demonstrate the ability of the EU to intervene directly in economic recovery, playing a role hitherto played only by nation states. This was embodied in the Delors White Paper of 1993, 'Growth, Competitiveness, Employment', in which it was calculated that substantial investment in infrastructural and environmental projects, largely paid for by loans and bonds, would create fifteen million new jobs by 2000 (*The Economist*, 11–17 December 1993: 27–8). This was largely dependent on the creation of an EU public borrowing facility hitherto available only to nation states, but the principle was rejected at Delors's final meeting as President in 1995 (Wilde 2007: 48–51).

The Social Europe project envisaged in the early 1990s has stalled, due partially to the economic recovery enjoyed in the years following the adoption of the single market, but also to the preoccupation of the EU with enlargement, the adoption of a common currency and then its defence, and the failed attempt to adopt a constitution. Nevertheless, the aspirations for a 'Social Europe' are still present in the Social Policy Agenda following the Lisbon Treaty of 2009, and in such things as the Working Time Directive and the right to have works councils. It is possible that tighter central control over economic practices within the eurozone may lead to renewed calls for the type of intervention suggested by Delors in the early 1990s. Even in the middle of economic crisis the social model still commands support, as, for example, when the EU summit in Brussels in January 2012 agreed to inject €23 billion from the Social Fund into a scheme to secure the right of all young people to be offered a job, training or education within four months of their unemployment.

The general response of European social democracy to economic globalization has been to accede to business pressure for low tax rates and market-friendly initiatives. When in power, the strategy has been to provide optimum conditions for profit accumulation while using the tax revenues from higher growth to ensure that key public services such as health and education are properly funded. Yet during the years of high growth from the mid-1990s unemployment remained stubbornly high, inequality grew, and chronic poverty developed in many neglected communities in most of the most affluent states. When a minister in the Labour government in Britain, Peter Mandelson, commented in 1998 that he was 'intensely relaxed about people getting filthy rich' (Rawnsley 2000) it reflected a wider malaise within social democracy, a willingness to believe in 'trickle down' economics without seriously addressing the problem of social exclusion.

Social democracy must live or die by eradicating social exclusion, and this will be possible only through redistributive taxation. This brings us back to Steinar Stjernø's definition of solidarity quoted near the beginning of this book, as 'the preparedness to share resources with others by personal contribution to those in struggle or in need and through taxation and redistribution organised by the state' (Stjernø 2005: 2). It is commonplace now to assume that making the eradication of poverty a central platform of party policy would be a vote loser, because it would have to rely on increasing personal taxation, something that would be resisted by an increasingly individualistic majority of the electorate. But how do we know this? Opinion polls are highly unreliable, because the responses on fairness are strongly dependent on the wording of the question (Horton and Gregory 2009: 104). This issue of preparedness to pay more tax to fight poverty is rarely put to electorates, who have become used to a process of 'bargaining down' the rate of personal taxation. In Britain, for example, the basic rate of income tax fell in stages from 33 per cent in 1979 to 23 per cent by 1997, and was then reduced to 20 per cent by the Labour government in 1998. A reversal of this trend would certainly provoke a fierce reaction from the parties of the Right and their allies in the media, but it is entirely possible to raise large extra revenue through progressive taxation by raising rates on incomes well above the national average, with three or four rising bands (Lansley 2012: 257–9).

One significant shift that should help social democracy is the considerable public anger at tax evasion and the continued growth of incomes among the most highly paid. Securing due taxes from rich individuals and corporations would be a popular policy, but it would require determination to face down the threats of corporate withdrawal. As Colin Crouch has commented,

> since it is impossible to envisage an economy that is not dominated by giant firms and in which they are unable to translate their economic power into political influence, governments cannot be trusted not to be exceptionally responsive to these firms' interests. (Crouch 2011: 171–2)

However, 'responsive' does not have to mean supine, and open debate about the real economic impact of redistributive measures is long overdue. It will be argued that increasing higher rates of personal taxation will deter investment and entrepreneurship, but there is no evidence for this, and it is an argument that can be exposed as a disingenuous defence of greed. Increasing tax revenues is a much surer way to guarantee investment, and could also be used to support small and medium-sized enterprises. Ultimately, only a radical redistributive economic policy can bring back something close to full employment, a *sine qua non* for social inclusion, and therefore for social solidarity.

The improvement in employment in the United States in 2011/12 as a result of government economic stimulus demonstrated the merit of continued public investment, in stark contrast to the austerity path followed in Europe (Allen 2012). However, in the world economy as a whole it is evident that the financial crisis of 2008 has not produced the death of neoliberalism, and the relative weakness of the financial regulatory measures taken since then do not rule out the possibility of a second crash. Not only does there need to be a return to Keynesianism, but it needs to be done with the thoroughness and drive of Roosevelt's New Deal in the 1930s if it is to regulate the market so that social needs are no longer ignored (Harvey 2009: 183–4; Lansley 2012: 255–6). It needs to be shown that the state can play a vital role as an enabling state, securing the material basis on which groups and communities can create solidaristic relations. Above all, social democracy cannot surrender to fear of the opposition that will be unleashed against programmes advocating redistribution and regulation. For this great historic movement, this is the line in the sand beyond which they cannot retreat, and they must be open to every possible alliance with greens and other parties of the Left who share the commitment to eradicating poverty and creating a sustainable future. If they are not immediately successful, the arguments must be mounted again and again with greater intensity. In addition, social democratic parties, with their global links in the Socialist International, are well placed to bring concrete proposals for global institutional change into the domestic agenda. If agreements among leading parties can be reached on issues such as a global financial transactions tax or cuts in greenhouse gas emissions, then promoting those policies at the global level can be presented in national programmes, rather than ignored or mentioned in passing as issues that can only be addressed 'elsewhere'.

Many global activists have long since given up on the old parties of the Left as if the 'men in suits' were irrelevant to the global causes discussed above. But states are still crucial actors in global politics and parties can secure access to state power (Crouch 2011: 177). It is therefore essential to the prospects of solidaristic politics that the civil society movements focused on global issues develop constructive relationships with those parties that may be in a position to bring the arguments about the regulation of corporate capital to the gaze of public debate. When progressive agreements have been made in the past, such as the Montreal Protocol of 1987 on CFC emissions, or the Kyoto Protocol of 1997 on greenhouse gas emissions, or the 2005 Gleneagles Agreement on debt cancellation, constructive relationships between global civil society activists and political elites have been significant. Social democracy needs to seek common cause with global activists, but to do so would require a revival of principled radical politics and a rejection of opportunism guided by 'spin doctors'.

An enabling state, then, would offer material support to national or local civil society groups to develop solidaristic projects across a range of areas that would promote the potentials of compassion, productive work and cooperation. Through conservation, reclamation, refurbishment and caring for the aged and disabled, as well as the promotion of local cultural and recreational initiatives, the productive efforts of individuals could be seen to be building a more humane society. The role of voluntary organisations is important here, provided that they are not substitutes for properly funded public provision. An enabling state would support the third sector in providing more sensitive care at local level (Jessop 2002: 159). There is great solidaristic potential in public support for third-sector delivery of a range of services that could play a vital role in building social inclusion. The state should also be prepared to regulate business to protect the public against practices such as money-lending at exorbitant rates of interest, marketing strong alcoholic drinks for teenagers, or advertisements directed at very young children.

There is evidence, for Europe at least, that whereas party and trade union membership is declining, participation in civil society groups is increasing, and more citizens are becoming involved in protest activities such as signing petitions, attending demonstrations and boycotting goods (Bale 2008: 241–5). Although participation may be more sporadic than party political activity, it shows that people do care, often intensely, about decisions that are taken on matters over which they have not been consulted. The anger felt by millions of people across the world at the impending invasion of Iraq by American and British forces led to massive demonstrations in February 2003. In Europe they were the largest demonstrations since the massive turnouts against the deployment of a new range of American nuclear weapons in the early 1980s. The rise of new social movements has mobilised people in causes that have been treated as marginal by political parties fixated on managing the economy. They have challenged the ordering of the political agenda by political and administrative elites with astonishing success, achieving immense social changes and helping to redefine the nature of politics itself. For example, the transformation of women's place in society was led not by political parties but by women campaigning at every level of social interaction, forcing society to confront traditional gender roles as a political issue. Green politics gained its impetus from civil society movements with such success that all mainstream parties were obliged to respond to the ecological issues raised. It has transformed the way we think about the relationship between humanity and the environment, and in alerting humanity to the precariousness of life on earth it has provided a material cause that cries out for human solidarity.

The reimagining of social relationships and the questioning of our interaction with nature that have been seen in the brief history of new social movements have been profound, but they have also been contained. That is to say that although many social-movement activities develop the potentials identified in Chapter 4 as being key to forging solidarity – compassion, rationality, productiveness and cooperation – the globalized economic system has exacerbated inequalities across the world and made it difficult to mobilise those solidaristic values into effective political action. Yet the existence of a solidaristic spirit in a relatively unorganised, spontaneous way is a source for hope among solidarists. The research of Liz Spencer and Ray Pahl has shown that by focusing on 'the nature and quality of people's informal personal relations', it is possible to identify strong solidaristic communities (Spencer and Pahl 2006: 191). Paul suggests that such 'hidden' solidarities span the globe (Pahl 2005). What is also noticeable is the enormous increase in ethical consumption through movements such as Fairtrade, as well as the expansion of work in groups concerned with environmental conservation, animal welfare and the protection of birds. Here is evidence of a deep concern with the quality of our collective life, and an important source of hope.

Prospects

In considering how a politics of solidarity can develop, the emphasis has been on breaking the grip that neoliberal principles continue to hold over the conduct of economic life. This requires the imposition of political will over economic practices actively sustained by global business and financial elites, in a way that will be seen to work effectively and quickly. Looking for some historical precedents for such bold transformation, perhaps the Marshall Plan offers the most promising example. Between 1948 and 1952 the United States poured almost $13 billion of aid into western Europe, securing the economic recovery of devastated societies so that all easily passed their pre-war levels of production by the time the funding ceased. It laid the foundation for the formation of the European Economic Community, which went on to become the European Union, and enabled the introduction of welfare state models. Republican opponents of the plan were appalled at the thought of state intervention of this sort that involved simply giving away money. In fact, the creation of a market for the export of American goods resolved the problem of surplus economic capacity once the war effort was over, and it cemented the rise of the USA to global hegemony (Van der Pijl 1984: 143–50). Setting to one side the fact that the plan was also an important weapon in the Cold War against the Soviet Union (Milward 1984: 113–25), its success as a technical 'fix' gives us a glimpse of what a global financial transaction tax could achieve.

Breaking with neoliberalism would not, of itself, deliver global solidarity, but it would open the way for it as a real historical possibility. In general, I accept Jamie Peck's caution that 'any successor to neoliberalism will have to be generated from the terrain that the market revolution has imperfectly shaped' (Peck 2010: 276). For that reason, I have avoided more sweeping prescriptions that, from our present position, would be regarded as utopian in the sense of being unattainable in the foreseeable future. So, for example, while it would truly be a great solidaristic act if the United Nations were to take into global public ownership the world's pharmaceutical industries and distribute free medicine for all, in the present situation it would be more realistic to think of providing incentives to get low-price medicines made available to the global poor, as suggested by Thomas Pogge in his proposal for a Health Impact Fund (Pogge 2008: 244–61). To consider, as

Walden Bello does, that radicals should be critical of global social democratic proposals such as those of David Held, on the grounds that if implemented they will sustain capitalism, is to play posture politics (Bello 2009: 57, 64). It is true that Held proposes taming global markets rather than replacing them, but the Keynesian measures he outlines would enable the development of a politics of global solidarity (Held 2004: 165). A more decisive breakthrough would be achieved by a global financial transactions tax, which Held sees only as a 'longer run' possibility (Held 2006: 65). However, the important point to be made here is that proposals that would reverse the logic of neoliberal globalization should be welcomed by all supporters of the ideal of global solidarity.

The starting point, then, is to bury neoliberalism, but how is it possible to imagine a reversal of the assault on solidarity that has held sway for so long? The first thing to point out is that not only has the project failed dismally, but repeat doses of the same medicine will not revive the patient. In this situation it will become clear that, despite the fascinating insights revealed by those researching the potential for a transnational ruling class, there is no homogenous, tightly disciplined economic elite. There remain big differences in the interests of the major players in international capital. A global tax on financial transactions might draw howls from finance capital, but manufacturing and extractive industries could be persuaded of the benefits of the raised levels of effective demand created by such redistributive measures. Nor should small and medium-sized enterprises be averse to public interventions to facilitate easier borrowing than is currently offered by banks still focused on financial trading.

The greatest impetus for global institutional reform is likely to come from the fast-growing BRICS states, which represent almost half the world's population. At their summit meeting in Delhi in March 2012 they agreed a declaration that affirmed a vision of 'a future marked by global peace, economic and social progress, and enlightened scientific temper'. The group committed itself to multilateral decision-making and a strengthened representation of developing countries in global economic governance (Gillespie

2012). The summit process that has been initiated recently by these states represents the first stirrings of a political cooperation determined to create more representative global decision-making and to overcome the market anarchy that produced the 2008 financial crash and continues to threaten economic stability. But can they reach agreement with the leaders of the United States and the European Union?

In the recent past the aggressive unilateralism of the United States government was seen as perhaps the most serious obstacle to the development of global solidarity. Peter Gowan once remarked that no scheme for universal harmony is credible if it tries to sidestep the fact of American power (Gowan 2003: 65). However, there has been a considerable shift in direction during the Obama presidency. Willingness to pump money into the economy and reassert the merits of progressive taxation indicate a more Keynesian response to economic recession. It is impossible to say whether this will be sustained, but it can be argued that it would be in the interests of the United States to be sympathetic to the development of greater multilateralism in world affairs, including the institutional reforms discussed above, in a world where its hegemony is clearly coming to an end. Building fairness into global politics and global economic governance is a more rational strategy than risking a punitive struggle for power with China.

China, is, of course, the greatest single 'variable' with regard to global solidarity. The imprisoned winner of the 2010 Nobel Peace Prize, Liu Xiaobo, urges caution when it comes to assessing the prospects of Communist Party rule, arguing that the 'dictatorial system will be with us for some time' and that 'China's road to a free society is going to depend on gradual improvements from the bottom up' (Liu 2012: 28). More disturbingly, he comments on the intensive and aggressive nationalism that is fostered by the dictatorship, drawing on the memories of foreign interventions of the nineteenth and twentieth centuries (Liu 2012: 62–84). If this were to fuel an aggressive struggle to achieve hegemonic status, then it would be as damaging for the prospects of global solidarity as the last great struggle for hegemony that produced two world wars. However, with China's economy opening up to the world market, the benefits of global cooperation are appreciated and exchanges develop beyond purely economic points of contact. Increased cultural and educational interaction develops mutual understanding and a growing awareness of the real losses to be suffered by resorting to an aggressive economic battle for hegemony. A democratic transition in China would almost certainly produce a United Nations of democratic states in a very short time and provide the greatest opening ever for global solidarity. It would also bring its own solidaristic traditions; deep-seated Confucian concepts such as *ren* (human-heartedness) and *shu* (reciprocity) appear to resonate with the radical humanist view of human solidarity presented in Chapter 4 (Smart 2000: 65–7; Lai 2008: 22–3). As Liu cautions, a democratic China is not something imminent, or something to depend upon, but those who would dismiss its possibility or its implications should think about other events that few believed could happen, such as the demise of the Soviet Union, the democratic transitions in eastern Europe, South Africa and Latin America, and the reunification of Germany.

8 Conclusion

On the final page of William Morris's utopian novel *News from Nowhere* William Guest finds himself awakening from a vivid dream of an idyllic, egalitarian society, and he tries to absorb the principal lesson he needs to apply in his own world: 'Go on living while you may, striving, with whatsoever pain and labour needs be, to build up little by little the new day of fellowship, rest, and happiness' (Morris 1995: 2000). Morris, who did not believe that radical change could be achieved through peaceful means, had imagined a workers' revolution leading to a mass movement back to the countryside and the development of a moneyless society in which peace and beauty prevailed. In the years since the first publication of that book in 1890, workers' revolutions have been tried and, in various ways, have failed, while the rural idyll was, even then, a romantic fantasy. The compelling attraction of the novel, however, does not depend on its programmatic soundness but rather lies in the compassion, productiveness and cooperation that shine through the social relations depicted. Morris makes the case that it is within the power of humanity to create social arrangements that promote the fulfilment of human potentials, transforming our relations with nature and fostering a strong sense of social solidarity. Readers can recognise the happiness that flows from a solidaristic society because, even in today's highly individualistic societies, they still experience the warm, reciprocated support of others, as family, friends, neighbours, club members or work colleagues. In all walks of life, in all parts of the world, these supportive relations shine through, defying the logic of instrumental rationality that drives the processes of economic competition and compels people to work harder and faster simply to survive.

Perhaps the most significant argument of this book is that poverty is not inevitable and that the slogan of 'make poverty history' is one that can be realised. I offer an ameliorative perspective that argues it is entirely possible for humanity to create a global, solidaristic society, in opposition to those who deny the possibility of radical alternatives. In recalling the tragic history of social divisions in Chapter 5, and presenting the grim figures on inequality and poverty at the beginning of Chapter 7, the intention was to show both how much conflict and suffering humanity has had to overcome in the past, and how much more it needs to overcome if it is to change direction towards a more solidaristic, cosmopolitan future. Only the sort of striving alluded to by Morris can create the political framework to promote global cooperation on fighting poverty, creating a sustainable environment and enforcing human rights.

Employing the rhetoric of individual freedom has been a key strategy in legitimating neoliberal policies, and it is imperative that it is exposed as a deception, an impoverished substitute for a productive social self. The parties that still adhere to a democratic socialist tradition need to be pushed into reasserting the pressing relevance of an enabling state that provides the opportunities for all people to develop the potentials described in Chapter 4. In place of the illusory individualism of an atomised society, solidaristic politics needs to offer the hope of an expanded individual freedom through the unfolding of human potentials. Individualism needs to be reclaimed from its specious and amoral form presented in neoliberal dogma, in which only the affluent few enjoy a semblance of its promise. Oscar Wilde was right when he wrote in 1891 that 'private property has crushed true individualism and set up an individualism that is false', and he was right to argue that not only must socialism ensure the 'material well-being of each member of the community' but must be a precondition for the development of 'true, beautiful, healthy individualism' (Wilde 1991: 258–63).

Conclusion

Neoliberalism's blinkered version of individualism operates from the principle that prosperity will flow from each individual pursuing his or her self-interest, and that fair distribution will flow from the 'invisible hand' of the market. This principle, dating back to Adam Smith in the late eighteenth century, became the ruling idea of the economic and political elites in nineteenth-century Britain, as it powered to its hegemonic position in the world economy. Just over 160 years ago, the British political establishment stood by its determination not to intervene against market forces when the potato blight hit Ireland and one million people were allowed to starve to death, with another million forced to leave their country (Kinealy 1994: 342–59). A modern neoliberal might argue that this was not market failure, for the market did what it was supposed to and rectified the imbalance between supply and demand, albeit at the cost of one million lives. They were victims of a market dogmatism that shows a callous disregard for the social cost of its nostrums. From a radical humanist perspective, such thinking is simply inhumane, and its prevalence is the greatest obstacle to the development of global solidarity.

Under the conditions of casino capitalism, in Western societies at least, a ruthless competitive spirit was encouraged, geared to 'incentivise' ever more efficient delivery of goods and services and cut out waste. At the same time the poor, rather than poverty, were seen as a burden, while the rich were vaunted as the successful vanguard of the new prosperity. Despite the breathtaking persistence of this ideology of inequality since the collapse of the banks in 2008, it has proved impossible to hide from people the extent to which the poor are paying the price for the bankers' crisis and the rich are immune to its costs. This is the moment at which the change of direction discussed in Chapter 7 can be accomplished. The arguments for a shift towards solidarity will need to develop not just in the political sphere, but in all areas of culture, in workplaces, schools and universities. Solidaristic movements need to confront, directly and incessantly, the myopic certitude of the arguments of the political economy of greed, demonstrating the human and environmental costs of unfettered capitalism. Solidaristic movements need to agitate for social justice at every level of social life in all parts of the world in an increasingly conscious pursuit of an empowering, humane form of globalization.

Politically, the quest for solidarity originated in the nineteenth-century struggles of working-class social movements for democratic rights and economic security. From the outset it was fired by an internationalist vision, but that was eclipsed by the development of popular nationalism. Now, in the era of globalization, a global political agenda has emerged at a time when many of the old social movements have suffered dispiriting setbacks. At the same time, new movements have developed to revive the hope that solidarity, a feeling of sympathy shared by subjects within and between groups, impelling supportive action and pursuing social inclusion, may yet be realised. These movements reflect a rich plurality of interests and causes. They sense that nothing less than the future of humanity is at stake unless we collectively agree on sustainable development. They sense that we can no longer shrug our shoulders and claim that nothing can be done to lift billions of people out of poverty, and they sense that it is possible to build a democratic world order that drives the human-rights abusers from the field. These movements, impelled by an ethical commitment to social justice, can succeed in consigning neoliberalism to the museum of grotesque ideas and proclaim a new direction, towards global solidarity.

References

Adorno, Theodor W. (1992), *The Culture Industry: Selected Essays on Mass Culture*, London: Routledge.

Adorno, Theodor W. and Horkheimer, Max (1986), *Dialectic of Enlightenment*, 2nd ed., London: Verso.

Agamben, Giorgio (2007), *Infancy and History: On the Destruction of Experience*, London: Verso.

Alesina, Alberto and Glaeser, Edward L. (2005), *Fighting Poverty in the US and Europe: A World of Difference*, Oxford: Oxford University Press.

Alexander, Michelle (2010), *The New Jim Crow: Mass Incarceration in the Age of Colorblindness*, New York: New Press.

Allen, Katie (2012), 'Stock markets rise on surprise US jobs boost and UK services optimism', *The Guardian*, 4 February.

Amnesty International (2012), available at www.amnesty.org.

An-Na'im, Abdullahi A. (1999), 'Political Islam in National Politics and International Relations' in Peter Berger (ed.), *The Desecularization of the World: Resurgent Religion and World Politics*, Grand Rapids, MI: Eerdmans, pp. 103–22.

Anderson, Benedict (1991), *Imagined Communities*, 2nd ed., London: Verso.

Appiah, Kwame Anthony (1996), 'Cosmopolitan Patriots' in Martha Nussbaum *et al.*, *For Love of Country: Debating the Limits of Patriotism*, Boston: Beacon Press, pp. 21–29.

Appiah, Kwame Anthony (2006), *Cosmopolitanism: Ethics in a World of Strangers*, London: Allen Lane.

Archibugi, Daniele (2008), *The Global Commonwealth of Citizens: Toward Cosmopolitan Democracy*, Princeton, NJ: Princeton University Press.
Arendt, Hannah (1969), *The Human Condition*, Chicago: University of Chicago Press.
Arendt, Hannah ([1963] 1984), *Eichmann in Jerusalem: A Report on the Banality of Evil*, Harmondsworth: Penguin.
Arendt, Hannah (1986), *The Origins of Totalitarianism*, London: André Deutsch.
Argyle, Michael (1991), *Cooperation: The Basis of Sociability*, London: Routledge.
Aristotle (1969), *Politics*, ed. Ernest Barker, Oxford: Clarendon Press.
Aristotle (1976), *Ethics*, Harmondsworth: Penguin.
Axelrod, Robert (2006), *The Evolution of Cooperation*, rev. ed., New York: Basic.
Bachofen, Johann Jakob (1992), *Myth, Religion and Mother Right: Selected Writings of J. J. Bachofen*, Princeton, NJ: Princeton University Press.
Badiou, A. (2003), *Saint Paul: The Foundation of Universalism*, Stanford, CA: Stanford University Press.
Bahro, Rudolf (1984), *The Alternative in Eastern Europe*, London: Verso.
Bakunin, Mikhail (1973), *Bakunin on Anarchy*, ed. Sam Dolgoff, London: Allen and Unwin.
Bakunin, Jack (1976), *Pierre Leroux and the Birth of Democratic Socialism, 1797–1848*, New York: Revisionist Press.
Baldwin, Peter (1999), *The Politics of Social Solidarity: Class Bases of the European Welfare State, 1875–1975*, Cambridge: Cambridge University Press.
Bale, Tim (2008), *European Politics: A Comparative Introduction*, Basingstoke: Palgrave Macmillan.
Balibar, Etienne and Wallerstein, Immanuel (1991), *Race, Nation, Class: Ambiguous Identities*, London: Verso.
Ball, James, Milmo, Dan and Ferguson, Ben (2010), 'Half of UK's young black males are unemployed', *The Guardian*, 9 March.

References

Balmer, Randall (2006), *Thy Kingdom Come: An Evangelical's Lament*, New York: Basic.

Barber, Benjamin (1996), 'Constitutional Faith' in Martha Nussbaum *et al.*, *For Love of Country: Debating the Limits of Patriotism*, Boston: Beacon Press, pp. 30–7.

Barker, Ernest ([1918] 1970), *Greek Political Theory: Plato and His Predecessors*, London: Methuen.

Bauman, Zygmunt (2000), *Modernity and the Holocaust*, Ithaca, NY: Cornell University Press.

Bauman, Zygmunt (2001), *Work, Consumerism and the New Poor*, Buckingham: Open University Press.

Baurmann, Michael (1999), 'Solidarity as a Social and as a Constitutional Norm' in Kurt Bayertz (ed.), *Solidarity*, Dordrecht: Kluwer, pp. 243–64.

Bayertz, Kurt (1999), 'Four Uses of Solidarity' in Kurt Bayertz (ed.), *Solidarity*, Dordrecht: Kluwer, pp. 3–28.

Baylis, John, Smith, Steve and Owens, Patricia (2011), 'Introduction' in John Baylis, Steve Smith and Patricia Owens (eds), *The Globalization of World Politics: An Introduction to International Relations*, 5th ed., Oxford: Oxford University Press, pp. 2–12.

Beauvoir, Simone de ([1953] 1993), *The Second Sex*, London: Everyman's Library.

Beck, Ulrich (2000), *The Brave New World of Work*, Cambridge: Polity.

Beck, Ulrich (2002), 'The Cosmopolitan Perspective: Sociology in the Second Age of Postmodernity' in Steven Vertovec and Robin Cohen (eds), *Conceiving Cosmopolitanism: Theory, Context, and Practice*, Oxford: Oxford University Press, pp. 61–85.

Beck, Ulrich (2006), *The Cosmopolitan Vision*. Cambridge: Polity.

Beckett, Francis (1998), *Enemy Within: The Rise and Fall of the British Communist Party*, 2nd ed., London: Merlin Press.

Beitz, Charles R. (1999), *Political Theory and International Relations*, 2nd ed., Princeton, NJ: Princeton University Press.

Bellamy, Edward ([1888] 1982), *Looking Backward, 2000–1887*, Harmondsworth: Penguin.

Bellamy, Richard (1992), *Liberalism and Modern Society: A Historical Argument*, University Park: Pennsylvania State University Press.

Bello, Walden (2009), 'Goodbye Washington Consensus, Hello Global Social Democracy?' in David Ransom and Vanessa Baird (eds), *People First Economics*, Oxford: New Internationalist, pp. 57–64.

Benton, Ted (1993), *Natural Relations: Ecology, Animal Rights and Social Justice*, London: Verso.

Bergson, Henri (1913), *An Introduction to Metaphysics*, London: Macmillan.

Bieler, Andreas, Lindberg, Ingemar and Pillay, Devan (2008), 'What Future Strategy for the Global Working Class? The Need for a New Historical Subject' in Andreas Bieler, Ingemar Lindberg and Devan Pillay (eds), *Labour and the Challenges of Globalization: What Prospects for Transnational Solidarity?*, London: Pluto Press, pp. 264–86.

Bignell, Peter (2007), 'The fallen and the forgotten: the Falklands War, 25 years on', *The Independent*, 25 March.

Billig, Michael (1995), *Banal Nationalism*, London: Sage.

Black, Maggie (2008), *The No-nonsense Guide to the United Nations*, London: New Internationalist.

Blackburn, Robin (2007), 'Plan For a Global Pension', *New Left Review*, September–October, pp. 71–92.

Blanc, Louis (1966), 'Socialism' (July 1851) in *The Red Republican and The Friend of the People*, London: Merlin Press.

Bloch, Ernst (1972), *Atheism in Christianity: The Religion of the Exodus and the Kingdom*, New York, Herder and Herder.

Block, Gay and Drucker, Malka (1992), *Rescuers: Portraits of Moral Courage in the Holocaust*, New York: Holmes and Meier.

Boucher, David (1998), *Political Theories of International Relations: From Thucydides to the Present*, Oxford: Oxford University Press.

Boucher, David and Vincent, Andrew (2000), *British Idealism and Political Theory*, Edinburgh: Edinburgh University Press.

Boulding, Elise (1988), *Building a Global Civic Culture: Education for an Interdependent World*, New York: Teachers College, Columbia University.

Bourdieu, Pierre and Eagleton, Terry (1994), 'Doxa and Common Life: An Interview' in Slavoj Žižek (ed.), *Mapping Ideology*, London: Verso, pp. 265–77.

Bourgeois, Léon ([1986] 2009), *Solidarité*, Charleston, SC: BiblioLife.

Bowcott, Owen (2011), 'Afghanistan worst place in the world for women, but India in top five', *The Guardian*, 15 June.

Bowles, Samuel and Gintis, Herbert (2011), *A Cooperative Species: Human Reciprocity and its Evolution*, Princeton, NJ: Princeton University Press.

Braunthal, Julius (1967a), *History of the International, volume 1, 1864–1914*, New York: Praeger.

Braunthal, Julius (1967b), *History of the International, volume 2, 1914–1943*, London: Nelson.

Braunthal, Julius (1980), *History of the International, volume 3, 1943–1968*, London: Victor Gollancz.

Brock, Gillian and Brighouse, Harry (eds) (2006), *The Political Philosophy of Cosmopolitanism*, Cambridge: Cambridge University Press.

Brooks, Thom (ed.) (2008), *The Global Justice Reader*, Oxford: Blackwell.

Brown, Donald (1991), *Human Universals*, New York: McGraw-Hill.

Brunkhorst, Hauke (2005), *Solidarity: From Civic Friendship to a Global Legal Community*, Cambridge, MA: MIT Press.

Burckhardt, Jacob (2004), *The Civilization of the Renaissance in Italy*, Harmondsworth: Penguin.

Caldwell, Christopher (2010), *Reflections on the Revolution in Europe: Immigration, Islam and the West*, London: Penguin.

Calhoun, Craig (1982), *The Question of Class Struggle: Social*

Foundations of Popular Radicalism during the Industrial Revolution, Chicago: University of Chicago Press.

Calhoun, Craig (2003), 'The Class Consciousness of Frequent Travellers: Towards a Critique of Actually Existing Cosmopolitanism' in Daniele Archibugi (ed.), *Debating Cosmopolitics*, London: Verso, pp. 86–116.

Caney, Simon (2006), *Justice Beyond Borders: A Global Political Theory*, Oxford: Oxford University Press.

Canovan, Margaret (2001), 'Sleeping Dogs, Prowling Cats and Soaring Doves: Three Paradoxes in the Political Theory of Nationhood', *Political Studies* 49(2), pp. 203–15.

Carroll, William K. (2010), *The Making of a Transnational Capitalist Class: Corporate Power in the Twenty-first Century*, London: Zed.

Carter, April (2006), *The Political Theory of Global Citizenship*, London: Routledge.

Carter, Neil (2007), *The Politics of the Environment: Ideas, Activism, Policy*, 2nd ed., Cambridge: Cambridge University Press.

Chandler, David (2005), *Constructing Global Civil Society: Morality and Power in International Relations*, Basingstoke: Palgrave Macmillan.

Charlton, John (1997), *The Chartists: The First National Workers' Movement*, London: Pluto Press.

Child Poverty (2012), End Child Poverty website, available at www.endchildpoverty.org.uk/.

Christensen, John (2009), 'Can't Pay, Won't Pay' in David Ransom and Vanessa Baird (eds), *People First Economics*, Oxford: New Internationalist, pp. 115–26.

Clark, Mary E. (2002), *In Search of Human Nature*, London: Routledge.

Cobban, Alfred (1974), *A History of Modern France, volume 3: France of the Republics, 1871–1962*, Harmondsworth: Penguin.

Cockburn, Cynthia (2009), 'Women in Black: The Stony Path to Solidarity' in Howard Clark (ed.), *People Power: Unarmed*

Resistance and Global Solidarity, London: Pluto, pp. 156–63.
Coicaud, Jean-Marc (2008), 'Conclusion: Making Sense of National Interest and International Solidarity' in Jean-Marc Coicaud and Nicholas J. Wheeler (eds), *National Interest and International Solidarity: Particular and Universal Ethics in International Life*, Tokyo: United Nations University Press, pp. 288–301.
Commission on Global Governance (1995), *Our Global Neighbourhood: The Report of the Commission on Global Governance*, Oxford: Oxford University Press.
Congressional Budget Office (2011), 'Trends in the Distribution of Household Income between 1979 and 2007', 25 October, at http://www.cbo.gov/doc.cfm?index=12485, accessed 6 July 2012.
Cooke, Deborah, 2001, 'The Talking Cure in Habermas's Republic', *New Left Review* 12, November–December, pp. 135–51.
Crabtree, John (2009), 'Bolivia: Playing by the New Rules' in Geraldine Lievesley and Steve Ludlam (eds.), *Reclaiming Latin America: Experiments in Radical Social Democracy*, London: Zed, pp. 91–108.
Crisp, Roger and Slote, Michael (eds) (2002), *Virtue Ethics*, Oxford: Oxford University Press.
Cronin, Ciaran (2003), 'Democracy and Collective Identity: In Defence of Constitutional Patriotism', *European Journal of Philosophy* 11(1), pp. 1–28.
Crouch, Colin (2011), *The Strange Non-death of Neoliberalism*, Cambridge: Polity.
Crow, Graham (2002), *Social Solidarities: Theories, Identities and Social Change*, Buckingham: Open University Press.
Dawisha, Karen (1984), *The Kremlin and the Prague Spring*, Berkeley: University of California Press.
Dawkins, Richard (2006), *The God Delusion*, London: Bantam Press.
Della Porta, Donatella and Tarrow, Sidney (eds) (2004),

Transnational Protest and Global Activism, Lanham, MD: Rowman and Littlefield.

Delors, Jacques (1989), 'Europe: A New Frontier for Social Democracy?' in Piet Dankert and Ad Kooyman (eds), *Europe without Frontiers: Socialists on the Future of the European Community*, London: Mansell/Cassell, pp. 31–44.

Dennett, Daniel C. (2006), *Breaking the Spell: Religion as a Natural Phenomenon*, London: Allen Lane.

Derrida, Jacques (1997), *The Politics of Friendship*, London: Verso.

Desai, Manisha (2005), 'Transnationalism: The Face of Feminist Politics Post-Beijing', *International Social Science Journal* 57(184), pp. 319–30.

Dewey, John ([1916] 2007), *Democracy and Education*, Teddington: Echo Library.

Diaz Alba, Carmen L. (2010), 'Building Transnational Feminist Solidarity in the Americas: The Experience of the Latin American Network of Women Transforming the Economy' in Pascal Dufour, Dominique Masson and Dominique Caouette (eds), *Solidarities beyond Borders: Transnationalizing Women's Movements*, Vancouver: UBC Press.

Dobson, Andrew and Eckersley, Robyn (eds) (2006), *Political Theory and the Ecological Challenge*, Cambridge: Cambridge University Press.

Dollar, David (2007), 'Globalization, Poverty and Inequality since 1980' in David Held and Ayse Kaya (eds), *Global Inequality: Patterns and Explanations*, Cambridge: Polity.

Dorling, Daniel (2010), *Injustice: Why Social Inequality Persists*, Bristol: Policy Press.

Dower, Nigel (2003), *An Introduction to Global Citizenship*, Edinburgh: Edinburgh University Press.

Dower, Nigel and Williams, John (eds) (2002), *Global Citizenship: A Critical Reader*, Edinburgh: Edinburgh University Press.

Dubois, Ellen (1991), 'Woman Suffrage and the Left: An International Socialist-Feminist Perspective', *New Left Review* 186, March–April, pp. 20–45.

Dufour, Pascal, Masson, Dominique and Caouette, Dominique (eds) (2010), *Solidarities beyond Borders: Transnationalizing Women's Movements*, Vancouver: UBC Press.

Dunne, Tim and Schmidt, Brian C. (2011), 'Realism' in John Baylis, Steve Smith and Patricia Owens (eds), *The Globalization of World Politics: An Introduction to International Relations*, Oxford: Oxford University Press, 5th ed., pp. 84–99.

Durkheim, Emile ([1893] 1964), *The Division of Labour in Society*, London: Collier Macmillan.

Edwards, Stewart (ed.) (1973), *The Communards of Paris, 1871*, London: Thames and Hudson.

Einstein, Albert (1982), *Ideas and Opinions*, 3rd ed., New York: Three Rivers Press.

Einstein, Albert (1984), *The Einstein Reader*, New York: Citadel Press.

Esping-Anderson, Gøsta (1990), *The Three Worlds of Welfare Capitalism*, Cambridge: Polity.

Falk, Richard (1995), *On Humane Governance: Toward a New Global Politics*, Cambridge: Polity.

Falk, Richard (2001), *Religion and Humane Global Governance*, Basingstoke: Palgrave.

Falk, Richard (2002), 'An Emergent Matrix of Citizenship: Complex, Uneven, and Fluid' in Nigel Dower and John Williams (eds), *Global Citizenship: A Critical Reader*, Edinburgh: Edinburgh University Press, pp. 15–29.

Falk, Richard and Strauss, Andrew (2001), 'Toward Global Parliament', *Foreign Affairs*, January–February, pp. 212–20.

Fanon, Frantz ([1961] 1985), *The Wretched of the Earth*, Harmondsworth: Penguin.

Fanon, Frantz ([1952] 2008), *Black Skin, White Masks*, London: Pluto.

Faux, Jeff (2006), *The Global Class War: How America's Bipartisan Elite Lost Our Future – And What It Will Take to Win It Back*, Hoboken, NJ: John Wiley.

Featherstone, Simon (2005), *Postcolonial Cultures*, Edinburgh: Edinburgh University Press.

Field, John (2008), *Social Capital*, 2nd ed., London: Routledge.
Fine, Robert (2007), *Cosmopolitanism*, London: Routledge.
Fine, Ben (2010), *Theories of Social Capital: Researchers Behaving Badly*, London: Pluto Press.
Fine, Robert and Smith, Will (2003), 'Jürgen Habermas's Theory of Cosmopolitanism', *Constellations* 10(4), pp. 469–87.
Fisher, Colin and Lovell, Alan (2008), *Business Ethics and Values: Individual, Corporate and International Perspectives*, Harlow: Financial Times/Prentice Hall.
Foot, Philippa (2002), 'Virtues and Vices' in Roger Crisp and Michael Slote (eds), *Virtue Ethics*, Oxford: Oxford University Press, pp. 163–77.
Foot, Philippa (2003), *Natural Goodness*, Oxford: Clarendon Press.
Francione, Gary L. and Garner, Robert (2010), *The Animal Rights Debate: Abolition or Regulation?*, New York: Columbia University Press.
Fraser, Derek (2009), *The Evolution of the British Welfare State: A History of Social Policy since the Industrial Revolution*, 4th ed., Basingstoke: Palgrave Macmillan.
Fraser, Ian (1998), *Hegel and Marx: The Concept of Need*, Edinburgh: Edinburgh University Press.
Fraser, Ian and Wilde, Lawrence (2011), *The Marx Dictionary*, London: Continuum.
Fraser, Nancy (1997), *Justice Interruptus: Critical Reflections on the 'Postsocialist' Condition*, New York and London: Routledge.
Fraser, Nancy (2003a), 'Social Justice in the Age of Identity Politics: Redistribution, Recognition, and Participation' in Nancy Fraser and Axel Honneth, *Redistribution or Recognition? A Political-philosophical Exchange*, London and New York: Verso, pp. 7–109.
Fraser, Nancy (2003b), 'Distorted beyond All Recognition: A Rejoinder to Axel Honneth' in Nancy Fraser and Axel Honneth, *Redistribution or Recognition? A Political-philosophical Exchange*, London and New York: Verso, pp. 198–236.

References

Fraser, Nancy (2008), *Scales of Justice: Reimagining Political Space in a Globalizing World*, Cambridge: Polity.

Fraser, Nancy (2009), 'Feminism, Capitalism and the Cunning of History', *New Left Review* 56, March–April, pp. 97–117.

Fraser, Nancy and Honneth, Axel (2003), 'Introduction' in Nancy Fraser and Axel Honneth, *Redistribution or Recognition? A Political-philosophical Exchange*, London and New York: Verso, pp. 1–5.

Freud, Sigmund (2001), 'The Ego and the Id' in *The Complete Psychological Works of Sigmund Freud, volume 19*, London: Vintage.

Freud, Sigmund ([1930] 2004), *Civilization and its Discontents*, London: Penguin.

Friends of the Earth (2012), available at www.foe.org.

Fromm, Erich (1964), *The Heart of Man: Its Genius for Good and Evil*, New York: Harper and Row.

Fromm, Erich ([1955] 1990), *The Sane Society*, New York: Owl.

Fromm, Erich ([1966] 1991), *You Shall Be As Gods: A Radical Interpretation of the Old Testament and its Tradition*, New York: Owl.

Fromm, Erich ([1956] 1995), *The Art of Loving*, London: Thorsons.

Fromm, Erich ([1973] 1997), *The Anatomy of Human Destructiveness*, London: Pimlico.

Fromm, Erich ([1976] 2002), *To Have or To Be?*, New York: Continuum.

Fromm, Erich ([1947] 2003), *Man For Himself: An Inquiry into the Psychology of Ethics*, London: Routledge.

Gaita, Raimond (2002), *A Common Humanity: Thinking About Love and Truth and Justice*, London: Routledge.

Gareis, Sven Bernhard and Varwick, Johannes (2005), *The United Nations: An Introduction*. Basingstoke: Palgrave Macmillan.

Geary, Dick (1992a), 'Introduction' in Dick Geary (ed.), *Labour and Socialist Movements in Europe before 1914*, Oxford: Berg.

Geary, Dick (1992b), 'Socialism in the German Labour Movement' in Dick Geary (ed.), *Labour and Socialist Movements in Europe before 1914*, Oxford: Berg.

George, Henry (2006), *Progress and Poverty: Why There Are Recessions and Poverty amid Plenty – And What to Do about It!*, New York: Robert Schalkenbach Foundation.

George, Susan (2004), *Another World Is Possible, if ...*, London: Verso.

George, Susan (2010), *Whose Crisis, Whose Future? Towards a Greener, Fairer, Richer World*, Cambridge: Polity.

Geras, Norman (1995), *Solidarity in the Conversation of Humankind: The Ungroundable Liberalism of Richard Rorty*, London: Verso.

Geras, Norman (1999), *The Contract of Mutual Indifference: Political Philosophy After the Holocaust*, London: Verso.

Giddens, Anthony (2006), 'Introduction' in Emile Durkheim, *Selected Writings*, ed. Anthony Giddens, Cambridge: Cambridge University Press.

Gilbert, Martin (1993), *The Dent Atlas of the Holocaust*, London: J. M. Dent.

Gildea, Robert (1996), *The Past in French History*, New Haven, CT: Yale University Press.

Gillespie, Paul (2012), 'Brics highlight skewed nature of global power', *Irish Times*, 31 March.

Gilligan, Carol (2000), *In a Different Voice: Psychological Theory and Women's Development*, Cambridge, MA: Harvard University Press.

Gilman, Charlotte Perkins (1999), *Herland, The Yellow Wall-paper, and Selected Writings*, ed. Denise D. Knight, Harmondsworth: Penguin.

Gilroy, Paul (2004), *Between Camps: Nations, Culture and the Allure of Race*, London: Routledge.

Gini Index (2011), World Bank website, http://data.worldbank.org/indicator/SI.POV.GINI, accessed 10 July 2012.

Glebe-Möller, Jens (1987), *A Political Dogmatic*, Philadelphia: Fortress Press.

References

Goldhagen, Daniel Jonah (1997), *Hitler's Willing Executioners: Ordinary Germans and the Holocaust*, London: Abacus.

Gorz, André (1999), *Reclaiming Work: Beyond the Wage-based Society*, Cambridge: Polity.

Gould, Stephen J. (2001), 'More Things in Heaven and Earth' in Hilary Rose and Steven Rose (eds), *Alas Poor Darwin: Arguments against Evolutionary Psychology*, London, Vintage, 85–105.

Gould, Carol C. (2004), *Globalizing Democracy and Human Rights*. Cambridge: Cambridge University Press.

Gould, Carol C. (2007), 'Transnational Solidarities', *Journal of Social Philosophy* 38(1), pp. 148–64.

Gould, Carol C. (2009), 'Varieties of Global Responsibility: Social Connection, Human Rights, and Transnational Solidarity' in Ann Ferguson and Mechthild Nagel (eds), *Dancing with Iris: The Philosophy of Iris Marion Young*, Oxford: Oxford University Press, pp. 199–212.

Gowan, Peter (2003), 'The New Liberal Cosmopolitanism' in Daniele Archibugi (ed.), *Debating Cosmopolitics*, London: Verso, pp. 51–66.

Graham, Gordon (2006), *Eight Theories of Ethics*, London: Routledge.

Grayling, A. C. (2007), *Against All Gods: Six Polemics on Religion and an Essay on Kindness*, London: Oberon.

Greenpeace (2010), available at www.greenpeace.org.

Grossman, Dave (2009), *On Killing: The Psychological Cost of Learning to Kill in War and Society*, rev. ed., Boston: Back Bay.

Guevara, Ernesto (1972), *Venceremos! The Speeches and Writings of Ernesto Che Guevara*, ed. John Gerassi, London: Panther.

Habermas, Jürgen (1988), *Legitimation Crisis*, Cambridge: Polity.

Habermas, Jürgen (1989), *The Theory of Communicative Action, volume two: Lifeworld and System – A Critique of Functionalist Reason*, Cambridge: Polity.

Habermas, Jürgen (1990), 'Justice and Solidarity: On the Discussion Concerning Stage Six' in Thomas E. Wren (ed.), *The Moral Domain: Essays in the Ongoing Discussion between*

Philosophy and the Social Sciences, Cambridge, MA: MIT Press, pp. 224–51.
Habermas, Jürgen (1992), *The Structural Transformation of the Public Sphere: An Inquiry into a Category of Bourgeois Society*, Cambridge: Polity.
Habermas, Jürgen (1996), *Between Facts and Norms*, Cambridge: Polity.
Habermas, Jürgen (1999), *The Inclusion of the Other: Studies in Political Theory*, Cambridge: Polity.
Habermas, Jürgen (2001), *The Postnational Constellation: Political Essays*, Cambridge: Polity.
Habermas, Jürgen (2002), *Religion and Rationality: Essays on Reason, God and Modernity*, Cambridge: Polity.
Habermas, Jürgen (2003), *The Future of Human Nature*, Cambridge: Polity.
Habermas, Jürgen (2006), *The Divided West*, Cambridge: Polity.
Habermas, Jürgen and Ratzinger, Joseph (2006), *The Dialectics of Secularization: On Reason and Religion*, San Francisco: Ignatius Press.
Hage, Ghassan (2003), *Against Paranoid Nationalism: Searching for Hope in a Shrinking Society*, London: Merlin Press.
Hands, Joss (2011), *@ is for Activism: Dissent, Resistance and Rebellion in a Digital Culture*, London: Pluto Press.
Hanhimäki, Juss M. (2008), *The United Nations: A Very Short Introduction*. New York: Oxford University Press.
Hannaford, Ivan (1996), *Race: The History of an Idea in the West*, Washington, DC: Woodrow Wilson Center Press.
Hannam, June (2012), *Feminism*, Harlow: Pearson Longman.
Hardt, Michael and Negri, Antonio (2000), *Empire*, Cambridge, MA: Harvard University Press.
Hardt, Michael and Negri, Antonio (2009), *Commonwealth*, Cambridge, MA: Belknap Press.
Harris, Sam (2006), *The End of Faith: Religion, Terror, and The Future of Reason*, London: Free Press.
Harvey, David (2000), *Spaces of Hope*, Edinburgh: Edinburgh University Press.

Harvey, David (2009), *A Brief History of Neoliberalism*, Oxford: Oxford University Press.
Haynes, Jeffrey (2008), *Development Studies*, Cambridge: Polity.
Hayward, J. E. S. (1959), 'Solidarity: The Social History of an Idea in Nineteenth Century France', *International Review of Social History* 4(2), pp. 261–84.
Hayward, J. E. S. (1961), 'The Official Social Philosophy of the French Third Republic: Léon Bourgeois and Solidarism', *International Review of Social History* 6(1), pp. 19–48.
Heater, Derek (2002), *World Citizenship: Cosmopolitan Thinking and its Opponents*, London: Continuum.
Hechter, Michael (1987), *Principles of Group Solidarity*, Berkeley: University of California Press.
Hegel, G. W. F. ([1807] 1971), *The Phenomenology of Mind*, London: Allen and Unwin.
Heins, Volker (2005), 'Orientalising America? Continental Intellectuals and the Search for Europe's Identity', *Millennium: Journal of International Studies* 34(2), pp. 433–48.
Heisenberg, Werner ([1958] 2000), *Physics and Philosophy: The Revolution in Modern Science*, London: Penguin.
Held, David (1995), *Democracy and the Global Order: From the Modern State to Cosmopolitan Governance*, Cambridge: Polity.
Held, David (2004), *Global Covenant: The Social Democratic Alternative to the Washington Consensus*, Cambridge: Polity.
Held, David and McGrew, Anthony (2007), *Globalization/Anti-Globalization: Beyond the Great Divide*, Cambridge: Polity.
Heyd, David (2007), 'Justice and Solidarity: The Contractarian Case against Global Justice', *Journal of Social Philosophy* 38(1), pp. 112–30.
Heywood, Andrew (2011), *Global Politics*, Basingstoke: Palgrave.
Hickley, Andrew (2012), 'Sarkozy to introduce French FTT in August', GFS News website, 30 January, www.gfsnews.com/article/4182/1/, accessed 6 July 2012.

Hitchens, Christopher (2007), *God is Not Great: The Case Against Religion*, London: Atlantic.
Hobbes, Thomas ([1651] 1991), *Leviathan*, Cambridge: Cambridge University Press.
Hobsbawm, Eric (1990), *Nations and Nationalism since 1870: Programme, Myth, Reality*, Cambridge: Cambridge University Press.
Hobsbawm, Eric (1996) 'Identity Politics and the Left', *New Left Review* 217, May–June, pp. 38–47.
Hobsbawm, Eric (2004), 'History: A New Age of Reason', *Le Monde Diplomatique*, December.
Holloway, John (1998), 'Dignity's Revolt' in John Holloway and Eloína Peláez, *Zapatista! Reinventing Revolution in Mexico*, London: Pluto, pp. 159–198.
Honneth, Axel (1996), *The Struggle for Recognition: The Moral Grammar of Social Conflicts*, Cambridge: Polity.
Honneth, Axel (1999), 'Reply to Andreas Kalyvas, "Critical Theory at the Crossroads: Comments on Axel Honneth's Theory of Recognition"', *European Journal of Social Theory* 2(2), pp. 249–52.
Honneth, Axel (2003), 'Redistribution as Recognition: A Response to Nancy Fraser' in Nancy Fraser and Axel Honneth, *Redistribution or Recognition? A Political-philosophical Exchange*, London and New York: Verso, pp. 110–97.
Honneth, Axel (2007), *Disrespect: The Normative Foundations of Critical Theory*, Cambridge: Polity.
Hooker, Juliet (2009), *Race and the Politics of Solidarity*, Oxford: Oxford University Press.
Hopper, Paul (2007), *Understanding Cultural Globalization*, Cambridge: Polity.
Horne, Alistair ([1965] 2002), *The Fall of Paris*, London: Pan.
Horton, Tim and Gregory, James (2009), *The Solidarity Society: Fighting Poverty and Inequality in an Age of Affluence, 1909–2009*, London: Fabian Society.
Horvat, Branko (1976), *The Yugoslav Economic System: The*

First Labor-managed Economy in the Making, New York: M. E. Sharpe.
Huntington, Samuel P. (1997), *The Clash of Civilizations and the Remaking of World Order*, New York: Simon and Schuster.
Hursthouse, Rosalind (1999), *On Virtue Ethics*, Oxford: Oxford University Press.
Hutchings, Kimberley (1999), *International Political Theory: Rethinking Ethics in a Global Era*, London: Sage.
Hutchings, Kimberley (2010), *Global Ethics: An Introduction*, Cambridge: Polity.
Hutchinson, John (2007), 'Warfare, Remembrance and National Identity' in Athena S. Leoussi and Steven Grosby (eds), *Nationalism and Ethnosymbolism: History, Culture and Ethnicity in the Formation of Nations*, Edinburgh: Edinburgh University Press, pp. 42–52.
Inglis, David and Robertson, Roland (2008), 'The Elementary Forms of Globality: Durkheim and the Emergence and Nature of Global Life', *Journal of Classical Sociology* 8(1), pp. 5–25.
ITUC (2012), International Trades Union Confederation, www.ituc-csi.org, accessed 6 July 2012.
Jessop, Bob (2002), *The Future of the Capitalist State*, Cambridge: Polity.
Kain, Philip J. (1991) *Marx and Ethics*, Oxford: Clarendon Press.
Kaldor, Mary (2003), *Global Civil Society: An Answer to War*, Cambridge: Polity.
Kalyvas, A. (1999), 'Critical Theory at the Crossroads: Comments on Axel Honneth's Theory of Recognition', *European Journal of Social Theory* 2(1), pp. 99–108.
Kamiński, Bartłomiej (1991), *The Collapse of State Socialism: The Case of Poland*, Princeton, NJ: Princeton University Press.
Kant, Immanuel (1992), *Political Writings*, ed. H. Reiss, Cambridge: Cambridge University Press.
Kautsky, Karl (1983), *Selected Political Writings*, Basingstoke: Macmillan.
Keane, John (2003), *Global Civil Society?*, Cambridge: Cambridge University Press.

Keller, Suzanne (2005), *Community: Pursuing the Dream, Living the Reality*, Princeton, NJ: Princeton University Press.

Kenny, Anthony (2000), *A Brief History of Western Philosophy*, Oxford: Blackwell.

Kershaw, Ian (2000), *Hitler, 1936–1905: Nemesis*, London: Allen Lane.

Kinealy, Christine (1994), *This Great Calamity: The Irish Famine 1845–52*, Dublin: Gill and Macmillan.

King, Michael R. and Rime, Dagfinn (2010), 'The $4 Trillion Dollar Question: What Explains FX Growth since the 2007 Survey?', *BIS Quarterly Review*, December.

Kingsley, Patrick (2012), 'Making the grade', *The Guardian*, 16 February.

Kingsnorth, Paul (2003), *One No, Many Yeses: A Journey to the Heart of the Global Resistance Movement*, London: Free Press.

Kingsolver, Barbara (1996), *Holding the Line: Women in the Great Arizona Mine Strike of 1983*, Ithaca, NY: ILR Press.

Kingsolver, Barbara (1998), *The Poisonwood Bible*, London: Faber and Faber.

Klein, Naomi (2002), *Fences and Windows: Dispatches fro the Front Lines of the Globalization Debate*, London: Flamingo.

Klein, Naomi (2004), 'Reclaiming the Commons' in Tom Mertes (ed.), *A Movement of Movements: Is Another World Really Possible?*, London: Verso.

Kumar, Manjit (2008), *Quantum: Einstein, Bohr and the Great Debate about the Nature of Reality*, London: Icon.

Küng, Hans (1997), *A Global Ethic for Global Politics and Economics*, London: SCM Press.

Lacroix, Justine, 2002, 'For a European Constitutional Patriotism', *Political Studies* 50(5), pp. 944–58.

Lai, Karyn L. (2008), *An Introduction to Chinese Philosophy*, Cambridge: Cambridge University Press.

Lamy, Pascal (2005), *Towards World Democracy*, London: Policy Network.

Lamy, Steven L. (2011), 'Contemporary Mainstream Approaches: Neo-realism and Neo-liberalism' in John Baylis, Steve Smith and Patricia Owens (eds), *The Globalization of World Politics: An Introduction to International Relations*, Oxford: Oxford University Press, 5th ed., pp. 116–29.

Lansley, Stewart (2012), *The Cost of Inequality: Why Economic Equality Is Essential for Recovery*, London: Gibson Square.

Lenin, V. I. (1977), *Selected Works, volume 3*, Moscow: Progress.

Lenin, V. I. (1992), *The State and Revolution*, Harmondsworth: Penguin.

Lentin, Alana (2008), *Racism: A Beginner's Guide*, Richmond: Oneworld.

Lentin, Alana and Titley, Gavan (2011), *The Crises of Multiculturalism: Racism in a Neoliberal Age*, London: Zed.

Leoussi, Athena S. and Grosby, Steven (2007) (eds) *Nationalism and Ethnosymbolism: History, Culture and Ethnicity in the Formation of Nations*, Edinburgh: Edinburgh University Press.

Lerner, Gerda (1986), *The Creation of Patriarchy*, New York: Oxford University Press.

Lerner, Gerda (1994), *The Creation of Feminist Consciousness: From the Middle Ages to Eighteen-seventy*, New York: Oxford University Press.

Leroux, Pierre (1985), *De l'humanité*, Paris: Fayard.

Levi, Primo ([1947] 2000), *If This Is a Man*, London: Folio Society.

Lichterman, P. (2005), *Elusive Togetherness: Church Groups Trying to Bridge America's Divisions*, Princeton, NJ: Princeton University Press.

Lister, Ruth (1997), *Citizenship: Feminist Perspectives*, Basingstoke: Macmillan.

Liu Xiaobo (2012), *No Enemies, No Hatred: Selected Essays and Poems*. Cambridge, MA: Belknap Press.

Long, A. A. (2001), *Stoic Studies*, Berkeley: University of California Press.

Lukes, Steven (1973), *Emile Durkheim, His Life and Work: A Historical and Critical Study*, London: Allen Lane.

Lukes, Steven (1985), *Marxism and Morality*, Oxford: Clarendon Press.

Luxemburg, Rosa (1971), *Selected Political Writings*, ed. Dick Howard, New York: Monthly Review Press.
McCrea, Christian (2009), 'Giorgio Agamben' in Felicity Colman (ed.) *Film, Theory and Philosophy: The Key Thinkers*, Durham: Acumen, pp. 349-57.
MacIntyre, Alasdair (1994) *After Virtue: Study in Moral Theory*, London: Duckworth.
MacIntyre, Alasdair (1999), *Dependent Rational Animals: Why Human Beings Need the Virtues*, London: Duckworth.
MacMaster, Neil (2001), *Racism in Europe, 1870-2000*, Basingstoke: Palgrave.
McNally, David (2011), *Global Slump: The Economics and Politics of Crisis and Resistance*, Oakland, CA: PM Press.
Magraw, Roger (1986), *France, 1815-1914: The Bourgeois Century*, New York: Oxford University Press.
Magraw, Roger (1992), 'Socialism, Syndicalism, and French Labour before 1914' in Dick Geary (ed.), *Labour and Socialist Movements in Europe before 1914*, Oxford: Berg.
Malatesta, Errico ([1891] 1974), *Anarchy*, London: Freedom Press.
Marcuse, Herbert (1978), *The Aesthetic Dimension: Toward a Critique of Marxist Aesthetics*, Boston: Beacon Press.
Marcuse, Herbert ([1964] 2002), *One-dimensional Man: Studies in the Ideology of Advanced Industrial Society*, London: Routledge.
Marshall, T. H. (1973), *Class, Citizenship, and Social Development*, Westport, CT: Greenwood Press.
Marx, Karl (1975), *Early Writings*, Harmondsworth: Penguin.
Marx, Karl ([1894] 1981), *Capital: A Critique of Political Economy, volume 3*, Harmondsworth: Penguin.
Marx, Karl ([1867] 1990), *Capital: A Critique of Political Economy, volume 1*, Harmondsworth: Penguin.
Marx, Karl (2009), *Selected Writings*, ed. David McLellan, Oxford: Oxford University Press.
Marx, Karl (2010a), *The Revolutions of 1848*, London: Verso.
Marx, Karl (2010b), *Surveys from Exile*, London: Verso.
Marx, Karl (2010c), *The First International and After*, London: Verso.

Mason, Paul (2007), *Live Working or Die Fighting: How the Working Class Went Global*, London: Harvill Secker.
Mason, Paul (2009), *Meltdown: The End of the Age of Greed*, London: Verso.
Mazzini, Giuseppe (1966), 'The Italian National Committee to the Italians', 16 November 1850, in *The Red Republican and Friend of the People*, London: Merlin Press.
Mazzini, Giuseppe (2010), *A Cosmopolitanism of Nations: Giuseppe Mazzini's Writings on Democracy, Nation Building, and International Relations*, ed. Stefano Recchia and Nadia Urbinati, Princeton, NJ: Princeton University Press.
Mertes, Tom (ed.) (2004), *A Movement of Movements: Is Another World Really Possible?*, London: Verso.
Meyer, Thomas and Hichman, Lewis (2007), *The Theory of Social Democracy*, Cambridge: Polity.
Milanovic, Branko (2007), 'Globalization and Inequality' in David Held and Ayse Kaya (eds), *Global Inequality: Patterns and Explanations*, Cambridge: Polity.
Miliband, Ralph (1969), *The State in Capitalist Society*, London: Weidenfeld and Nicolson.
Milner, Henry (1989), *Sweden: Social Democracy in Practice*, Oxford: Oxford University Press.
Milward, Alan S. (1984), *The Reconstruction of Western Europe, 1945–51*, London: Methuen.
Modood, Tariq (2007), *Multiculturalism: A Civic Idea*, Cambridge: Polity.
Monroe, Kristen Renwick (1996), *The Heart of Altruism: Perceptions of a Common Humanity*. Princeton, NJ: Princeton University Press.
More, Thomas ([1516] 1991), *Utopia*, Cambridge: Cambridge University Press.
Morris, William ([1890] 1995), *News from Nowhere or an Epoch of Rest*, Cambridge: Cambridge University Press.
Müller, Jan-Werner (2007), *Constitutional Patriotism*, Princeton, NJ: Princeton University Press.

Munck, Ronaldo (2002), *Globalisation and Labour: The New 'Great Transformation'*, London: Zed.

Mutnick, Deborah (2011), 'Occupy Wall Street and the rhetoric of equality', *Forbes*, 1 November.

Nasr, Seyyed Hossein (2002), *The Heart of Islam: Enduring Values for Humanity*, San Francisco: HarperSanFrancisco.

Norman, Richard (2004), *On Humanism*, London: Routledge.

Norris, Pippa and Inglehart, Ronald (2011), *Sacred and Secular: Religion and Politics Worldwide*, 2nd ed., Cambridge: Cambridge University Press.

Noys, Benjamin (2004), 'Gestural Cinema? Giorgio Agamben on Film', *Film Philosophy* 8(22), www.film-philosophy.com/vol8-2004/n22noys.html, accessed 9 July 2012.

Nussbaum, Martha (1992), 'Human Functioning and Social Justice: In Defense of Aristotelian Essentialism', *Political Theory* 20(2), pp. 202–46.

Nussbaum, Martha (1996), 'Patriotism and Cosmopolitanism' in Martha Nussbaum *et al.*, *For Love of Country: Debating the Limits of Patriotism*, Boston: Beacon Press, pp. 2–20.

Nussbaum, Martha (1997), 'Kant and Stoic Cosmopolitanism', *Journal of Political Philosophy* 5(1), pp. 1–25.

Nussbaum, Martha (2000), *Women and Human Development: The Capabilities Approach*, Cambridge: Cambridge University Press.

Nussbaum, Martha (2001), *Upheavals of Thought: The Intelligence of Emotions*, Cambridge: Cambridge University Press.

Nussbaum, Martha (2006), *Frontiers of Justice: Disability, Nationality, Species Membership*, Cambridge, MA: Belknap Press.

Nussbaum, Martha (2010), *Not For Profit: Why Democracy Needs the Humanities*, Princeton. NJ: Princeton University Press.

Nussbaum, Martha (2011), *Creating Capabilities: The Human Development Approach*, Cambridge, MA: Belknap Press.

OECD (2011), *Divided We Stand: Why Inequality Keeps Rising*, Paris: OECD.
Offe, Claus (1984), *Contradictions of the Welfare State*, London: Hutchinson.
Olesen, Thomas (2005), *International Zapatismo: The Construction of Solidarity in the Age of Globalization*, London: Zed Books.
Oneworld (2012), 'Official Poverty Statistics', Oneworld website, www.oneworld.net/guides/poverty#statistics, accessed 9 July 2012.
Onfray, Michel (2007), *In Defence of Atheism: The Case against Christianity, Judaism, and Islam*, London: Serpent's Tail.
Özkirimli, Ulmut (2000), *Theories of Nationalism: A Critical Introduction*. Basingstoke: Macmillan.
Pagel, Mark (2012), *Wired for Culture: The Natural History of Human Cooperation*, London: Allen Lane.
Pahl, Ray (2005), 'Hidden solidarities that span the globe', *New Statesman*, 17 January.
Palast, Greg (2002), *The Best Democracy Money Can Buy*, London: Pluto Press.
Parekh, Bhikhu (2000), *Rethinking Multiculturalism: Cultural Diversity and Political Theory*, Basingstoke, Palgrave.
Parker, George and Masters, Brooke (2011), 'Cameron pours cold water on Tobin tax', *Financial Times*, 2 November.
Patomäki, Heikki and Teivanen, Teivo (2004), *A Possible World: Democratic Transformation of Global Institutions*, London: Zed.
Peck, Jamie (2010), *Constructions of Neoliberal Reason*, Oxford: Oxford University Press.
Peet, Richard (2009), *Unholy Trinity: The IMF, World Bank and WTO*, 2nd ed., London: Zed.
Pensky, Max (2008), *The Ends of Solidarity: Discourse Theory in Ethics and Politics*, Albany: State University of New York Press.
Pierson, Christopher (1991), *Beyond the Welfare State: The New Political Economy of Welfare*, Cambridge: Polity.

Pilbeam, Pamela (2000), *French Socialists before Marx: Workers, Women and the Social Question in France*, Teddington: Acumen.

Pleyers, Geoffrey (2010), *Alter-Globalization: Becoming Actors in the Global Age*, Cambridge: Polity.

Pogge, Thomas W. (1989), *Realizing Rawls*, Ithaca, NY: Cornell University Press.

Pogge, Thomas (2008), *World Poverty and Human Rights: Cosmopolitan Responsibilities and Reforms*, 2nd ed., Cambridge: Polity.

Pontusson, Jonas (2005), *Inequality and Prosperity: Social Europe versus Liberal America*, Ithaca, NY: Cornell University Press.

Potel, Jean-Yves (1982), *The Summer before the Frost: Solidarity in Poland*, London: Pluto Press.

Poverty (2012), 'United Kingdom: Income Inequalities', The Poverty Site, www.poverty.org.uk/09/index.shtml, accessed 9 July 2012.

Price, Roger (1975), *1848 in France*, London: Thames and Hudson.

Proudhon, Pierre-Joseph ([1851] 1971), 'General Idea of the Revolution in the Nineteenth Century' in Marshall S. Shatz (ed.), *The Essential Works of Anarchism*, New York: Bantam, pp. 81–122.

Putnam, Robert D. (2000), *Bowling Alone: The Collapse and Revival of American Community*, New York: Simon and Schuster.

Rattansi, Ali (2007), *Racism: A Very Short Introduction*, Oxford, Oxford University Press.

Rawls, John (1999), *A Theory of Justice*, rev. ed., Oxford: Oxford University Press.

Rawls, John (2003), *The Law of Peoples*, Cambridge, MA: Harvard University Press.

Rawnsley, Andrew (2000), 'The Fall of Mandelson', *The Observer*, 17 September.

Recchia, Stefano and Urbinati, Nadia (2009), 'Introduction' in

Giuseppe Mazzini, *A Cosmopolitanism of Nations: Giuseppe Mazzini's Writings on Democracy, Nation Building, and International Relations*, ed. Stefano Recchia and Nadia Urbinati, Princeton, NJ: Princeton University Press, pp. 1–30.

Redford, Robert (2007), interview, *The Motorcycle Diaries* DVD, Channel 4.

Rehg, William (2007), 'Solidarity and the Common Good: An Analytic Framework', *Journal of Social Philosophy* 38(1), pp. 7–21.

Renan, Ernest ([1882] 2010), 'What is a Nation?' in Homi K. Bhabha (ed.), *Nation and Narration*, London: Routledge, pp. 8–22.

Robertson, Roland (1992), *Globalization: Social Theory and Global Culture*, London: Sage.

Rorty, Richard (1996), *Contingency, Irony, and Solidarity*, Cambridge: Cambridge University Press.

Rorty, Richard (1998), *Truth and Progress*, Cambridge: Cambridge University Press.

Rorty, Richard (1999), *Philosophy and Social Hope*, London: Penguin.

Rorty, Richard (2011), *An Ethics for Today: Finding Common Ground between Philosophy and Religion*, New York: Columbia University Press.

Rothleder, Dianne (1999), *The Work of Friendship: Rorty, His Critics, and the Project of Solidarity*, Albany: State University of New York Press.

Rousseau, Jean-Jacques ([1762] 1993), *Emile*, London: Everyman.

Rudolph, Susanne Hoeber (2005), 'Religious Transnationalism' in Mark Juergensmeyer (ed.), *Religion in Global Civil Society*, Oxford: Oxford University Press.

Salles, Walter (2004), interview, Then It Must Be True website, July, www.thenitmustbetrue.com/salles/salles1.html, accessed 9 July 2012.

Salles, Walter (2007), interview, *The Motorcycle Diaries* DVD, Channel 4.

Sanford, George (ed.) (1990), *The Solidarity Congress, 1981: The Great Debate*, Basingstoke: Macmillan.
Schattle, Hans (2008), *The Practices of Global Citizenship*, Lanham, MD: Rowman and Littlefield.
Schwartz, Joseph M. (2007), 'From Domestic to Global Solidarity: The Dialectic of the Particular and Universal in the Building of Social Solidarity', *Journal of Social Philosophy* 38(1), pp. 131–47.
Sen, Amartya (2009), *The Idea of Justice*, London: Allen Lane.
Sennett, Richard (1998), *The Corrosion of Character: The Personal Consequences of Work in the New Capitalism*, New York: W. W. Norton.
Sennett, Richard (2012), *Together: The Rituals, Pleasures and Politics of Co-operation*, London: Allen Lane.
Sewell, William H. Jr (1997), Work and Revolution in France: The Language of Labor from the Old Regime to 1848, Cambridge: Cambridge University Press.
Shaxson, Nicholas (2011), Treasure Islands: Tax Havens and the Men Who Stole the World, London: Bodley Head.
Simon, Rick (2007), 'Eurocommunism' in Daryl Glaser and David M. Walker (eds), *Twentieth Century Marxism: A Global Introduction*, London: Routledge, pp. 81–94.
Sinclair, Andrew (2006), *Viva Che!: The Strange Death and Life of Che Guevara*, Stroud: Sutton.
Singer, Peter (1972), 'Famine, Affluence, and Morality', *Philosophy and Public Affairs* 1, pp. 229–43.
Singer, Peter (1995), *Animal Liberation*, 2nd ed., London: Pimlico.
Singer, Peter (2005), *In Defense of Animals: The Second Wave*, Oxford: Blackwell.
Singer, Peter (2009), *The Life You Can Save: Acting Now to End World Poverty*, London: Picador.
Sklair, Leslie (2003), *The Transnational Capitalist Class*, Oxford: Blackwell.
Slote, Michael (1992), *From Morality to Virtue*, New York: Oxford University Press.

Slote, Michael (2007), *The Ethics of Care and Empathy*, London and New York, Routledge.
Smart, Ninian (2000), *World Philosophies*, London: Routledge.
Smith, Anthony D. (1991), *National Identity*, Harmondsworth: Penguin.
Smith, Roger (2007), *Being Human: Historical Knowledge and the Creation of Human Nature*, Manchester: Manchester University Press.
Smock, David R. (ed.) (2002), *Interfaith Dialogue and Peacebuilding*, Washington, DC: United States Institute of Peace Press.
Sorel, Georges ([1908] 1999), *Reflections on Violence*, Cambridge: Cambridge University Press.
Spencer, Liz and Pahl, Ray (2006), *Rethinking Friendship: Hidden Solidarities Today*, Princeton, NJ: Princeton University Press.
Statman, Daniel (ed.) (1997), *Virtue Ethics: A Critical Reader*, Edinburgh: Edinburgh University Press.
Stedman Jones, Gareth (1983), *Languages of Class: Studies in English Working Class History, 1832–1982*, Cambridge: Cambridge University Press.
Stedman Jones, Susan (2001), *Durkheim Reconsidered*, Cambridge: Polity.
Steenson, Gary P. (1991), *After Marx, before Lenin: Marxism and Socialist Working-class Parties in Europe, 1884–1914*, Pittsburgh: University of Pittsburgh Press.
Steger, Manfred (1997), *The Quest for Evolutionary Socialism: Eduard Bernstein and Social Democracy*, Cambridge: Cambridge University Press.
Steger, Manfred (2008), *The Rise of the Global Imaginary: Political Ideologies from the French Revolution to the Global War on Terror*, Oxford: Oxford University Press.
Stenger, Victor J. (2007), *God, the Failed Hypothesis: How Science Shows that God Does Not Exist*, Amherst, NY: Prometheus.
Stjernø, Steinar (2005), *Solidarity in Europe: The History of an Idea*, Cambridge: Cambridge University Press.
Sultana, Farhana and Loftus, Alex (2011), *The Right to*

Water: Politics, Governance and Social Struggles, London: Routledge.

Swift, Jonathan ([1726] 1997), *Gulliver's Travels*, London: Folio Society.

Tamir, Yael (1993), *Liberal Nationalism*, Princeton, NJ: Princeton University Press.

Tan, Kok-Chor (2004), *Justice without Borders: Cosmopolitanism, Nationalism and Patriotism*, Cambridge: Cambridge University Press.

Tännsjö, Torbjörn (2008), *Global Democracy: The Case for a World Government*, Edinburgh: Edinburgh University Press.

Tax Justice Network (2008), 'Obama and the Stop the Tax Haven Abuse Act', 5 November, http://taxjustice.blogspot.com/2008/11/obama-and-stop-tax-haven-abuse-act.html, accessed 10 July 2012.

Taylor, Antony (1999), 'Commemoration, Memorialisation and Political Memory in Post-Chartist Radicalism: The 1885 Halifax Chartist Reunion in Context' in Owen Ashton, Robert Fyson and Stephen Roberts (eds), *The Chartist Legacy*, Woodbridge: Merlin Press, pp. 255–85.

Taylor, Charles (1996), 'Why Democracy Needs Patriotism' in Martha Nussbaum *et al.*, *For Love of Country: Debating the Limits of Patriotism*, Boston: Beacon Press, pp. 119–21.

Taylor, Charles (2007), *A Secular Age*, Cambridge, MA: Belknap Press.

Thomas, Hugh (1997), *The Slave Trade: The Story of the Atlantic Slave Trade, 1440–1870*, New York: Simon and Schuster.

Thomas, Caroline and Evans, Tony (2011), 'Poverty, Development, and Hunger' in John Baylis, Steve Smith and Patricia Owens (eds), *The Globalization of World Politics: An Introduction to International Relations*, Oxford: Oxford University Press, 5th ed., pp. 460–76.

Thompson, Dorothy (1984), *The Chartists: Popular Politics in the Industrial Revolution*, Aldershot: Wildwood House.

Tibi, Bassam (2005), *Islam between Culture and Politics*, 2nd ed., Basingstoke: Palgrave Macmillan.

Tomlinson, John (1991), *Cultural Imperialism: A Critical Introduction*, London: Pinter.
Tomlinson, John (1999), *Globalization and Culture*, Cambridge: Polity.
Tormey, Simon (2004), *Anti-capitalism: A Beginner's Guide*, Oxford: Oneworld.
Touraine, Alain (2000), *Can We Live Together? Equality and Difference*, Stanford, CA: Stanford University Press.
Touraine, Alain (2007), *A New Paradigm For Understanding Today's World*, Cambridge: Polity.
Touraine, Alain (2009), *Thinking Differently*, Cambridge: Polity.
Touraine, Alain, Dubet, François, Wieviorka, Michel and Strzelecki, Jan (1983), *Solidarity: Poland 1980–81*, Cambridge: Cambridge University Press.
Townshend, Jules (1996), *The Politics of Marxism: The Critical Debates*, London: Leicester University Press.
Tronto, Joan C. (1994), *Moral Boundaries: A Political Argument for an Ethic of Care*, New York and London: Routledge.
UN News Centre (2011), 'Ban presents budget proposal of nearly $5.2 billion for next two years', 27 October, http://www.un.org/apps/news/story.asp?NewsID=40224&Cr=budget&Cr1=, accessed 16 July 2012.
Unger, Roberto Mangabeira (1998), *Democracy Realized: The Progressive Alternative*, London: Verso.
Unger, Roberto Mangabeira (2005), *What Should the Left Propose?*, London: Verso.
Unger, Roberto Mangabeira (2007), *The Self Awakened: Pragmatism Unbound*, Cambridge, MA: Harvard University Press.
Van der Pijl, Kees (1984), *The Making of an Atlantic Ruling Class*, London: Verso.
Van Hooft, Stan (2009), *Cosmopolitanism: A Philosophy for Global Ethics*, Durham: Acumen.
Vertovec, Steven and Cohen, Robin (eds) (2002), *Conceiving Cosmopolitanism: Theory, Context, and Practice*, Oxford: Oxford University Press.

Vout, Malcolm and Wilde, Lawrence (1987), 'Socialism and Myth: The Case of Sorel and Bergson', *Radical Philosophy* 46, pp. 2–7.

Wallerstein, Immanuel (1991), *Unthinking Social Science: The Limits of Nineteenth-century Paradigms*, Cambridge: Polity.

Wallerstein, Immanuel (1999), *The End of the World as We Know It: Social Science for the Twenty-first Century*, Minneapolis: University of Minnesota Press.

Waterman, Peter (2001), *Globalization, Social Movements and the New Internationalisms*, London: Continuum.

Waterman, Peter (2008), 'A Trades Union Internationalism for the 21st Century: Meeting the Challenges from Above, Below, and Beyond' in Andreas Bieler, Ingemar Lindberg and Devan Pillay (eds), *Labour and the Challenges of Globalization: What Prospects for Transnational Solidarity?*, London: Pluto Press, pp. 248–63.

Weber, Max ([1922] 1978), *Economy and Society, volume one*, Berkeley: University of California Press.

Wilde, Oscar (1991), *Plays, Prose Writings and Poems*, London: Everyman's Library.

Wilde, Lawrence (1994a), *Modern European Socialism*, Aldershot: Dartmouth.

Wilde, Lawrence (1994b), 'Swedish Social Democracy and the World Market' in Ronen P. Palan and Barry Gills (eds), *Transcending the State–Global Divide: A Neostructuralist Agenda in International Relations*, Boulder, CO and London: Lynne Rienner.

Wilde, Lawrence (1998), *Ethical Marxism and Its Radical Critics*, Basingstoke: Macmillan.

Wilde, Lawrence (2000), '"The Creatures, Too, Must Become Free": Marx and the Animal/Human Distinction', *Capital and Class* 72, pp. 37–54.

Wilde, Lawrence (ed.) (2001), *Marxism's Ethical Thinkers*, Basingstoke: Palgrave.

Wilde, Lawrence (2004), *Erich Fromm and the Quest for Solidarity*, New York: Palgrave Macmillan.

References

Wilde, Lawrence (2007), 'Europe and the "re-regulation of world society": a critique of Habermas', *Capital and Class* 93, pp. 47–66.

Wilde, Lawrence (2009), 'The Cry of Humanity: Dylan's Expressionist Period' in David Boucher and Gary Browning (eds), *The Political Art of Bob Dylan*, 2nd ed., Exeter: Imprint Academic, pp. 104–35.

Wilde, Lawrence (2010), 'The Antinomies of Aggressive Atheism', *Contemporary Political Theory* 9(3), pp. 266–83.

Wildt, Andreas (1999), 'Solidarity: Its History and Contemporary Definition' in Kurt Bayertz (ed.), *Solidarity*, Dordrecht: Kluwer, pp. 209–22.

Willetts, Peter (2011a), *Non-Governmental Organizations in World Politics: The Construction of Global Governance*, Abingdon: Routledge.

Willetts, Peter (2011b), 'Transnational Actors and International Organizations in Global Politics' in John Baylis, Steve Smith and Patricia Owens (eds), *The Globalization of World Politics: An Introduction to International Relations*. Oxford: Oxford University Press, 5th ed., pp. 326–45.

Wollstonecraft, Mary ([1792] 1992), *A Vindication of the Rights of Woman*, Harmondsworth: Penguin.

Woodcock, George (1977), *Anarchism: A History of Libertarian Ideas and Movements*, Harmondsworth: Penguin.

World Hunger Education Service (2012), '2012 World Hunger and Poverty Facts and Statistics', Hunger Notes website, http://www.worldhunger.org/articles/Learn/world%20hunger%20facts%202002.htm, accessed 10 July 2012.

World Social Forum (2012), 'Charter of Principles', Fórum Social Mundial website, http://www.forumsocialmundial.org.br/main.php?id_menu=4&cd_language=2, accessed 10 July 2012.

World Values Survey (2005), 2005 Wave Data Files, available at http://www.wvsevsdb.com/wvs/WVSData.jsp, accessed 10 July 2012.

Young, Iris Marion (1990) *Justice and the Politics of Difference*, Princeton, NJ: Princeton University Press.

Index

Adorno, Theodor, 194, 196
advertisements, 194, 249
Agamben, Giorgio, 209, 212–13, 216
aggression, 121, 123, 177
alienation, 91, 11–12, 116, 127, 135, 155, 178, 212
Allen, Theodore, 163
alter-globalization movement, 97, 133, 239–43
Amnesty International, 66
An Na'im, Abdullahi, 178
anarchism, 15, 27, 29, 30, 31, 34, 243
Anderson, Benedict, 42
animal welfare, 63–4, 123
anthropocentrism, 125
anthropology, 98, 117
anti-capitalist movement, 65, 74, 146, 238, 242
anti-Semitism, 159–60
Aquinas, Thomas, 108
Arab Spring, 196
Arendt, Hannah, 160–1
Archibugi, Daniele, 8, 12, 101, 234
Ardey, Robert, 128–9
Aristotle, 6, 104, 106–7, 109, 110–11, 113, 114, 118, 122, 126, 134–5
atomisation, 256
Augustine of Hippo, 120
authoritarianism, 46, 198
Averroes, 108
Axelrod, Robert, 133

Bachofen, Johann Jacob, 182–3
Badiou, Alain, 172
Bakunin, Mikhail, 29–30
Baldwin, Peter, 54, 57–8, 219–20

Balibar, Etienne, 156
Balmer, Randall, 177
Barber, Benjamin, 11
Bauman, Zygmunt, 61, 162
Bayertz, Kurt, 60
Beauvoir, Simone de, 181–2, 183, 189
Beck, Ulrich, 12–13, 192, 194
Beckett, Samuel, 213
Behan, Brendan, 195
being mode, 116
Beitz, Charles, 5
Bellamy, Edward, 55
Bello, Walden, 252
Bentham, Jeremy, 113
Bernal, Gael García, 211
Bergson, Henri, 1
Beveridge Report, 56
Billig, Michael, 151
Blackburn, Robin, 230
Blanc, Louis, 22, 24
Blanqui, Louis Auguste, 26–7
Bloch, Ernst, 173
Blumenbach, J.-F., 158
Bogarde, Dirk, 196
Bohr, Niels, 172
Bonapartism, 57
Booth, Charles, 55
Boulding, Elise, 10
Bourgeois, Léon, 35, 39, 228
Bourdieu, Pierre, 154
Bowles, Samuel, 129
Brown, Gordon, 227
British Labour Party, 26, 246
British Liberal Party, 25
Brown, Donald, 118
Bush, George W., 235

Index

Caldwell, Christopher, 192–3
Calhoun, Craig, 237
Canovan, Margaret, 106
care, 4, 49, 58, 60, 65, 70, 99, 100–1, 111, 122–5, 177, 183–6, 198, 234, 249; see also ethics of care
Carroll, William, 147–8
Chandler, David, 241
Charcot, Jean-Martin, 212
charity, 21, 23, 24, 61, 122, 123, 141, 194, 196, 215
Chartism, 25
Chilean Miners, 103
class, 17, 18, 19, 22, 23, 28, 37, 41, 43, 50, 54, 57, 58, 59, 61, 62, 74, 81, 143–9, 163, 186, 200, 210, 214, 217, 219, 220, 229, 240, 252, 258
class struggle, 19, 23, 26, 30–5, 37, 44, 45, 57, 68, 143, 145, 148, 208, 223–5
Clark, Mary, 122, 129
Cockburn, Cynthia, 187
Coicaud, Jean-Marc, 134
Cold War, 2, 49, 154, 232, 240, 251
communication, 12, 91, 93–6, 103, 132, 196, 198
communism, 44–53
communitarianism, 93, 94–6, 98, 242
community, 4, 5, 8, 12, 36–7, 49, 59, 61, 75, 77, 80, 82, 84, 85, 93, 104, 110, 132, 151, 156, 161, 172, 199, 200, 214, 218, 224, 237, 240, 251, 256
compassion, 16, 122–6, 128
Comte, Auguste, 36
constitutional patriotism, 82–7
cooperation, 16, 73, 86, 100, 115, 118, 124, 128–34, 137, 141, 146, 184, 191, 222, 225, 235, 249
cosmopolitan democracy, 7–8, 87, 101, 233, 234
cosmopolitanism, 1–13, 90, 138, 151, 155, 156, 194, 237
culture, 8, 10, 11–12, 16, 17, 42, 71, 72, 78, 82, 93–4, 109, 117–18, 120, 135, 140, 145, 146, 151, 152, 155, 156, 163, 186, 188, 190, 191–9, 217, 233, 257
Cynics, 2–3

Dahl, Robert, 99
Darwin, Charles, 159
Darwinism, 159
Dawkins, Richard, 168–72
Dearden, Basil, 196
Debord, Guy, 213
Delors, Jacques, 244–5
Dennett, Daniel, 168, 178–9
dependency, 194, 200, 206–7
Derrida, Jacques, 86, 122
destructiveness, 120–1, 140, 142
Dewey, John, 71, 75, 197
difference, 5, 27, 64, 161, 174, 175, 179, 182, 184, 189, 193, 206, 207, 229, 230
disability, 59, 189, 200, 207, 215
Dreifuss, Arthur, 195
Drumont, Edouard, 160
Dubček, Alexander, 50
Duncan, Isadora, 212
Dürer, Albrecht, 213
Durkheim, Emile, 1, 2, 13, 15, 35–41, 53–4, 58
duty, 3, 19, 21, 39, 41, 55, 108, 162
Dylan, Bob, 196

Edgerton, Robert, 129
education, 38, 39, 41, 42, 49, 54, 60, 65, 85, 136, 140, 151, 163, 169, 184, 191, 194, 196–9, 201, 221, 235, 245
Einstein, Albert, 169, 170–1, 172
empathy, 71, 99, 100, 101, 103, 122–4, 187, 192, 214
Engels, Friedrich, 23, 33, 45
environmentalism, 7, 10, 63, 65, 79, 94, 112, 125–6, 136, 176, 194, 218, 224, 225, 233, 238, 250, 256
equality, 11, 22, 59, 63, 73, 84, 93, 100, 177, 178, 181, 182, 184, 198, 220
Esping-Anderson, Gøsta, 54
essentialism, 16, 73, 104, 106, 109, 117, 134, 139, 141
ethics of care, 100–1, 122–5, 183–4
eudaemonia, 107, 110
evil, 110, 114, 121, 160–2, 168, 170, 206

291

faith, 32, 116, 168, 170–2, 174, 176–8, 180
Falk, Richard, 7, 168, 175
family, 3, 11, 22, 37, 56, 59, 133, 138, 150, 180, 185, 201–5, 255
Fanon, Frantz, 163–6
fascism, 42–4, 47–8
Faux, Jeff, 148
Featherstone, Simon, 193
feminism, 63, 180–1, 183–6, 188, 238
Feuerbach, Ludwig, 111
financial crash, 90, 223, 225–6, 230, 247, 253
Fitzpatrick, Jim, 216
Fourier, Charles, 20
Fraser, Derek, 56
Fraser, Nancy, 79, 90–1, 188
freedom, 23, 29, 43, 51, 52, 56, 71, 77, 93, 96–100, 106, 113, 120, 134, 150, 164–6, 173, 188, 194, 198, 200, 224, 256
French Revolution (1789), 22, 27, 72, 84, 153
French Revolution (1848), 23–5, 27
Freud, Sigmund, 120–1
Friedman, Milton, 130
friendship, 76, 98, 122, 199, 210
Fromm, Erich, 16, 113–18, 121, 122, 126, 127–8, 150, 171, 173
Fukuyama, Francis, 154
fundamentalism, 14, 168, 177

Gaita, Raimond, 166
Galton, Francis, 159
gender, 17, 59, 72, 80, 124, 141, 143, 180–9, 199, 243, 250
George, Henry, 55
George, Susan, 228
Geras, Norman, 73, 161–2
German Greens, 63
German Social Democratic Party (SPD), 26
Gilligan, Carol, 123–4
Gilman, Charlotte Perkins, 183–5
Gilroy, Paul, 167
Gintis, Herbert, 129
Glebe-Möller, Jens, 175
global citizenship, 8–11, 66, 146, 151, 197, 218, 241–2

global governance, 168, 218–19, 225, 229, 232–5, 238
global justice, 5–7, 12–13, 66, 89–90, 92, 101, 107, 134, 137–9, 176, 188, 196, 199, 224, 240, 243
global pension plan, 230
Gobineau, Arthur de, 159
Golden Rule, 176
Goldhagen, Daniel, 160
Gorbachev, Mikhail, 50
Gorz, André, 131
Gould, Carol, 16, 69, 98–10
Gould, Stephen J., 124, 170
Gournay, M. le Jars de, 181
Gowan, Peter, 253
Granado, Alberto, 209–11, 213–16
Grayling, A. C., 168
greed, 110, 120, 226, 247, 258
Green, T. H., 41
Greenham Common peace camp, 64
Greenpeace, 65
Group of Twenty (G20), 9, 226, 236, 244, 246
guaranteed income, 131, 234
Guevara, Ernesto Che, 209–17

Habermas, Jürgen, 13, 16, 68–9, 77, 80–92, 96, 99, 105, 117, 133, 175
Hage, Ghassan, 147
Hands, Joss, 133, 196
Hannaford, Ivan, 157
Harnay, Julian, 22
Harris, Sam, 168
Hart, Michael, 145–6, 131–2
Harvey, David, 121–2, 223–4
hatred, 52, 157, 159
Hechter, Michael, 103
Hegel, G. W. F., 75–6, 78
Heisenberg, Werner, 172
Held, David, 7–8, 101, 233–4, 252
Heyd, David, 14
Hitchens, Christopher, 168
Hitler, Adolf, 47–8
Hobbes, Thomas, 120
Holocaust, 83, 160–2
Honneth, Axel, 16, 68, 75–80, 97
Hooker, Juliet, 167

Index

hope, 14, 19, 89, 120, 124, 142, 147, 151, 157, 167, 191, 196, 204, 205, 250, 256, 258
Hopper, Paul, 199
Horkheimer, Max, 194, 196
human nature, 16, 21, 68–70, 73, 80, 91–2, 96, 104–6, 107–9, 110–17, 118, 120–1, 122, 125, 127, 134, 138–41, 195
human potentials, 16, 91, 104, 105, 107, 112, 116, 135, 138–40, 172, 222, 255, 256
human rights, 9, 10, 65–6, 71–2, 79, 88, 99–101, 103, 134, 138, 168, 178, 179, 218, 225, 223, 224, 242, 256, 258
humanism, 98, 108, 125, 167, 173; see also radical humanism
Hume, David, 108, 109
Huntington, Samuel, 12, 192
Hurricane Katrina, 102
Hursthouse, Rosalind, 122

identity, 42, 75, 78, 79, 82, 85–9, 94, 95, 98, 120, 143, 148, 149, 151, 153–4, 156, 167, 178, 208
inequality, 37–8, 61, 90, 123, 131, 154, 167, 185, 190, 194–5, 219–23, 229, 246, 256, 257
Inglis, David, 40
International Monetary Fund (IMF), 2, 9, 232, 234, 235
Internet, 10, 133, 196
Irish famine, 257

Jones, Henry, 41
justice, 5–7, 12–13, 18, 52, 66, 68, 78–82, 84–6, 89–90, 92, 97, 98–102, 107, 110, 123–5, 134, 136–9, 150, 166, 173, 175, 176–7, 180, 185, 188, 195, 196, 199, 206, 219, 224, 225, 232, 236, 239, 240, 242, 243, 258

Kain, Philip, 109
Kalyvas, Andreas, 77–8
Kant, Immanuel, 2–4, 72, 88, 108
Kautsky, Karl, 46, 53
Keane, John, 9
Keynesianism, 60, 67, 247, 252

Khrushchev, Nikita, 50
Kidd, Benjamin, 159
Kingsolver, Barbara, 17, 200–8
Klein, Naomi, 238
Knox, Robert, 159
Korda, Alberto, 216
Küng, Hans, 176

labour, 1, 24, 25, 31, 35–8, 46, 53, 54, 57, 94, 112, 128, 131–2, 144, 145–6, 164, 182–3, 188, 220, 235, 237, 240, 255
Lamy, Pascal, 235
Las Casas, Bartolomé, 158
Lassalle, Ferdinand, 26
Le Pen, Jean-Marie, 154
Le Pen, Marine, 154
Lee, Harper, 195
Lenin, V. I., 45–6, 33, 74
Lennon, John, 196
Leroux, Pierre, 15, 18, 20–2, 24, 27
liberal solidarity, 35–41
liberation, 21, 22, 42, 43, 46, 49, 113, 150, 155, 166, 173
Lichterman, Paul, 177
Loach, Ken, 195
Lorenz, Konrad, 129
love, 21, 73, 76, 98, 116, 117, 122, 136, 150, 164, 183, 204–5
Luxemburg, Rosa, 44–5

McCarthyism, 74,
MacIntyre, Alasdair, 108–10
McNally, David, 66
Maimonides, 108
Malatesta, Errico, 30
Mandela, Nelson, 152, 166
Mandelson, Peter, 246
Marcuse, Herbert, 116, 197, 199–200
Marr, Wilhelm, 159
Marshall, T. H., 54, 59, 219
Marshall Plan, 251
Marx, Karl, 16, 23, 30–4, 45, 53, 74, 104, 107, 110–13, 116, 118, 125–6, 127, 130–1, 134–5, 138–9, 144, 146, 148, 163, 173, 217, 223, 224, 228–9
Marxist, 26, 30, 34, 91, 113, 116, 118, 139, 146
Mason, Paul, 145–6, 226

293

mass media, 3, 71, 103, 133, 147, 150, 160, 191, 194–6, 209–17, 223, 236, 242, 246
Mazzini, Giuseppe, 19, 43
Meade, George Herbert, 75–6, 78
Metz, J.-B., 175
Miliband, Ralph, 59
Mill, John Stuart, 41
Millennium Development Goals, 9, 66, 89, 186, 199, 227, 232
Montesquieu, Charles, 158
Morales, Evo, 67
morality, 58, 72, 78, 108–9, 118, 122, 124, 172
More, Thomas, 122, 125, 126–7
Morris, William, 255
Mulligan, Robert, 195
multiculturalism, 69, 94, 141, 174, 175, 178–9, 193, 198
Mussolini, Benito, 43

Nabokov, Vladimir, 71
Nasr, Sayyed Hossein, 178
nation, 1, 2, 13, 17, 19, 40, 41–4, 65, 82–3, 85, 87, 88, 90, 105, 136, 143, 149–57, 160, 202, 215, 218, 220, 241, 242, 245, 253, 258
National Health Service, 56
nature (non-human), 37, 63, 113, 114, 115, 120, 125–7, 136, 169, 170, 172, 181, 190, 207, 250, 255
Nazism, 43, 159, 160–2
Negri, Antonio, 145–6, 131–2
neoliberalism, 14–15, 60, 65, 67, 89, 119, 130, 140, 146, 188, 219, 222, 224, 226, 236, 238, 242, 244, 247, 250–2, 256–8
New Deal, 247
new social movements, 2, 20, 63–7, 97, 240, 249–50
Nietzsche, Friedrich, 71, 212
North American Free Trade Association, 148, 187, 243
Nussbaum, Martha, 6, 16, 104, 107, 122, 123, 134–40, 151, 155, 197, 217

Obama, Barack, 63, 230
Occupy Movement, 196, 221

O'Connor, Feargus, 25
Onfray, Michel, 168, 178
Orwell, George, 71

Pahl, Ray, 132
Parekh, Bhikhu, 179
Paris Commune, 27–9, 33
patriarchy, 59, 180, 182–3
patriotism, 39–40, 73, 74, 83–6, 150, 151–2, 153–5
peace, 3–4, 18, 57, 64, 79, 121, 144, 174, 176, 183, 187, 218, 252, 255
Pearson, Karl, 159
Peck, Jamie, 226, 251
Pensky, Max, 92
Plato, 74
Pleyers, Geoffrey, 239, 242–3
Pogge, Thomas, 229–30, 252
Pollitt, Harry, 48
Pope John Paul II, 52
Pope Benedict XVI, 175
post-fordism, 131
poverty, 6, 7, 21, 55, 61–3, 66, 79, 88, 103, 123, 139, 147, 156, 176–7, 188, 194, 210, 219–23, 225, 227, 229, 230, 239, 242, 246, 248, 256–8
privatisation, 66–7, 91, 187
productiveness, 16, 116–18, 126–8, 141, 189, 222, 250, 255
Proudhon, Pierre-Joseph, 26–7
Proust, Marcel, 212
Putnam, Robert, 132

race, 17, 18, 43, 59, 61–2, 63, 72, 94, 126, 136, 141, 143, 152, 156–67, 186, 195, 225, 243
radical humanism, 6–7, 69, 92, 96–8, 105, 106–34, 140–1, 173, 254
rationality, 8, 70, 71, 82, 104, 109, 118–22, 132, 137, 141, 162, 168, 172, 175, 189, 191, 198, 222, 224, 225, 250, 256
Rattansi, Ali, 157, 162
Rawls, John, 5, 96, 99, 136, 138
Reagan, Ronald, 244
reconciliation, 16–17, 86, 108, 120, 142, 152, 175, 187
Redford, Robert, 212, 217

Index

redistribution, 6, 15, 38, 39, 68, 79, 82, 139, 188, 214, 219, 228, 230, 246, 248
religion, 17, 21, 36, 59, 70, 79, 108, 118, 136, 143, 144, 149, 153, 154, 167–80, 182, 186
Renan, Ernst, 42, 149
Renaud, Hyppolyte, 21
revolution, 29, 31, 32, 33, 53, 126, 132, 143, 211, 251, 255
Rivera, José, 211
Robertson, Roland, 11, 40
Roosevelt, Franklin D., 247
Rorty, Richard, 16, 68–75, 102, 105
Ross, Gary, 195
Rothleder, Diane, 71
Rousseau, Jean-Jacques, 181–2
Rowntree, Seebohm, 55
Rudolph, Susanne, 176
Russian Revolution (1917), 19, 46, 53, 144

Salles, Walter, 17, 209–17
Sandford, Jeremy, 195
Santaolalla, Gustavo, 211
Sarkozy, Nicolas, 227
Scholtz, Sally, 102
Seattle protests, 65, 146, 237–8, 239
self-realisation, 77, 96, 142
Sen, Amartya, 6
Senna, Rodrigo de la, 211
Sennett, Richard, 129
Sepulveda, Gines de, 158
Sewell, William, 23
sexism, 18, 126, 134, 181, 185
sexual orientation, 43, 59, 63, 72, 136, 186, 189
Shaxson, Nicholas, 231
Singer, Peter, 6
Sklair, Leslie, 147, 197
social democracy, 11, 56, 57, 148, 226, 234, 237, 244–8
social inclusion, 1, 14, 15, 16, 21, 22, 23, 32, 43, 59, 62, 64, 100, 141, 147, 154, 180, 194, 222, 241, 147, 249, 258
social partnership, 131
socialism, 15, 20–2, 27, 34–5, 39, 41, 44–7, 50, 52, 74, 256

Socrates, 2
Soderbergh, Steven, 216
solidarity
  definition, 1, 258
  global, 2, 5, 7. 10, 12, 13–17, 18, 20, 62, 65, 66, 68, 69, 87, 91, 101, 104, 105, 107, 118, 119, 139, 141, 142, 146, 149, 152, 153, 155, 156, 160, 168, 180, 186, 187, 199, 218, 219, 220, 229, 230, 241, 251, 252, 253, 254, 258
  human, 1, 5, 16–18, 32, 68, 69–73, 75–80, 92, 93, 101–5, 115, 117, 118, 139, 140, 141, 150, 151, 168, 169, 180, 189, 192, 193, 194, 200, 213, 250, 254
  mechanical, 36
  organic, 1, 36, 37
  social, 1, 2, 13–15, 19, 20, 23, 26, 35–8, 40, 44, 53–60, 79, 84, 85, 147, 153, 219, 237, 247, 256, 260
Sorel, Georges, 28
species being, 111
Spencer, Herbert, 167
Spencer, Liz, 132
Spinoza, Baruch, 113
Stalin, J. V., 46–7, 50
Steger, Manfred, 225, 236
Stenger, Victor, 168
Stoics, 2–3
sustainability, 7, 10, 64, 184, 224
Swift, Jonathan, 142

taxation, 38, 55, 59, 60, 82, 194, 219, 225–9, 231, 235–6, 244, 246–7, 253
Taylor, Charles, 151, 171
teleology, 107–8, 114, 219
Thatcher, Margaret, 244
Theunissen, Michael, 175
Tibi, Bassam, 177–8
Tobin Tax, 226–9
Touraine, Alain, 16, 69, 92–8, 105, 197–8
Tourette, Georges de la, 212
trades unions, 240–1, 249
Tronto, Joan, 125, 185
tsunami (2004), 102

295

unemployment, 49, 56, 58, 60–2, 132, 144, 222–3, 226, 236, 245–6
Unger, Roberto, 198
United Nations, 9, 162, 186, 221, 224, 227, 229, 233, 235, 240, 251, 254
universalism, 41, 64, 69, 88, 96, 104
utilitarianism, 6, 108–9
utopianism, 80

Van Hooft, Stan 149
virtue ethics, 16, 106–10, 117, 125

Wallerstein, Immanuel, 12, 119
war, 3, 4, 6, 42, 49, 57, 74, 75, 90, 115, 120, 121, 142, 150, 160, 177, 178, 184, 205, 218, 251
Weber, Max, 119, 172
welfare state, 2, 15, 20, 41, 53–62, 144, 151, 219–20, 251
Welles, Orson, 213

Wilde, Oscar, 256
Wollstonecraft, Mary, 181–2
women's movements, 185–9, 225
workers' self-management, 51, 130–1
World Bank, 9, 65, 232, 234–5
World Economic Forum, 148, 238
World Social Forum, 65, 187, 238–9
World Trade Organization (WTO), 2, 9, 65, 101, 146, 148, 232, 234, 235, 237–8
World War I, 18, 19, 25, 33–5, 39–41, 44, 54, 56, 121, 228
World War II, 19, 47, 48, 54, 56, 57, 160, 163

xenophobia, 115, 155
Xiaobo, Liu, 253–4

Young, Iris Marion, 52, 99, 106, 147

Zapatistas, 243